THE
CLIMAX
OF THE
Bible

22 Sermons and Notes on Revelation

MILO HADWIN

Table of Contents

Preface

T his book is a collection of twenty-two sermons on the book of Revelation, by Milo Hadwin, preached in Wheeling, West Virginia, in the United States, from January through June of 1980. There is one sermon on each chapter of the book. The sermons were taped, transcribed, and, with a minimum of editing, are presented here as they were preached. This book contains additional material on Revelation.

The book of Revelation provides an exciting and encouraging message for the people of God. It is hoped these sermons will convey that sense of excitement and provide a great encouragement for all who read them. The Scripture quotations in the sermons are from *New International Version*. Grand Rapids, Michigan: Zondervan Bible Publishers, 1978.

Quotations in the supplemental material are from *New Revised Standard Bible*. Nashville: Thomas Nelson Publishers, 1989.

Introduction to Revelation

Author – God

Writer – John, the Apostle

Date – c. 95 A.D.

Destination – The original recipients were the seven churches in the province of Asia (Asia Minor) (1:4). It was written for God's servants (1:1) and was designed to bless everyone who will read, hear, and keep the things written in it (1:3; 22:7). It will bring a curse to anyone who adds to or takes away from the words written in it (22:18-19). Even the parts addressed specifically to a church in one place (e.g. 2:1) were intended for everyone in all the churches of Christ in every place (e.g. 2:7). It is a revelation to God's servants (1:1), and there is no guarantee it will reveal anything to anyone else nor is there any assurance it will bless anyone except those who will keep its teaching (1:3).

Purpose – To *reveal* (1:1) in such a way as to bless all God's servants who read it (1:3). It is the only book in the Bible that pronounces a blessing on those who read, hear, and obey its words. It is not written just for historians, theologians, scholars, and intellectuals. Yet the difficulty of the book is frequently stressed to the discouragement of the would-be reader. For example, a recent commentator wrote:

Because of its symbolism, its saturation with Old Testament passages and themes, the various schemes of interpretation that have developed concerning this book through the ages, and the profundity and vastness of the subjects that are here unveiled, I believe that the Apocalypse, above every book of the Bible, will yield its meaning only to those who give it prolonged and careful study" (Wilbur Smith, *The Wycliffe Bible Commentary*, p. 1500).

Surely, the more one studies the more one is apt to learn, but even a beginner is bound to learn something and may even see something the scholar has missed. A pertinent question here is "How much did God intend to reveal in his Revelation? Are we expecting it to have more meaning than God intended for it?"

To illustrate, the same writer referred to quoted these words regarding Revelation from a man he said is generally acknowledged to have been the most gifted Biblical expositor in the first quarter of the 20th century. "There is no book in the Bible which I have read so often, no book to which I have tried to give more patient and persistent attention….There is no book in the Bible to which I turn more eagerly in hours of depression than to this, with all its mystery, all the details of which I do not understand" (G. Campbell Morgan, *Westminster Bible Record*, Vol. 3 (1912), 105, 109). Could it be this scholar was looking for meanings in the details which the details were never intended to convey? Might it not have been sufficient that through these details God was able to convey a message sufficiently powerful to overcome his depression?

As another writer expressed it: "Whenever there is a world crisis, whenever the State exalts itself and demands an allegiance which Christians know they cannot pay without abandoning their very souls, whenever the church is threatened by destruction, and faith is dim and hearts are cold, then the Revelation will admonish and exhort, uplift and encourage all who heed its message" (Martin Kiddle in *Moffatt Commentary*, p. xlix).

How can we know what Revelation means? How do we interpret the Bible? How do we interpret any literature?

1. Allow it to explain itself (2:11; 20:14).

2. Interpret the part in light of the whole. (Recognize unity of Bible. Part must harmonize with whole.)

3. Consider historical background, purpose (don't make it say more than it intends to say), and style of writing (prose and poetry are interpreted differently).

4. Interpret the complex by the simple, the confusing by the clear, the ambiguous by the unambiguous. Do not change the clear meaning of a simple passage to fit one possible meaning of a difficult passage.

What more should we consider in interpreting Revelation specifically?

1. Approach it with humility. One of the most respected Bible scholars in the world said very simply in the preface to his commentary on Revelation: "Some of the problems of this book are enormously difficult and I certainly have not the capacity to solve them" (Leon Morris, *The Revelation of St. John*, p. 13). That does not mean we can understand nothing nor be certain about anything. It is to approach Revelation with the kind of attitude Peter had toward some of Paul's writings (2 Peter 3:15-18).

2. Recognize that it is highly symbolic. This does not mean we enter a world of unreality. As J.B. Phillips, who produced a popular translation of the New Testament, said: "He is carried, not into some never-never land of fancy, but into the Ever-ever land of God's eternal Values and Judgments" (J.B. Phillips, *The Book of Revelation*, 1960, p.9, as quoted by Morris, op. cit., p. 15). Or as C.S. Lewis said in his book *Mere Christianity*,

> There is no need to be worried about facetious people who try to make the Christian hope of "Heaven" ridiculous by saying they do not want "to spend eternity playing harps." The answer to such people is that if they cannot understand books written for grown-ups, they should not talk about them. All the scriptural imagery (harps, crowns, gold, etc.) is, of course, a merely symbolical attempt to express the inexpress-

ible. Musical instruments are mentioned because for many people (not all) music is the thing known in the present life which most strongly suggests ecstasy and infinity. Crowns are mentioned to suggest the fact that those who are united with God in eternity share this splendour and power and joy. Gold is mentioned to suggest the timelessness of Heaven (gold does not rust) and the preciousness of it. People who take these symbols literally might as well think that when Christ told us to be like doves, He meant that we were to lay eggs (p. 121).

That in Revelation we are dealing with some symbolic language can be seen from a few sample passages (3:18; 6:13; 8:10; 12:3-4). The rich imagery of Revelation introduces us to a whole menagerie of animals: horses, lions, leopards, bears, lambs, calves, locusts, scorpions, eagles, vultures, fish, and frogs.

Revelation comes to us in living color with white symbolizing purity, black – distress, red – death (blood), purple – royalty and luxurious ease, and pale yellow – expiring life and the kingdom of the dead.

Numbers are important symbols in Revelation. The number seven leads the way with fifty-four occurrences in Revelation. It symbolizes completeness, fullness or perfection. Three and a half is a broken number that appears in various forms (42 months, 1260 days, "a time, times and half a time") symbolizing distress or tribulation. Ten also is a symbol of completeness or perfection (Ten Commandments, the Holy of Holies was a cube, each side being of ten cubits—symbolic of heaven, according to Hebrews 9:3, 24). Twelve is symbolic of God's people, the church or the kingdom. So, we have twelve tribes, twelve apostles, twice twelve being the number of elders representing the redeemed church (4:4), the new Jerusalem has twelve gates, and the walls of the city have twelve foundations—all of this associated with God's people.

Multiples of these numbers are common, as the cube of ten which is a thousand. Certainly, one could turn Revelation into a bizarre mathematical nightmare with numerological games, but it is well to be aware of the possible symbolism that is often suggested and sometimes demanded by the context. We must not force into a symbol a meaning it does not naturally bear, or Revelation will become merely a playground for our own wild fantasies.

3. Recognize the Biblical context. Revelation was not a work produced in some sublime isolation, but it breathes the atmosphere of the whole Bible of which it is the climax. It has been concluded by the research of two Bible scholars, Westcott and Hort, that of the 404 verses in Revelation, 265 contain lines embracing approximately 550 references to Old Testament passages. A thorough knowledge of the Old and New Testaments will surely enrich one's study and understanding of Revelation. Similarities to the language and symbolism of Daniel, Ezekiel, Zechariah, Matthew 24, Mark 13, Luke 21, and other prophecies and portions of scripture are found in abundance.

    While these comparisons can be helpful, they can also cause one to seriously distort the message and meaning of Revelation if the rest of the Bible is used as a kind of dictionary for assigning meanings to symbols. This assumes Revelation is a kind of cryptogram or code message to be deciphered by treasure hunting through all the Bible for hints and meanings. It is natural that Revelation would express itself in the familiar phrases of the rest of scripture since it is the summing up of God's purpose in the history of his people.

    However, it would be a mistake to assume that a symbol used in one part of scripture will have the same meaning as the same symbol used in another place. (Consider the serpents in Eden and the wilderness; also, the cross, once a symbol of shame, became the symbol of salvation.) This mistake can be seen in some attempts to apply the symbolism of

Revelation which refers to the glorified kingdom in its perfected state which is yet to come.

4. Recognize it is not a book written to titillate or to gratify the curiosity of men anxious to tear aside the veil from the future (see Matthew 24:35, 42, 44). Revelation was never intended to be a celestial timetable of what is to come. It becomes tiring to listen to the frantic ravings of those who see in Bible prophecies forecasts of imminent disasters.

Two prominent religious groups noted for such activity proved themselves false prophets in 1975 (for those who didn't already know it). One group's magazine of October 8, 1966, specifically declared that the seventh millennium would begin in Autumn, 1975. It read: "*All* the many, many parts of the great sign of the 'last days' are here, together with verifying Bible chronology...." (*Awake*).

The other religious group's leader published a book in 1957 called *1975 in Prophecy*. Here is what it said:

> While modern science and industry strive to prepare for us a push-button leisure-luxury-world by 1975, United States Assistant Weather chief, I.R. Tarrahill, warns us unofficially to really fear *"the big drought of 1975."* But the indications of prophecy are that this drought will be even *more* devastating than he foresees, and that it will strike *sooner* than 1975—probably between 1965 and 1972!...Here is exactly *how* catastrophic it will be: ONE-THIRD OF OUR ENTIRE POPULATIONS will DIE in the famine and disease epidemic! (p. 12).

To use that writer's favorite adjectives, that is Amazing, Astounding, Incredible, and Fantastic!! On page 14 of the same work, he declared that another one-third would be killed by hydrogen bombs, and the remaining one-third would be sold into slavery!

Jeremiah had the best comment on that (Jeremiah 14:14). (Herbert W. Armstrong was the author of aforesaid document. Refer also to Kirban's I

Predict.) While Revelation was not designed to tear back the curtain on some chronological countdown of Jesus' return, it does "draw veils aside and open up a vista of God's actions and his ways; for it proclaims the kingdom of God, which is here and now and yet is still to come in its fullness, bringing with it the overthrow of all that is against him" (W.C. van Unnik, The New Testament, 1964, p. 161, as quoted by Morris, p. 20).

The methods by which commentators have tried to interpret Revelation tend to fall into four categories:

1. Preterist – According to this view, all or nearly all, of the book had its fulfillment in the first century or, at most, the first three hundred years of the history of the church. Supposedly, the book deals primarily with the persecution inflicted on Christians by the Roman government. For example, J.W. Roberts maintained in his commentary that Revelation 6:1-16:21 predicts the history of the church from John's time until the conversion of Constantine and the Edict of Toleration (A.D. 311). The three and a half years of the rule of the beast and the prostitute represent this "little season" of Roman dominance. The binding of Satan represents the downfall of the persecuting power in which the cause of the saints (6:9 ff.) is "resurrected" (the first resurrection) and the thousand years is the longer period of the triumph of the Biblical faith.

2. Continuous Historical or Chronological School – This view says Revelation is a prophetic history of the church from the first century to the end of time. This view attempts to match up significant historical events with the various symbols in Revelation. The book is seen as one continuous series of historical events.

3. Futurist – This interpretation says most of Revelation is yet to be fulfilled. It usually says chapters 4-22 have not yet been fulfilled. Chapters 14-19 are supposed to describe events in a three and a half year period immediately preceding the second coming of Christ. This is supposed to be followed by a literal thousand year reign of Christ on earth.

4. Philosophy of History (sometimes called Spiritual, Symbolic, Idealist, or Poetic) – This view says the book is not dealing with historical events at all. It is simply a symbolic representation of principles, ideas, and spiritual truths.

Is the task of interpreting Revelation hopeless? Not if it is a *revelation*. Surely the proper way to interpret Revelation is to read the book and, insofar as possible, allow it to explain itself and interpret it in harmony with the rest of scripture. When this is done, what impressions are made on the mind? Here are some that are helpful in seeing how the book is structured. Four groups of "sevens" cover more than half the book suggesting this much of a tentative and incomplete outline as a starting point:

> Chapters: 1-3 – Seven Lampstands
> 4-7 – Seven Seals
> 8-11 – Seven Trumpets
> 12-14 – ?
> 15-16 – Seven Bowls
> 17-22 – ?

A comparison of the seven trumpets and the seven bowls suggests that in some sense they are dealing with the same things. Notice:

- 1st trumpet (8:7) and bowl (16:2) affect the earth
- 2nd trumpet (8:8) and bowl (16:3) affect the sea
- 3rd trumpet (8:10) and bowl (16:4) affect the rivers
- 4th trumpet (8:12) and bowl (16:8) affect the sun
- 5th trumpet (9:1-11) and bowl (16:10-11) affect the Abyss where the throne of the beast is (see 13:11)
- 6th trumpet (9:14) and bowl (16:12) pertain to the *Euphrates River*
- 7th trumpet (11:15, 19) and bowl (16:17-21) produce lightning, rumblings, peals of thunder, earthquakes, and great hailstorms

A kind of repetition, as seen in the case of the trumpets and bowls, is characteristic of the whole book. The end of time, especially the coming of Christ to final judgment, seems to be described at various intervals throughout the book (6:12-17 with 7:9-17; 11:15-18; 14:14-20; 16:13-21; 19:11-21; 20:11-15). Four of these passages occur at the ends of the four central divisions of the tentative outline suggested above.

This begins to indicate that Revelation does not present a continuous sequence of events, but may contain sections which each cover somewhat the same material. This is emphasized by the fact that the last three passages mentioned each include the identical expression in the Greek text, "the battle" (16:14; 19:19; 20:8). This is surely not referring to three different battles, but the same battle is described in three different places. "The battle" (war) in 19:19 suggests that one section closes with the end of chapter 19, just as previous sections had closed with God's final judgment.

This enables us to see a completed outline of the book of Revelation which further analysis will confirm as the way the book naturally divides itself.

Chapters: 1-3 – Seven Lampstands (the church in the world)
4-7 – Seven Seals (the church suffering trials)
8-11 – Seven Trumpets (the church protected and avenged)
12-14 – Christ opposed by the dragon and his helpers
15-16 – Seven Bowls (final wrath on impenitent)
17-19 – Fall of Babylon and the Beasts
20-22 – Dragon's Doom and Christ's Victory

The sections of Revelation appear to be somewhat parallel, but with the emphasis progressing from section to section toward the events that bring this age to a climax. For example, chapters 1-3 discuss Christ among the lampstands which represent the churches. While chapters 2 and 3 are letters addressed to seven specific churches in Asia Minor, they also are designed to be speaking to the churches in general and are generally representative of the problems and glories of the church in every period of time.

While a letter is addressed to one church (2:1, 8, 12, 18; 3:1, 7, 14), the instruction in each case is to "hear what the Spirit says to the *churches*" (2:7, 11, 17, 29; 3:6, 13, 22). The picture of Christ among the churches reminds one of his statement in Matthew 28:20: "And surely I will be with you always, to the very end of the age."

While the first three chapters are considering the church in general throughout the whole age, they are focused particularly on the churches of that time.

The second section calls our attention to the crucified Christ with the picture of the slain Lamb (5:5-6) before the seals are opened, but the scenes revealed by the opened seals carry us forward to the persecuted church, even to the final judgment (11:15-18).

The third section is more concerned with the end of the age. However, there is a major dividing line in the middle of the book at which point, in chapter 12, we are carried back to the beginning again with the birth, death, ascension, and coronation of Christ before we are carried ahead to see the behind-the-scenes working of Satan trying to destroy God's people.

There is then an intensification of the action as we progress through the next sections. While we see the nature of the conflict between God and Satan throughout the age of the church, we move forward in emphasis to the wrath of God on the impenitent in the fifth section, the destruction of Babylon and the beasts in the sixth section, and the destruction of Satan, death, and Hades in the last section, with an extended look at the world which is to come.

This interpretation of Revelation seems to be the one the Bible itself is suggesting and which harmonizes most readily with the rest of scripture. It has been called "progressive parallelism" by William Hendricksen who, in his book on Revelation called *More Than Conquerors*, elaborates extensively on what we have only briefly sketched here.

Synopsis of Revelation

In chapters 1-3 we see the church as the light of the world—a light shining brightly in some places at some times and sometimes barely flickering, but nevertheless, a light. But light and darkness cannot co-exist. And so, the church will inevitably face persecution. "In fact, everyone who wants to live a godly life in Christ Jesus will be persecuted" (2 Timothy 3:12). But, let us see things in their proper perspective. First, then, we must see Jesus.

And see him we do in chapters 4-5—the head of the church is the King on the throne who controls the destiny of history. Knowing who is ultimately controlling our world, the Lamb who was slain to show his love and draw us to him, we are ready to face the persecution which comes with chapter 6.

Here we find that those who die in the Lord go to be in his presence. This reassurance provides us with courage to view the awesome judgment finally to be inflicted on the world. Even then, the Church Triumphant is seen rejoicing before the throne of God. But, will the persecuted be avenged? Yes! The seals of persecution give rise to the trumpets of judgment.

In 8:1-5, God is seen constantly sending his judgment in response to the prayers of his people. Here we are introduced to the warning (trumpet) judgment of God designed to cause men to repent and persecutors to relent. But, for the most part, it doesn't work (9:21).

Consequently, we see in chapters 10-11 the gospel-proclaiming, cross-bearing church being afflicted but emerging victorious. But the book does not end here. Two questions cry out for answers: Why is the church being so vigorously persecuted? And what will be the ultimate fate of the impenitent? So far, we have seen the surface and the conflict on the earth. Now, let us see what is behind it all. Behind the struggle on earth between the church and the world is the cosmic struggle between Christ and Satan!

In chapter 12, we see the dragon, Satan, trying to destroy the male child, Christ. Failing in this, he directs his persecution against Christ's people, the church.

In chapters 13-14, we see Satan employing the beast out of the sea (representing anti-Christian persecution concentrated in government) and the beast out of the earth (representing anti-Christian religion) and the great prostitute, Babylon, (representing anti-Christian seduction of the world) to destroy the church. But Satan fails, and in chapter 14 we see the Lamb standing victoriously on Mount Zion initiating the harvest of God's final judgment. And what is the fate of those who, being warned by the trumpets of judgment, remain impenitent?

In chapters 15-16, we see the bowls of God's wrath given to the angels and poured out on the wicked. But what of the great prostitute, Babylon, and the two beasts?

In chapters 17-18, we see Babylon described and destroyed.

In chapter 19, we see the beasts cast into the lake of fire and brimstone.

In chapter 20, the devil, death, and Hades are all thrown into the fiery lake of burning sulfur.

In chapters 21 and 22, the great Revelation closes with the vision of the new heaven and earth where the saints are seen reigning with God and the Lamb forever and ever!

REVELATION 1:

The Super Drama of Revelation

Tonight we begin our study of the book of Revelation, and I hope this evening that under the special tension that many of you are experiencing, I can lift you somewhat out of Super Bowl fever into the super drama of the book of Revelation. I know that in preparation for the lesson tonight that the excitement I felt in simply delving into the great things that John was trying to reveal to us far exceeded what I have been able to generate myself over the Super Bowl, and I hope I can convey that in a small way to you this evening. We are this evening going to be looking beyond the shallow superficiality of this life into the great realities that underlie our experience. We are going to be looking at those great causes that produce the problems that have troubled our world since man was created.

The Revelation came to John in the last decade of the first century during the reign of the Roman emperor Diocletian. It was a trying time for Christians. They were facing the imperial power of Rome and the persecution and the effort to make them bow their knees to Caesar. Yet they had committed their lives unreservedly to the Lord Jesus Christ, and now they had to make the decision as to whether they would succumb to the power and pressure of Rome or hold true to the one who said, "Be faithful, even to the point of death, and I will give you the crown of life." To whom would allegiance be given? That was the issue then; that is the issue today.

Perhaps the forces that challenge us today are not the forces of political pressure and perhaps not of physical persecution. Yet, there is before us the power of a seductive world order, the seduction of the world that would lead us away from a firm commitment and allegiance to Jesus Christ. We, too, must daily face that challenge of allegiance, whether it be to Caesar or to Christ, whether it be to Satan or to God. These people were confronted with a tremendous burden. They were a people who could easily have become depressed and discouraged, a people who were seeing those whom they loved being put to death and, perhaps, their faith was on the verge of weakening. Not only for that day did the book of Revelation come as a tremendous inspiration, but for each of us, in our time, it can do the same thing.

One commentator on Revelation said:

> Whenever there is a world crisis, whenever the state exalts itself and demands an allegiance which Christians know they cannot pay without abandoning their very souls, whenever the church is threatened by destruction, and faith is dim and hearts are cold, then the Revelation will admonish and exhort, uplift and encourage all who heed its message.

One of the more effective expositors of the Bible in the early part of the 20th century said of the book of Revelation: "There is no book in the Bible which I have read so often, no book to which I have tried to give more patient and persistent attention....There is no book in the Bible to which I turn more eagerly in hours of depression than to this, with all its mystery...." The book does have some mystery. But it is, in fact, a revelation. God is saying something to us, and what he is saying to us above all else is that God's people will be victorious, that things are not as they seem. That is the single great message and theme of Revelation.

It may seem to us as though Satan is in control of our world. It may seem to us that God has hidden himself from the problems and pressures of our time and there is no one to whom we can turn. Yet Revelation 17:14 describes graphically and symbolically the message of the book: "They will make war against the Lamb, but the Lamb will overcome them because he is Lord of lords and King of kings—and with him will be his called, chosen and faithful followers." God will be victorious! The Lamb that was slain has become King of kings and Lord of lords. Jesus reigns, and with him his people who are called and chosen and faithful will reign and have dominion. That's the message and theme of the book. But let's look at it as we enter the first chapter of Revelation.

After the opening words, John says in verses 4-5:

> John,
>
> To the seven churches in the province of Asia:
>
> Grace and peace to you from him who is, and who was, and who is to come, and from the seven spirits before his throne, and from Jesus Christ, who is the faithful witness, the firstborn from the dead, and the ruler of the kings of the earth.

We're introduced immediately to God, the Father, to the Son, and to the Holy Spirit, and it is from them that this Revelation comes.

We are introduced to Jesus Christ in verse 5 who is presented to a discouraged people as prophet, priest, and king. It would be an encouragement to know they have paid their allegiance to the one who is really in charge. Jesus Christ is spoken of as the faithful witness in his capacity as prophet, and his statements are true. In John 8:14 Jesus said, "…my testimony is valid…." In a world of conflicting and uncertain voices, there is one Voice we can listen to and know with certainty that we are hearing reality expressed, that this is the way things really are. Jesus is a faithful witness. He alone can be depended on to tell you the truth. Satan would deceive us and blind us to the realities of life. But God is saying to us that through Jesus Christ there is a clear vision of what is true and what is to come and what our destiny is to be.

Jesus is presented not only as a prophet, but as a priest. He is referred to as the firstborn from the dead. That does not mean that he is the first person who was ever raised from the dead, because the term "firstborn" is primarily a title of pre-eminence. Jesus, among all those who have risen from the dead, is pre-eminent. That's the thought that is expressed in Colossians 1:18 where the Apostle

Paul says: "And he is the head of the body, the church; he is the beginning and the firstborn from among the dead, so that in everything he might have the supremacy." And Jesus Christ has the supremacy as the firstborn from among the dead in the realm of priesthood. In Hebrews 2:14-3:1, the writer said:

> Since the children have flesh and blood, he too shared in their humanity so that by his death he might destroy him who holds the power of death—that is, the devil—and free those who all their lives were held in slavery by their fear of death. For surely it is not angels he helps, but Abraham's descendants. For this reason he had to be made like his brothers in every way, in order that he might become a merciful and faithful high priest in service to God, and that he might make atonement for the sins of the people. Because he himself suffered when he was tempted, he is able to help those who are being tempted. Therefore, holy brothers, who share in the heavenly calling, fix your thoughts on Jesus, the apostle and high priest whom we confess.

Jesus Christ suffered and died enabling us to realize that he has been tempted in every way, just as we are—yet was without sin, that he is one who can sympathize with our weaknesses. He understands us. He has been in the flesh. He has been tempted and tried and tormented, and he knows our anguish, he knows our needs. Jesus is the one who truly can serve as our high priest.

Jesus is not only presented to a troubled people as a prophet and as a priest, but he is presented as king. And this passage in Revelation 1:5 says not only that he is the faithful witness and the firstborn from the dead, but he is ruler of the kings of the earth. That is an amazing statement, and it violates the most popular interpretation of Revelation that is heard in our times. Jesus Christ is not one who one day is going to return to the earth and set up a kingdom and reign here for a thousand years. We are informed by the Revelation of Almighty God that Jesus Christ, today, now, is the ruler of the kings of the earth. He doesn't have to wait until some future date to become the ruler. God is in charge, and he has placed Jesus Christ in charge.

In Jesus, God fulfilled his promise spoken in Psalm 89:27:

> I will also appoint him my firstborn,
>
> the most exalted of the kings of the earth.

Jesus rules now and he reigns now. In 1 Peter 3:22 Peter speaks of Jesus Christ who "is at God's right hand—with angels, authorities and powers in submission to him." The world is subject to Christ. We're not under the ultimate dominion of the leaders of our nation. We are under the authority and dominion and power of Almighty God through his son, Jesus Christ.

In Ephesians 1:20-21 the apostle Paul speaks of Jesus Christ, that God "seated him at his right hand in the heavenly realms, far above all rule and authority, power and dominion, and every title that can be given, not only in the present age but also in the one to come." Jesus has already been put in dominion, and he is far above all rule and authority. That is true now, and that's the reason why in Acts 2:29-35, after Jesus had risen from the dead and ascended into heaven, the apostle Peter said:

> Brothers, I can tell you confidently that the patriarch David died and was buried, and his tomb is here to this day. But he was a prophet and knew that God had promised him on oath that he would place one of his descendants on his throne. Seeing what was ahead, he spoke of the resurrection of the Christ, that he was not abandoned to the grave, nor did his body see decay. God has raised this Jesus to life, and we are all witnesses of the fact. Exalted to the right hand of God, he has received from the Father the promised Holy Spirit and has poured out what you now see and hear. For David did not ascend to heaven, and yet he said,
>
> > "The Lord said to my Lord:
> >
> > "Sit at my right hand
> >
> > until I make your enemies
> >
> > a footstool for your feet."

Jesus Christ now reigns at the right hand of God and he will continue to reign until every enemy is put under his feet. So in 1 Corinthians 15:24-26 Paul said: "Then the end will come, when he hands over the kingdom to God the Father after he has destroyed all dominion, authority and power. For he must reign until he has put all his enemies under his feet. The last enemy to be destroyed is death." God has already done it. Jesus reigns and rules now! We don't need to wait until some future time.

Some people say, "Well, if Jesus is reigning and ruling in the nations of men, why is it there is so much trouble in the world?" Well, it's because not all men have submitted to the reign of Jesus. The same was true in the Old Testament. God was reigning in the kingdoms of men, but there were those who failed to realize it and failed to submit themselves to the reign of Almighty God. But the fact continued to be that God was in charge. King Nebuchadnezzar was the most powerful ruler the world had ever known to his time. But Daniel 4:28-37 says:

> All this happened to King Nebuchadnezzar. Twelve months later, as the king was walking on the roof of the royal palace of Babylon, he said, "Is not this the great Babylon I have built as the royal residence, by my mighty power and for the glory of my majesty?"
>
> The words were still on his lips when a voice came from heaven, "This is what is decreed for you, King Nebuchadnezzar: Your royal authority has been taken from you. You will be driven away from people and will live with the wild animals; you will eat grass like cattle. Seven times will pass by for you until you acknowledge that the Most High is sovereign over the kingdoms of men and gives them to anyone he wishes."
>
> Immediately what had been said about Nebuchadnezzar was fulfilled. He was driven away from people and ate grass like cattle. His body was drenched with the dew of heaven until his hair grew like the feathers of an eagle and his nails like the claws of a bird.

At the end of that time, I, Nebuchadnezzar, raised my eyes toward heaven, and my sanity was restored. Then I praised the Most High; I honored and glorified him who lives forever.

His dominion is an eternal dominion;

his kingdom endures from generation to generation.

All the peoples of the earth

are regarded as nothing.

He does as he pleases

with the powers of heaven

and the peoples of the earth.

No one can hold back his hand

or say to him: "What have you done?"

At the same time that my sanity was restored, my honor and splendor were returned to me for the glory of my kingdom. My advisers and nobles sought me out, and I was restored to my throne and became even greater than before. Now I, Nebuchadnezzar, praise and exalt and glorify the King of heaven, because everything he does is right and all his ways are just. And those who walk in pride he is able to humble.

Nebuchadnezzar learned that God rules in the kingdom of men and he said "I…raised my eyes toward heaven, and my sanity was restored." I am convinced that we have to take our eyes off the political intrigue and conflict and chaos of our world and lift our eyes to heaven to see that God rules and reigns in the kingdoms of men and that he is the one who will bring his people triumphant to the end. We are not people who are slaves and servants to the world powers of this age. God has placed Jesus Christ on the throne.

Satan himself did not quite understand the picture. In Matthew 4, Satan came to Jesus in the wilderness to tempt him. And in verses 8 through 10 it says:

Again, the devil took him to a very high mountain and showed him all the kingdoms of the world and their splendor. "All this I will give you," he said, "if you will bow down and worship me."

Jesus said to him, "Away from me, Satan! For it is written: 'Worship the Lord your God, and serve him only.'"

Jesus made himself subject to the Father. Consequently, when he broke the bonds of death and rose to life again he said, "All authority in heaven and on earth has been given to me." Jesus Christ had gained the victory despite the temptations of Satan. By following the word of God, he came to be the one who has all authority in heaven and on earth.

But God's power is not to make us cower. John could only burst into praise when he heard and expressed the truth of Jesus Christ as prophet and priest and king, and he could only say: "To him who loves us and has freed us from our sins by his blood, and has made us to be a kingdom and priests to serve his God and Father—to him be glory and power for ever and ever! Amen." "To him who loves us"—he who rules the world loves us! He freed us from our sins. He washed us from our sins.

We're told in 1 Corinthians 6:11 about some who had been bound by sin and who had found themselves slaves of sinful ways. Paul said, "And that is what some of you were. But you were washed, you were sanctified, you were justified in the name of the Lord Jesus Christ and by the Spirit of our God." Paul tells us that Jesus Christ is the one who cleanses us of all sins. He himself in Acts 22:16 was told by Ananias to "Get up, be baptized and wash your sins away, calling on his name." That washing occurred in the blood of the Lamb.

In Hebrews 10:22 the writer said, "…let us draw near to God with a sincere heart in full assurance of faith, having our hearts sprinkled to cleanse us from a guilty conscience and having our bodies washed with pure water." We know our hearts are sprinkled by the blood of Jesus Christ because in verse 19 we are told to boldly "…enter the Most Holy Place by the blood of Jesus." Jesus shed his blood to cleanse us from our sins. He loved us. He washed us.

Jesus freed us from our sins, but he made us also to be a kingdom. Back in the Old Testament in Exodus 19:5-6, as the people of Israel approached Sinai there was a promise that God made to the people who were about to enter a covenant relationship with him. God said: "'Now if you obey me fully and keep my covenant, then out of all nations you will be my treasured possession. Although the whole earth is mine, you will be for me a kingdom of priests and a holy nation.' These are the words you are to speak to the Israelites." He made them a kingdom of priests, and when God established a new covenant through Jesus Christ with all mankind, he did it so he might establish a kingdom of priests. He made us to be a kingdom, and we enter that kingdom now, in this life. In John 3:5 Jesus said: "...unless a man is born of water and the Spirit, he cannot enter the kingdom of God." But you can enter the kingdom now if you are born again, born into the kingdom.

But he not only made us a kingdom, he made us to be priests. In 1 Peter 2:9-10, Peter expresses the grandeur of the whole thing when he says: "But you are a chosen people, a royal priesthood, a holy nation, a people belonging to God, that you may declare the praises of him who called you out of darkness into his wonderful light. Once you were not a people, but now you are the people of God; once you had not received mercy, but now you have received mercy." He who rules in the affairs of men and the kingdoms of men freed us from our sins and made us to be a kingdom and priests.

Priests in the Old Testament were ones who stood between the people and God. But there is no one standing between us and God now. He has elevated us to the position of priesthood so that we now offer our bodies as living sacrifices, holy and pleasing to God—which is our spiritual worship. You see, we are now able to have immediate access to God because he loves us. The king of the universe is one that you may address tonight as you go to bed and call him not, "the imperial majesty of the universe," but "my Father," because he loves you and because the king of the ages is your Father in heaven. In Revelation 5:9-10 we see a vision of heaven itself:

And they sang a new song:

"You are worthy to take the scroll

and to open its seals,

because you were slain,

and with your blood you purchased men for God

from every tribe and language and people and nation.

You have made them to be a kingdom and priests to

serve our God,

and they will reign on the earth."

We now reign on the earth as a kingdom and priests.

You say, "I don't understand." It's because we have been so caught up in the world's conception of power and authority and sovereignty that we do not even understand what happens to the spirit. When we allow our lives to come under the dominion of God, whether we are faced with trouble or hardship or persecution or famine or nakedness or danger or sword, we are more than conquerors through him who loves us. In him is the power to reign, the power to transcend earthly power and to actually enjoy that dominion with God himself where we reign with him. We are not slaves and servants in this earth to the powers of this world. But, rather, we are sons of God. That's what Paul is trying to tell us in Galatians chapter 4 when he says, beginning with verse 3:

So also, when we were children, we were in slavery under the basic principles of the world. But when the time had fully come, God sent his Son, born of a woman, born under law, to redeem those under law, that we might receive the full rights of sons. Because you are sons, God sent the Spirit of his Son into our hearts, the Spirit who calls out, "*Abba,* Father." So you are no longer a slave, but a son; and since you are a son, God has made you also an heir.

You are not slaves to this world. You are sons of God, and you are heirs of what he has provided for you of his promises and his blessings.

Go back to the Old Testament, in Daniel 7:13-14, and there is a prophecy concerning Jesus Christ. Listen to the words:

> "In my vision at night I looked, and there before me was one like a son of man, coming with the clouds of heaven. He approached the Ancient of Days and was led into his presence. He was given authority, glory and sovereign power; all peoples, nations and men of every language worshiped him. His dominion is an everlasting dominion that will not pass away, and his kingdom is one that will never be destroyed."

It was when Jesus, one like a son of man, came to the Ancient of Days, to the Father, that he was given dominion and glory and a kingdom, and his kingdom will last forever. When Jesus ascended into heaven and began to reign as King of kings and Lord of lords, he established the kingdom, a kingdom that will never be shaken, a kingdom in which you can be a participant and where you can reign.

One like a son of man is now seen in Revelation once again. This time as he is walking among the lampstands. In Revelation 1:12-13 John said:

> I turned around to see the voice that was speaking to me. And when I turned I saw seven golden lampstands, and among the lampstands was someone "like a son of man," dressed in a robe reaching down to his feet and with a golden sash around his chest.

We're told in verse 20 that the lampstands represent the churches. And so we see in Revelation chapter 1, Jesus walking among the churches. The one like a son of man, who now reigns at the right hand of God, has condescended to walk with his people in his church.

Right now you can walk hand in hand with the one who is the Savior of mankind, the one who is the creator of the universe, the one who is King of kings and Lord of lords and rules in the kingdoms of men. He is the one who is able to take you through life and lead you, finally, to an eternity with God. In Matthew 28:20 Jesus said, "And surely I will be with you always, to the very end of the age," because as long as the church continues in the world, Jesus continues to walk among his people, the church.

And right now we invite you to allow yourself to be washed in the blood of the Lamb, to allow the cleansing blood of Jesus to come and cleanse your conscience, that you might be born again of water and the Spirit, having your body washed with pure water and your heart sprinkled to cleanse you from a guilty conscience. Jesus will purchase you from among men, that you might be one of the people belonging to him, that you might reign with him on earth and, finally, be granted inheritance in the everlasting kingdom.

REVELATION 2:

The Overcomers

───────────✦───────────

Through the resurrection of Jesus Christ from the dead, he overcame death and made it possible for us, too, to become overcomers. As we come now to the 2nd chapter of Revelation, we read about how you can become overcomers.

In Revelation chapter 2, Jesus Christ is addressing a group of churches. These were very real churches that existed in some of the leading cities of Asia Minor in the first century. I believe that in the letters that are addressed to these churches we can see lessons applicable to the churches today and to us as individuals. We would like to look for a few minutes at some of the lessons I think are to be found in the letters to the churches of Asia Minor.

In chapters 2 and 3 of Revelation there are letters written to seven different churches. I believe it is significant that there are seven churches selected. There were more churches than that in Asia Minor. Through the New Testament we have references to other churches in the province of Asia that are not included here, but could well have been. But I believe that Jesus intentionally chose seven churches, and John reveals to us his words to seven churches, because the number seven itself is significant. It is used fifty-four times in the book of Revelation. It is a symbol of completeness. I believe we are seeing here an evidence of Jesus' conveying to us the idea that these words are for all the churches of all times.

The message was addressed specifically to specific problems that existed in each of these seven churches then, but I believe they are typical of the kinds of problems that are to be found in churches throughout the ages. Certainly, while they were addressed to churches in the first century in one part of the world, the message of these letters is clearly for all of us, because at the conclusion of each of these letters it is said, "He who has an ear, let him hear what the Spirit says to the churches." So, if you have an ear, then you're to hear this! Jesus wants you to get the message that is being spoken to these churches because it is also a message being spoken to us today.

As we look at these churches, one thing we notice immediately is that there is no particular ecclesiastical hierarchy indicated in these letters to these churches. They each stand alone. They are autonomous churches. There is no evidence of any kind of organization linking them together. The thing that ties these churches together is submission to the Spirit of God, not to some human hierarchy. The Spirit who regulated each one of them regulated all of them.

I believe it is also significant that while there are those today who say that we ought to hear the church, that is not what Revelation is saying to us. It is saying, "Let us hear what the Spirit says to the church." The church has no authority to make laws. The church has no authority to originate doctrines. The church is a body that receives the message of the Spirit of God, a message that has long ago been revealed, and it is our responsibility as a church today to hear the message of the Spirit. If every church on the face of this earth would permit itself to hear what the Spirit says to the churches, we would all be doing the same things, we would be speaking the same things and practicing the same things. Religious division would not exist. We are to hear what the Spirit says to the churches.

Now as we look at these churches, we don't have time to look at every detail about all that was said to each of them. However, we want to look at certain teachings that seem to be presented as of special importance. I believe these can be seen in certain expressions that are given by the Lord to each one of these seven churches. The first of these is, "I know." Seven times to the seven churches Jesus said, "I know." "I know your deeds." "I know your afflictions." "I know where you live." Jesus was saying to them, "I know all about you. You are my people. I know you like I know the palm of my hand. I am well aware of your circumstances," and that should be reassuring to all of us that Jesus knows and Jesus cares.

As we see these expressions of "I know," in some cases Jesus is saying, "I know the things you're doing that you shouldn't be doing." That may be a bit scary, but he also says, "I know your patience. I know your love. I know your deeds." He knows all about us. He understands. He knows our tribulations. He knows about where we are. He said, "I know where you live." "I know where you are." Jesus knows, he understands.

The second expression that is used to every one of these churches is, "To him who overcomes." There are several things he says about those who overcome. He says, for example, "To him who overcomes, I will give the right to eat from the tree of life, which is in the paradise of God." "He who overcomes will not be hurt at all by the second death." "To him who overcomes, I will give some of the hidden manna. I will also give him a white stone with a new name written on it, known only to him who receives it." "To him who overcomes and does my will to the end, I will give authority over the nations—'He will rule them with an iron scepter;'... I will also give him the morning star." Now even if we don't understand for sure what some of these details mean, the basic picture is clear. Jesus is saying to those who overcome, "I will give my reward. I will extend my blessings to those who overcome."

Those who overcome are explained to us in verse 26 of chapter 2 as those who do his will to the end. That's what overcoming means. Those people who keep the commandments of Jesus are overcomers, the ones who have the victory. So, we need to give attention to what Jesus teaches and what he commands, because those who do these things to the end are the ones who overcome, and over those, Jesus says, the second death will have no power.

We need not be uncertain about what he means there, because later on, toward the end of Revelation, he reveals to us that the second death means the fiery lake of burning sulfur. In other words, the second death is hell, and those who overcome will never experience hell. Those who overcome will escape the second death, which is separation from God. We are all going to experience the first death, unless Jesus should come first. We will all experience that separation of body and soul that we think of as death. But those who overcome will not experience that second separation, which is the separation from God himself.

Those who overcome will be given the hidden manna. I believe that refers to Jesus Christ himself, because in John 6 Jesus speaks of himself as the bread of life, comparing himself to the manna which was given to the people of Israel as they wandered in the wilderness. Here Jesus is saying he is the hidden manna. He is hidden from the world because the world does not accept him, but he is not hidden from those who do accept him. Jesus is saying in essence, "I am the bread of life. If you eat of me, then you will never hunger."

Jesus said, "I will also give him a white stone." This is for the overcomers too, and on the stone a new name is written "known only to him who receives it." I believe Jesus is saying the same thing as he is when he speaks of giving the hidden manna. Giving a white stone is saying in another way, "I am giving you myself," because a new name is written on the stone. In the Bible when you have that expression, that new name is referring to Jesus. The expression, "known only to him who receives it" is to say again that the world does not know Jesus. Jesus said, "The world does not know me, but my sheep hear my voice. They know me," and those who overcome the world are the ones who have Jesus in their lives.

Then, in 1 John 5:4-5, John said: "…for everyone born of God has overcome the world. This is the victory that has overcome the world, even our faith. Who is it that overcomes the world? Only he who believes that Jesus is the Son of God." These are the overcomers, those who believe that Jesus Christ is the Son of God and who keep his commandments. Jesus said to those who were his, in John 14 through 16 when he was speaking to his disciples, "I will come to you." Jesus comes to those who are his people with comfort, with strength that they need. He is the one who provides for our well-being.

But Jesus also says to the one who overcomes, "I will give authority over the nations—'He will rule them with an iron scepter.'" I would like you to look more carefully at this one in Revelation 2:26. Jesus said that

To him who overcomes and does my will to the end, I will give authority over the nations—

'He will rule them with an iron scepter.'"

he will dash them to pieces like pottery'—

just as I have received authority from my Father. I will also give him the morning star.

Last week we pointed out that those who are God's people rule and reign with him now. I think one of the most tragic misconceptions that has dominated the thinking of modern religion is the idea that someday Jesus is going to come back to earth and set up a throne in Jerusalem, and he is going to reign over the nations here on earth for a thousand years, and we're going to be over there reigning with him, etc. I believe that that is just as serious a misconception of what Revelation is talking about as was the Jews' misconception of the Messiah who came the first time.

The Jews, taking the Old Testament prophecies in the same light that many modern religionists take the prophecies of Revelation, assumed that Jesus, when he came the first time, was going to set up a throne in Jerusalem, and he was going to literally reign as a political leader among the nations of the earth and literally drive out the Roman occupation armies from Palestine. It is the same misunderstanding of the nature of prophecy that has caused many today to make the mistake the Jews made and think Jesus is going to come back here to earth and set up some kind of a political empire.

That isn't the case at all, but the fact is that Jesus is now already reigning in his kingdom, and those prophecies that are dealing with the kingdom are prophecies dealing with God's church or, ultimately, with heaven itself, the eternal kingdom. In Revelation 1, Jesus is spoken of as the ruler (present tense) of the kings of the earth. Revelation 1:6 says he, "…made us to be a kingdom and priests." The King James Version says he "made us kings." That also is true. We are a kingdom of kings. We are a royal priesthood. We reign right now. Romans 5 says that God's people right now are involved in a reign here on earth. It's already happening. We share in the reign of Jesus Christ.

In Romans 5:17 Paul said, "For if, by the trespass of the one man, death reigned through that one man, how much more will those who receive God's abundant provision of grace and of the gift of righteousness reign in life through the one man, Jesus Christ." We reign now. In life. Through Jesus Christ. We share in his reign. I think that's exactly what Jesus was trying to say in Revelation chapter 2 and verses 26 and 27 when he said to the one who overcomes:

> To him who overcomes and does my will to the end, I will
> give authority over the nations—
>
> 'He will rule them with an iron scepter;
>
> he will dash them to pieces as pottery'—
>
> just as I have received authority from my Father.

Jesus said, "I have received (past tense) authority from my Father." In other words, "I have already received authority and dominion over the nations, and to him who overcomes, I will give the same authority, and he will reign with me now here on this earth."

You say, "Well, I don't see myself as a king reigning over Afghanistan or Tibet or Germany—where's my kingdom?" Where is it? You're reigning over your own spirit, aren't you? And what is more important, that you should be able to rule your own spirit or that you should be able to rule France or Italy? You think about it. In the Old Testament there is a beautiful proverb that ought to put things in better perspective for us. Proverbs 16:32 says:

> Better a patient man than a warrior,
>
> a man who controls his temper than one
>
> who takes a city.

There are too many worldly-minded people who, when they think of reigning and ruling, think of some kind of a political empire and having some power over other people. God wants you to have power over your own passions. He wants you to learn to control your life. He wants you to be able to overcome those bad habits. The man who is able to overcome those bad habits, and the man who is able to control his temper, is greater, the scripture says, than one who takes a city. And surely, he is greater than one who rules a whole nation.

If we have the mind of Christ, and if we have any spiritual discernment at all, we ought to be able to see that what Jesus is trying to create is a people belonging to God, a people who are a holy nation, a royal priesthood. He wants a holy people. He doesn't necessarily want people with political power. He wants you to learn to control and to rule and to reign in your own life, in your own heart, and you can do that through his power. I believe what we are seeing is that we do reign in this life.

But if we see the battles in Revelation and we start thinking about Russia going to war against countries in the Middle East, we have missed what Revelation is all about. If we are so materially-minded and worldly-minded that we can only think in terms of world politics, then we have missed what Jesus came into this world to do. He wants to create a people who are a holy and righteous people, and that's what he is trying to accomplish in this world. When we read of the battles in Revelation, we're not seeing prophecies about what's going to happen to Israel and Egypt and Lebanon and Syria. Nor are we to watch the newspapers against the background of Revelation to see the significance of the movement of troops into Afghanistan. That isn't what Revelation is talking about.

Revelation is talking about something infinitely more profound and eternal than that. It's talking about the souls of men. It's talking about the conflict between God and Satan, between goodness and evil. It's talking about the battle for the minds of men. It's talking about the battle where Satan is overcoming so many people, causing them to live lives of slavery to sin. But God wants us not to be slaves, he wants us to be kings. He wants us to be able to rule our passions, to rule our lives, to have dominion over ourselves. He wants to give us the power to overcome the world, and you don't overcome the world by going out with a sword and defeating some great, impressive power. You overcome the world by being able to look Satan in the eye and say, "I won't do what you want me to do because Jesus is my Lord." There's the man who is the overcomer.

Remember, Jesus said when he came out of the grave, "All authority in heaven and on earth has been given to me." All right, what was the authority to be used for? Was it to drive the Romans out or someday two thousand years in the future to drive Russia out of someplace? That's not what his authority and power in heaven and on earth is for. It is to take men and make them disciples.

On the basis of his authority as King of kings and Lord of lords, he says to his people, "…go and make disciples of all nations; you're going to rule them with an iron scepter." How? By allowing Jesus to control and dominate the lives of the people, by letting him be the Lord, by letting him be the Master of their lives, not letting Satan have dominion anymore. So, you go and "…make disciples of all nations, baptizing them in the name of the Father and of the Son and of the Holy Spirit, and teaching them to obey everything I have commanded you. And surely I will be with you always, to the very end of the age." These are the overcomers. These are the ones who will have a part in the tree of life in the paradise of God. Hebrews 1:3 says about Jesus, "After he had provided purification for sins, he sat down at the right hand of the Majesty in heaven." Jesus already reigns. Verse 13 says,

> To which of the angels did God ever say,
>
> "Sit at my right hand
>
> until I make your enemies
>
> a footstool for your feet"?

Jesus is reigning while he is sitting on the throne. His sitting on the throne is simultaneous with his reign over his enemies, and so it is with the Christian.

I want you to look now and compare that with Ephesians chapter 2 beginning at verse 4. I want you to see the part the Christian has in all of this. Paul said,

> But because of his great love for us, God who is rich in mercy, made us alive with Christ even when we were dead in transgressions—it is by grace you have been saved. And God raised us up

with Christ and seated us with him in the heavenly realms in Christ Jesus....

We sit with Christ in the heavenly realms. That's present tense. He's done that for us. He said that we reign with him here on the earth now. So, as we sit with him on the throne, we too share in his reign "in order that in the coming ages he might show the incomparable riches of his grace, expressed in his kindness to us in Christ Jesus" (Ephesians 2:7).

That all fits in with Revelation 5:9-10, where in heaven itself:

> ...they sang a new song:
>
> > "You are worthy to take the scroll
> >
> > and to open its seals,
> >
> > because you were slain,
> >
> > and with your blood you purchased men for God
> >
> > from every tribe and language and people and nation.
> >
> > You have made them to be a kingdom and priests...."

They reign with Jesus who sits at the right hand of the majesty on high, and we sit with him and share in that reign. So in Ephesians 1:20-23 Paul speaks of what God

> ...exerted in Christ when he raised him from the dead and seated him at his right hand in the heavenly realms, far above all rule and authority, power and dominion, and every title that can be given, not only in the present age but also in the one to come. And God placed all things under his feet and appointed him to be head over everything for the church, which is his body, the fullness of him who fills everything in every way.

What this is really saying is that God put all things under Jesus' feet and appointed him to be head over everything *for the benefit of the church*, because the church is God's kingdom and we are his people.

We share with him in his reign and in his rule today. When we overcome Satan in this life—I don't care if you're in a prison, I don't care if you're bound in chains—you have overcome if you're able to say to Satan, "I will not yield to your temptations." Then you have been able to show that Jesus reigns in your life, and you share with him in that reign and dominion over Satan, because sin is not your master. You were bought at a price, and therefore you honor God with your body. I want us to understand that Jesus Christ is providing for us now, in this time, power to rule, the power to one day be able to enjoy the presence of Jesus forever.

Finally, Jesus says to the one who overcomes, "I will give him the morning star." The beautiful part about that is that in Revelation 22:16 he says, "I am… the bright Morning Star." He will come and live in us and reign in us and bless our lives. Let us never think of ourselves as mere slaves and servants and ones who are put down, but let us hold our heads high because Jesus has given to us authority and power and dominion over sin and over Satan so that we can reign, not only now, but forever, and share in the reign of Jesus Christ.

If you're not a Christian, then you are overlooking something that is missing in your life, because Jesus wants you to have this power to overcome. So he says, "Be faithful, even to the point of death, and I will give you the crown of life." That's for you: blessings now, in this time, and in the world to come, eternal life with the Father. If you believe in Jesus and will repent of your sins and confess your faith in him, won't you come now and be baptized into Christ to begin a new life with him?

REVELATION 3:
The Christian Endurance Race

There are three letters in the 3rd chapter of Revelation that are addressed from Jesus to three different churches. There are several lessons that are taught in each of these letters, and we do not have time in the space of a single lesson to look at all there is to be found in these letters. So we must limit ourselves, and what I have tried to do is to see what lesson predominates. What is there that seems to be central in the messages to these churches?

As I was studying the 3rd chapter there was one thing that seemed to strike me particularly, and then as I went back and looked at the 2nd chapter again I noticed it occurring again and again, and that theme is one that can be expressed in several ways. One way of putting it is that the Christian life is a long distance race. It is not a sprint. Maybe with the Olympics coming up, we can express some of these in track terms, and that's one of them. The Christian life is a life of endurance. Practically all the teachings of scripture are designed in such a way as to build us up for the long haul. They try to give us stamina, try to give us strength for a lifetime of service and a lifetime of activity that will be against great pressures and great difficulties.

Jesus never tried to make anyone think that the Christian life is easy. His own life led to a cross, and he says that you, too, will suffer persecution. If that is the case, it means that we have got to have fortitude. We have got to have endurance. This is a theme that is found in the message to each of these churches, which then should be taken as a message to the church as a whole for all times, and a message we very much need. So I would like to call your attention to certain portions of these letters that I think emphasize this point. Hopefully we can pick up a point or two that will help us to gain this kind of endurance.

In Revelation 3:2, in the letter to the church in Sardis, Jesus said, "Wake up! Strengthen what remains and is about to die, for I have not found your deeds complete in the sight of my God." I think the word "complete" calls our attention to the fact that it is easy for people to begin well. If you are like I am, you started quite a lot of projects in your lifetime that you never did really finish for one reason or another. They just died. And from time to time in the church you try to initiate various programs and activities, and in the passing of time they just seem to die. They do not just come to a screeching halt. They just die a slow death. And I believe that I've seen, and you've probably seen, that happen to many Christian lives. It's not so often that you see a Christian all fired up and enthusiastic who then, one day, drops it all and that's the end of it. Usually the spark and enthusiasm slowly die and spiritual life vanishes.

Jesus says here that you need to "strengthen what remains." It reminds me somewhat of the thought that you see in the first Psalm where the man who is the blessed man is one who is looking into the law of God and meditating on it day and night. He is the one who

…is like a tree planted by streams of water,

which yields its fruit in season

and whose leaf does not wither.

Whatever he does prospers.

One gets the picture of a tree that has put down roots that are solid and is drinking up the moisture and bearing fruit. A man like this is meditating day and night on the law of God. This is something that we must do, I am convinced, if we are going to survive in this Christian experience. If we are going to excel, we have to allow God's word to be our meditation constantly. It is our source of strength, our source of guidance and direction.

Then Jesus says also in that 3rd chapter of Revelation, in verse 2, that "I have not found your deeds complete." We need to work on the business of beginning those things that are good and then continuing in them and not slacking up. Now, how are we going to be able to do that? I believe the next verse gives us a clue. He says, "Remember, therefore, what you have received and heard; obey it, and repent." After discussing the fact that they were lacking in this matter of endurance, he says, "I want you to remember." Memory is a powerful device if it is properly used and disciplined. He wants them to remember the beginning of their Christian life, the enthusiasm, commitment, and conviction with which they entered it, to remember what it was that caused that conviction.

What did you see at that time? What was there that you noticed about the Christian life that attracted you to it? Remember? Think. Think back to the good times, the times when you were filled with enthusiasm. What was happening then that was creating that enthusiasm? If we remember and will think and look back and keep those things before our minds, then, perhaps, we can latch on to that same enthusiasm again and we can see and possess those things that created that initial conviction and enthusiasm for God's purpose.

The matter of endurance is mentioned again in verse 5. Jesus says, "He who overcomes will, like them, be dressed in white. I will never erase his name from the book of life, but will acknowledge his name before my Father and his angels." He says of him who overcomes, I will "never erase his name from the book of life."

And later in Revelation you will see the great scene of the judgment where the books were opened and another book was opened which was the book of life. The names of God's righteous people had been written in that book, and the dead were judged according to what they had done as recorded in the books. I take that to be the books of the Bible, because the only fair way that judgment could be done would be by comparing our lives with what God had already revealed to us. It is not fair for a teacher to give a test from material the students have not studied, and I think God is fair. He is not going to bring us to the judgment and open up another set of books we have never seen before and say,

"Here is what you are going to be judged by." No, he is going to open books he has given us all along, and we are going to be judged by them.

Those who gain entrance into the eternal kingdom are those whose names are written in the book of life. But what he says here is that he will not erase the name of the one who overcomes from the book of life. Your name will stay there if you overcome, if you endure to the end. Essentially what he is saying is, "Endure, or else." And this, along with many other verses in the New Testament, says clearly and unequivocally that a Christian can be lost. A person who has experienced the grace of God and salvation and who has been born again is not automatically guaranteed a ticket into heaven. He must be faithful, even to the point of death, if he is to receive the crown of life. That is why exhortations are continually given to the church to be faithful, to endure, to hold fast, to keep on, because we need that or we won't. We must have this kind of encouragement.

In verse 11, in the next letter, the one to the church in Philadelphia, Jesus says, "I am coming soon. Hold on to what you have, so that no one will take your crown." Here is the same message again. Hold on to what you have so no one will take your crown away from you—that is, the crown of life. That's a conditional thing. The crown of life is for those who hold on to what they have, and if you don't hold on, you lose that reward.

Let's back up for a moment to the 2nd chapter. I just want to quickly show you that this thing is taught to every one of these churches. Let's look again at the short letter to the church in Ephesus in chapter 2, verse 3: "You have persevered and have endured hardships for my name, and have not grown weary." He is commending the people in the church in Ephesus because they had perseverance. That means steadfastness. You just keep on. You have borne the burden of the work and the heat of the day. Here are people then who have not grown weary.

We are told in Galatians 6:9, "Let us not become weary in doing good, for at the proper time we will reap a harvest if we do not give up." The time is coming. That is an absolute guarantee of God. That's the beauty of this. That's the thing that I think can help us to keep on. That which God promises us is the one certainty in the whole universe, that if you are faithful to God to the day you die, you will receive heaven. There is no way it can be otherwise. If you want a one-hundred percent guarantee on anything in life, that is it! All you have to do is just keep on living faithfully to God, and you are going to receive the crown of life. That's the assurance the Christian has. Now, granted, that is easier said than done. But, still, the fact remains that God has assured you that what you have to do is not something spectacular, just something steady. Just keep at it. That's what God wants of us.

Now look at Revelation 2:10, this time to the church in Smyrna: "Do not be afraid of what you are about to suffer. I tell you, the devil will put some of you in prison to test you, and you will suffer persecution for ten days. Be faithful, even to the point of death, and I will give you the crown of life." He's saying to them, "Look, you people are in serious trouble. You've got some problems coming; you've got some tremendous suffering to go through." That doesn't encourage anybody. So, immediately he adds: "Look, just be faithful until death, and I will give you the crown of life."

That's worth it all. What more could you want out of life than to be able to live forever with God and enjoy all the blessings of God forever, without any of the curses of life? That's the greatest thing that could ever happen. You take all the pleasures of this life and all the thrills and temporary excitements that the world can give you, and nothing can compare to this one thing. And it doesn't take a man who is a millionaire to do it, it doesn't take a man who has an I.Q. of 180, it doesn't take a man who has four doctoral degrees, it doesn't take a man who is the most skillful athlete in the world. All it takes is an ordinary person, anybody who will just stick with it and keep on going. Anyone! All it takes is will. It takes the will and determination to keep on going for God.

Now notice what Jesus said to the church in Pergamum in Revelation 2:13: "I know where you live—where Satan has his throne. Yet you remain true to my name. You did not renounce your faith in me, even in the days of Antipas, my faithful witness, who was put to death in your city—where Satan lives." Here the church had undergone a terrible ordeal where one of their number was actually put to death for his faith. But Jesus said, "You held fast to my name and you did not deny my faith." That's what God wants, people who will stand up for him and stick with him all the way.

Now look at Revelation 2:19, to the church in Thyatira: "I know your deeds, your love and faith, your service and perseverance, and that you are now doing more than you did at first." Now look at verse 25: "Only hold on to what you have until I come." You say, "You keep saying the same thing over and over again." Sure, I am. That's what Jesus kept saying over and over again. He wants you to get that message. You have to hang in there; you can't give up. You've got to keep after it. Don't slack up, don't give in, don't compromise, but just keep on with God.

Now let's go to chapter 3 again. Look at verses 15 through 16, this time to the church in Laodicea. Jesus says, "I know your deeds, that you are neither cold nor hot. I wish you were either one or the other! So, because you are luke-warm—neither hot nor cold—I am about to spit you out of my mouth." The one thing God does not want is lukewarm church members. He does not want somebody who is just complacent and sitting back and watching everybody do whatever they do. He wants people who are hot, and that word is a word that—sometimes, at least—means boiling. It means a person who is on fire, blazing with fervor and zeal for God.

Now that doesn't mean you have to jump up and down and clap your hands twenty-four hours a day to be zealous and on fire. But it means you're to be a person who really has a burning desire and concern for the advancement of the purposes of God. It means you are to be devoted and dedicated to doing all that you can with the talents God has given you to contribute what you can to furthering the cause of God in our world. He wants people who are hot, people who are burning and on fire for God. Jeremiah said,

> …his word is in my heart like a burning fire,
>
> shut up in my bones.
>
> I am weary of holding it in;
>
> indeed, I cannot. (Jeremiah 20:9)

The Christian has a message that must be spoken to others.

Now, unfortunately, there was something wrong with the church in Laodicea: they were lukewarm. Part of the reason they did not have this zeal which they needed to endure and hold fast was, as is said in verse 17: "You say, 'I am rich; I have acquired wealth and do not need a thing.' But you do not realize that you are wretched, pitiful, poor, blind and naked." Here were people who were blind to realities.

There were some things they were not seeing, and they weren't seeing those things because they had forgotten certain important things. What is it that causes spiritual blindness? Well, let's go back to 2 Peter 1:5. Peter says: "For this very reason, make every effort to add to your faith goodness; and to goodness, knowledge; and to knowledge, self-control; and to self-control, perseverance; and to perseverance, godliness; and to godliness, brotherly kindness; and to brotherly kindness, love." In other words, just keep on throughout your life adding and growing and developing all of these qualities and characteristics. Peter continues: "For if you possess these qualities in increasing measure, they will keep you from being ineffective and unproductive in your knowledge of our Lord Jesus Christ." Now notice verse 9: "But if anyone does not have them, he is nearsighted and blind." Why is he blind? Because he "has forgotten that he has been cleansed from his past sins."

Do you remember what it was like when you lived in fear from day to day knowing that you might die at any moment? You realized, "There is no hope for me; I have no confidence or assurance whatsoever that God is pleased with me, that God can accept me. If I died today I would be lost, and I would spend eternity in hell." You can't live that way, with that kind of realization. Somewhere down deep inside of every man who is in that condition there is that knowledge and, in the back of the mind, an awareness that takes the pleasure out of life because there is a realization that "I am alienated from God and there is something wrong with me. My life is twisted out of shape. It's bent out of shape. I'm not what I ought to be. There is a sickness in my soul. There is something missing. There is a vacuum that God must fill."

But these people had forgotten the cleansing from their sins and what it means to have that relief and to know that, "if I were to die tonight when everything is well with my soul, I know that God loves me. He has forgiven me." He loves us all but, unfortunately, not all of us have accepted the expression of his love to us, and done that which provides for us the cleansing of our sins. So there will always be that misery and knowledge that something is wrong because "I am not right with God." Here were people who did not have zest for life and zeal for God, having forgotten the cleansing of their own sins.

Now, reading on in that passage of 2 Peter 1, in verse 10 he says: "Therefore, my brothers, be all the more eager to make your calling and election sure." Don't let your life go on with this kind of half-heartedness and this uncertainty about your relationship to God. Make that calling and election sure. He says, "For if you do these things, you will never fall, and you will receive a rich welcome into the eternal kingdom of our Lord and Savior Jesus Christ." He is lavishly providing for you the kingdom that is everlasting, but it requires, on your part, diligence and faithfulness and fidelity.

Now, returning to our text again in Revelation chapter 3, look at verse 19. Jesus says, "Those whom I love I rebuke and discipline. So be earnest, and repent." We must have zeal for God.

Next comes one of the more famous passages from the Bible. In verse 20 of Revelation 3, Jesus said, "Here I am! I stand at the door and knock. If anyone hears my voice and opens the door, I will go in and eat with him, and he with me." Contrary to the way it is commonly used, this is not an invitation to those who have never begun to live with God. This is a statement written to Christians. Jesus is speaking to Christians. He is speaking to people in the church. "I am standing at your door, the door of your heart, and I am knocking and I want to come in." He is not talking about men who are alienated from God, who have never known the cleansing of their sins.

He is talking to lukewarm church members, and he says, "I want to fill you with my own presence in your life, and I am knocking at the door of your heart. Let me come in." Now the broader application, of course, would still be true. Jesus wants to come into the hearts of those who have never made a commitment to him. But, unfortunately, many of us have driven Jesus out of our lives and our hearts and have become an indifferent people. Jesus wants to come back into our hearts and our lives, and so he says to us—those who are in the church, "Here I am! I stand at the door and knock. If anyone hears my voice and opens the door, I will go in and eat with him, and he with me."

I heard a story about a father who took his little girl to an art gallery, and there was hanging on one of the walls a picture that many of you might have seen. It's a picture of a man who is standing at the door of a house, and he is in a posture of knocking on the door. In the picture it is obvious that the person who is there is Jesus. But the little girl was not familiar with this kind of art work and couldn't quite get what this was about. So she said, "Daddy, who is that man in the picture?"

And he said, "That is Jesus."

And the little girl said, "What's he doing?"

And he said, "Well, he's knocking at the door of that person's house."

And she said, "Daddy, why aren't they opening the door? Why aren't they letting him come in?"

Now the father was getting kind of irritated because he wanted to get on his way, and the little girl tugged at him and again said, "Daddy, don't you know why they would do this?"

Again he just shrugged it off and said, "No, I don't know."

That night the little girl, seeming not to be able to get that thing out of her mind, brought it up again. Little children do this. I don't know why, but they just get stuck on something that we don't think is important when it really is important to them. So that little girl said again that night, "Daddy, remember that picture we saw this afternoon?"

And he thought to himself, "Oh, no, here we go again."

And she said, "Daddy, why wouldn't they let Jesus into their house?"

Well, nothing else seemed to work, so he finally just said, "I guess they were mean and mad," and that seemed to make sense to her, and that was the end of the conversation. But he went to bed that night and couldn't get that out of his mind, and he lay in bed and tossed and turned. Finally, as it began to work on him, he began to think more seriously about that picture and began asking himself, "Why don't I let Jesus come into my heart?"

Sometimes it takes strange things like that to make an impression on us. But why would you keep Jesus out of your life? Is it because you're mean and mad? Is there any good reason not to let the loveliest person who ever lived enter your life and try to make something beautiful out of it? What are you making of your life? You are making a temple, or you are making a tomb. Is your heart filled with lovely things and the goodness and the love of God that overflows in kindness toward others, or is your life totally dominated with self-ishness and self-centeredness and interest only in yourself? Jesus continues to stand at the door and knock, and we continue either to refuse entrance or to allow him to come in.

But, hopefully, we are like those that Jesus speaks of in the very next verse: "To him who overcomes, I will give the right to sit with me on my throne, just as I overcame and sat down with my Father on his throne." Think of that. Jesus Christ wants to take you and to bring you to the throne where he sits with his Father, Almighty God, and he invites you to sit down there and share a place at home with him where you will reign with him forever and ever. Would you shut him out of your life? He invites you to him, and we encourage you to come to him, to believe in him, to repent of your sins, and to be baptized into him to begin that great life that never ends.

REVELATION 4:

From the Footstool to the Throne

We are studying the 4th chapter of Revelation. Homer Hailey, in his commentary on Revelation, made this statement:

> To the literalistic mind, lacking the power of imagination, Revelation will forever be a sealed book; to the speculative and visionary mind the book will provide fuel to inflame far-fetched assumptions and conjectures which totally miss the truth. But to the mind prepared by the rest of the Bible for reality in picture and action, impressions of truth will be made that give strength for victory in every conflict of life.

I believe that's a fine statement of the way in which Revelation should be approached. It is not a book designed to fuel far-fetched conjectures. It's not a book in which everything is to be taken literally, because it's a book of symbols. It is a book that is to be read against the background of the whole Bible and interpreted in the context of the Bible. It is a book that is designed to give us inspiration to face the trials and problems of day-to-day living.

We have seen in Revelation chapters 2 and 3 a portrayal of seven churches of Asia in their triumphs and tragedies. We have seen the churches being exhorted to overcome, because God knew they were going to face trials. God knew it would be very easy to become weary in doing good and to give up, to slacken their efforts to please God. So something was needed to lift their spirits, to boost their morale, and to encourage people under pressure. I believe that Revelation always has been and always will be a solution and answer to the needs of a weary people who are struggling against the forces of evil and against Satan himself in order to overcome and receive the crown of life.

I want to introduce the 4th chapter of Revelation by reading to you the 1st chapter of the book of Ezekiel. That will be followed immediately with the reading of the 4th chapter of Revelation. I believe when I have finished reading you will understand why I have read them together. [Please read Ezekiel 1 and Revelation 4 before continuing.]

John is attempting to express for us that which is virtually inexpressible. He is trying to say to us in the most poetic language, the language of symbols and imagery, something of the majesty and glory of God. This is something that cannot be accomplished in a simple statement, but something that might be painted with pictures of words to try to convey to us the majesty of God.

It is easy for us, bound as we are by the flesh and living in a sinful world, to have our minds constantly preoccupied with the problems and troubles and the suffering and the strife and the tensions and pressures that are about us. But from time to time, out of the middle of this, and with frequency, we need to lift our eyes and see that beyond the problems of this world there is a God who is in charge. There is a God who created us, who loves us, and who has prepared for us things that words cannot describe. And we must always keep before us the reality of the throne of God and of his power and his majesty so that we will not be overwhelmed by the difficulties that face us day by day.

In chapters 2 and 3 of Revelation, John has shown us the churches with all their weaknesses, with all their troubles and struggles. Now we need to brace ourselves for what is to come, because, shortly, as we move into the central portion of Revelation, we are going to be faced with all those nightmarish spectacles of terrors and horrors that are going to be inflicted on the whole world. God's people are going to be among those who suffer many of the calamities and difficulties that are to be seen, and God's people need strength. There are going to be times when we will be tempted to say, "It's no use, Satan is the victor." Then we need to keep before us that which is central and is of supreme importance to us. And that is to keep in mind that God still reigns, that he is still on the throne, that his people are going to be protected and preserved, and that, finally, Satan himself will be destroyed, and God's people will gain the victory.

So, as we come to chapter 4, before we get into the horrible conflicts and struggles that we are soon to see in chapter 6 and following, we are lifted up and the door of heaven is open and we see the throne of God. And John said, "After this I looked, and there before me was a door standing open in heaven. And the voice I had first heard speaking to me like a trumpet said, 'Come up here, and I will show you what must take place after this.' At once I was in the Spirit." You recall that back in the 1st chapter we are told that John was in the Spirit on the Lord's day. John is now about to see a remarkable vision.

You know, Stephen, as he was being stoned to death, as we read in the 7th chapter of the book of Acts, saw Jesus standing at the right hand of the throne of God. Yet, all the while, he was also conscious of the struggle that was around him and of the stones that were being hurled at his body. So, even while he was gazing into heaven, he could still speak of those about him and say, "…do not hold this sin against them."

But, now, John seems to be lifted to a higher plane than that, because it's just as though all the surroundings have been taken away and shut off from him. Now he is caught up in the Spirit, and his total vision is of the splendor of the throne of God. So he speaks and says,

> …and there before me was a throne in heaven with someone sitting on it. And the one who sat there had the appearance of jasper and carnelian. A rainbow, resembling an emerald, encircled the throne. Surrounding the throne were twenty-four other thrones, and seated on them were twenty-four elders. They were dressed in white and had crowns of gold on their heads. From the throne came flashes of lightning, rumblings and peals of thunder. Before the throne, seven lamps were blazing. These are the seven

spirits of God. Also before the throne there was what looked like a sea of glass, clear as crystal.

In the center, around the throne, were four living creatures, and they were covered with eyes, in front and in back.

John could have said, "I saw a throne, and on the throne was God," but he didn't say that. That would be simple, prosaic. It would get the matter out of the way, and we could move on. But John wants us to stand in awe, to gaze on that scene for a while, to drink it in and see its beauty. He wants to say something more than simply, "God was on the throne," so he paints word pictures for us. He says there's one sitting on the throne, and he looks like jasper and carnelian—beautiful, white and clear and red. Here's one who is altogether beautiful, altogether lovely to behold.

Then he goes on and says there was a rainbow around the throne. It reminds us of the rainbow that we saw once before in the Bible when Noah was made a promise, a promise which we now know was a faithful promise of God. For when we see the rainbow, we are reminded that God's promise that he would never again destroy the world with a flood has continued to be true even to our present time. And so, when John speaks of God, he is not just saying, "There's God," but he is saying, "Here is one who is beautiful, and here is one who is faithful to his promises." Here we see the rainbow suggesting the faithfulness and fidelity and care of God and the concern for his people.

But then we see another picture. Out of the throne come flashes of lightning and rumblings and peals of thunder. God is also a God of judgment, a God who puts terror into the hearts of those who would oppose him, a God who overcomes those who oppose him, a God who will send his son, Jesus, in flaming fire, taking vengeance on those who disobey God. Out of the throne come flashes of lightning, rumblings and peals of thunder. It's an awesome scene that John has been privileged to view, and he has tried to convey to us something of its splendor and majesty so we might be caused to exclaim with those before the throne,

"Holy, holy, holy

is the Lord God Almighty,

who was, and is, and is to come."

Now notice in verse 4: "Surrounding the throne were twenty-four other thrones, and seated on them were twenty-four elders. They were dressed in white and had crowns of gold on their heads." Who were these twenty-four elders sitting on the thrones around the throne of God? I believe they represent the righteous ones under both the old and new covenants. They represent the holy ones of Israel and the holy ones of the new Israel. These are the redeemed. These are God's people from every age who are sitting around the throne on thrones themselves, because they reign with God, as we have suggested before.

In Revelation, the 21st chapter, we see the new Jerusalem. In verse 12 we are told: "It had a great, high wall with twelve gates, and with twelve angels at the gates. On the gates were written the names of the twelve tribes of Israel." Verse 14 says, "The wall of the city had twelve foundations, and on them were the names of the twelve apostles of the Lamb." Here, on the gates and on the foundations of the wall of the new Jerusalem, are the names of the twenty-four representatives of the old covenant that God made through Moses and the new covenant that God made through Christ. No wonder in Revelation 15:3 the redeemed of all the ages gather around the throne of God, and they sing the song of Moses and the Lamb.

Now we see another picture in verses 6-7 of our text:

Also before the throne there was what looked like a sea of glass, clear as crystal.

In the center, around the throne, were four living creatures, and they were covered with eyes, in front and in back. The first living creature was like a lion, the second was like an ox, the third had a face like a man, the fourth was like a flying eagle.

Who are these strange creatures? I read earlier from Ezekiel chapter 1 because I wanted you to see that John is borrowing the language that was being used by a prophet of the Old Testament, Ezekiel. The heavens were opened to him, and he saw visions of God and he saw four creatures corresponding to the four creatures in Revelation 4. You see a rainbow in Ezekiel 1, and you see a rainbow in Revelation 4. You see the creatures around the throne in each place. Who were these creatures in Ezekiel? Well, we turn now to Ezekiel the 10th chapter, because Ezekiel does not leave us speculating too long. In Ezekiel 10 and verse 20 he says, "These were the living creatures I had seen beneath the God of Israel by the Kebar River, and I realized that they were cherubim." These were the cherubim, the angels of God, and that's what John was seeing before the throne.

Now John could have said to us, "I saw God on the throne and I saw angels around the throne," and then he could have moved on. But he wants us to spend some time surveying the majesty of God and being filled with awe as we see the spectacle. And so he paints a word picture for us to try to help us see that there is something spectacular here, something that is simply beyond expression. Here the holy angels of God are described, and they are awesome. The first creature was like a lion, probably suggesting strength. The second was like an ox, suggesting, perhaps, the idea of strength also. The third had a face like a man, perhaps suggesting intellect. And the fourth was like a flying eagle, perhaps suggesting swiftness, swiftness to do the will of God.

It almost reminds us of the prayer that Jesus said ought to be prayed:

"Our Father in heaven,

hallowed be your name,

your kingdom come,

your will be done

on earth as it is in heaven."

And in heaven we see the will of God being done swiftly. When God, as we will see later in Revelation, is ready to make his move against the oppressors of God's people, there is no delay. But, at once, fire is thrown to the earth as God responds to his people's pleas. And the cry, "How long?" is finally answered in God's time. And when he is ready, there is no longer a delay, but the angels of God respond at once in obedience to him.

Why do they do so? Because they have lived with God from the creation. They have been in the very presence of God and they understand what we can, only in our wildest dreams, begin to imagine of the greatness of God. They know that he is one to be loved and adored and worshiped and served for ever and ever. And so we are told that these creatures, these angels of God,

Day and night…never stop saying:

"Holy, holy, holy

is the Lord God Almighty,

who was, and is, and is to come."

Here we see God surrounded in heaven by the representatives of the redeemed of all the ages and surrounded by the heavenly beings, and all of heaven and all of earth bow before the throne of God and ascribe to him glory and honor and power and they say, "Holy, holy, holy is the Lord God Almighty."

And then we see that:

Whenever the living creatures give glory, honor and thanks to him who sits on the throne and who lives for ever and ever, the twenty-four elders fall down before him who sits on the throne, and worship him who lives for ever and ever. They lay their crowns before the throne and say:

"You are worthy, our Lord and God,

to receive glory and honor and power,

for you created all things,

and by your will they were created

and have their being."

It is as though from eternity they existed as an idea in the mind of God, but, finally, God brought into reality that which existed ideally and now, not only they were, but they were created. Now God has granted to them a position of honor and glory before the very throne of God where they ascribe honor to him.

In this great scene of heaven opened, the center of the scene is God himself, and all else around him focus attention on him. He is the one worthy of honor and glory. He is not only the one who created, but he is the one who bought them from among all the tribes and languages and nations by the blood of the Lamb. So they throw their crowns before him and say, "You are worthy, our Lord and God, to receive glory." It's an amazing scene, and we need to realize in the middle of all our petty problems and struggles that Almighty God sits on his throne. He is well aware of our needs and our troubles and our trials, and he cares. He is the God of power who created us all, a God of majesty and holiness and a God who will not let his people down. He is a God who has reserved for his people a crown of life which will be given to all who have longed for his appearing and to all those who are faithful, even to the point of death.

If you are not one of God's children, then surely you have missed out on what life is really about. The Christian life is not a strange and meaningless struggle against all odds here on earth, but is a triumphant life lived in hope and anticipation because of the certainty of the faithfulness and the truthfulness of Almighty God. He loves you, and he let Jesus die for you. In the next lesson, we are going to see one join God who sits on the throne, and then you are going to find something even more marvelous yet about the power and the majesty and the greatness of that throne. Let us simply say now, "Why not give your life to this one, the only one who really can bring you satisfaction and victory?" If you believe in Jesus, won't you surrender your life to him and be baptized into him?

REVELATION 5:

"Weep Not; Behold the Lamb"

We have finally come to the climax of the Bible, the book of Revelation. We are in the middle of studying Revelation, and we have come to the 5th chapter. Here is where the drama really begins. We have seen enough already to excite us. We have seen the church—with all its tribulations, difficulties, triumphs, victories, hardships, and persecutions—experiencing all the ordeals that have been common to the people of God from the beginning. But we have also seen a church that can easily become discouraged, a church that has seen persecution come so often. And, I am sure, on the part of many there must be the question as to whether or not God is really in control of things. So, in chapter 4 we are lifted out of the worldly scene and taken into heaven. There we see the throne of God, and we see one sitting on the throne who is described in all his majesty. We see the living creatures around the throne day and night saying,

> "Holy, holy, holy
>
> is the Lord God Almighty,
>
> who was, and is, and is to come."

Now we come to chapter 5 of Revelation, and if we were to pick a single phrase out of Revelation chapter 5 that might very well serve as the theme of the chapter it would be the words that are found in verse 5: "Do not weep! See the Lion." Those six words suggest something very exciting, and I believe we will see it as we work our way through this 5th chapter.

In verse 1 of chapter 5, John said: "Then I saw in the right hand of him who sat on the throne a scroll with writing on both sides and sealed with seven seals." Of course, books in those days were not put together the same way books are today. This was a scroll, and it was sealed with seven seals. It was an unusual scroll, because usually scrolls had writing only on one side. But this one had writing on the front and back, suggesting, it seems to me, a book that is crammed with information and completely filled. As we move along, we see why. As the seals are removed one by one we see unveiled the purpose and the plan of God for his people and for the destiny of the universe. We see God acting in our world, and we see the forces of Satan trying to defeat the purpose of God.

In chapter 4 and verse 1 John had been promised: "Come up here, and I will show you what must take place after this." So it seems John is now about to see those things as the book is about to be opened. But a problem arises, as John says in Revelation 5:2-3: "And I saw a mighty angel proclaiming in a loud voice, 'Who is worthy to break the seals and open the scroll?' But no one in heaven or on earth or under the earth could open the scroll or even look inside it." So in verse 4 John said, "I wept and wept because no one was found who was worthy to open the scroll or look inside."

John was, at this point, terribly disappointed because he had been promised that he was going to be able to see the things that were to take place, and now the scroll which was going to show him these things could not be opened. There was no one worthy to open the scroll. Now, apparently, the one who would be worthy to open the scroll would be one who had sufficient moral worth, because what we are going to see revealed in this scroll are the moral judgments of God. And, apparently, the one who would be able to open the scroll and reveal the future would be one who could and would determine what the future would be.

So John was weeping and weeping, but in verse 5 he said: "Then one of the elders said to me, 'Do not weep! See, the Lion of the tribe of Judah, the Root of

David, has triumphed. He is able to open the scroll and its seven seals.'" What a sense of relief and joy! Now we do find at last that there is one who is worthy to open the scroll, and this one who is worthy to open the scroll is revealed to us, first, as being "the Lion," the Lion of the tribe of Judah. I believe that the expression originates in what occurred back in the beginning of the Bible, in Genesis chapter 49, beginning at verse 9, where Jacob was blessing his sons. He was, in his blessing, prophesying what was going to happen in the case of each of his sons, and he gives a description of the characters of his sons. In Genesis 49:9, Jacob finally comes to Judah, and he says:

> You are a lion's cub, O Judah;
>
> you return from the prey, my son.
>
> Like a lion he crouches and lies down,
>
> like a lioness—who dares to rouse him?
>
> The scepter will not depart from Judah,
>
> nor the ruler's staff from between his feet,
>
> until he comes to whom it belongs
>
> and the obedience of the nations is his.

Judah is identified in terms of a lion and then, in his prophecy, Jacob speaks in terms of one who would rule: "The scepter will not depart from Judah, nor the ruler's staff from between his feet." So, we are introduced now to the one who is the ultimate of what Judah is supposed to be. We see one who is described as "the Lion of the tribe of Judah."

"The root of David" is the second term to describe the one John sees. The prophecy of Isaiah seems to be the background for that expression, because it is used nowhere else in the New Testament. But Isaiah 11:1 says:

> A shoot will come up from the stump of Jesse;
>
> from his roots a Branch will bear fruit.

What we are seeing here is a description of Jesse's greater son. He is the one who is not only the Lion of the tribe of Judah, but one who is a branch out of the root of David, a descendant of David. So we have one who is a descendant of Judah and one who is a descendant of David.

Now an Old Testament expectation of the coming Messiah, as seen in Psalm 2:9, was one who would rule with an iron scepter. There was the Messianic expectation portrayed in the prophets and in the Psalms that the Messiah who was to come would be someone like David, who would sit on David's throne. To the Jew, David was the greatest king. David was the mighty warrior. He was the one who extended the empire to its furthest limits on the earth. He was the great hero, king of Israel. Now we see one who is going to rule the nations with an iron scepter. This was the expectation the Jews had of their Messiah who was to come.

There was another expectation, however, that was found among the prophets. That was of a suffering servant as seen, for example, in Isaiah 53:7:

> He was oppressed and afflicted,
>
> yet he did not open his mouth;
>
> he was led like a lamb to the slaughter,
>
> and as a sheep before her shearers is silent,
>
> so he did not open his mouth.

Here is Isaiah's very graphic portrayal of the suffering of Jesus Christ on the cross, prophesied in terms of a suffering servant of God.

Well, this, too, was the Messiah who was to come, and yet the Jews had difficulty putting the two ideas together. How could he be the king who rules with an iron scepter, and yet a suffering servant, one who is led like a lamb to the slaughter? The Jews of Jesus' day could only see their Messiah as a great ruler, the one who would sit on David's throne and drive the oppressive Roman armies out of the conquered land of Palestine. The Jewish mind simply could not harmonize that idea with the idea of a suffering servant, but Jesus in his ministry and in his life blended the two together.

In fact, God seems to have combined these two ideas of the kingship of David, on the one hand, and the suffering servant, on the other, when, at the baptism of Jesus, God said from heaven: "This is my Son, whom I love; with him I am well pleased." In Psalm 2:7 God had said: "You are my Son." That Psalm is one that emphasizes the concept of the Messiah as king, one with great power. But in Isaiah 42:1, God spoke of "my chosen one in whom I delight." And that particular passage in Isaiah 42 is speaking about the servant of the Lord. So God speaks about Jesus at his baptism in terms seemingly drawn from the Psalm portraying the Messiah as king and from the prophet speaking of the Messiah as a servant. Even at the beginning of Jesus' ministry, God seems to be pulling together what would have been familiar passages in the Jewish mind showing that this man Jesus is, in fact, the Messiah who fulfills both of the expectations of the prophets.

The one who is presented in this scene in Revelation as being worthy to open the scroll was announced first of all as "the Lion," but when John looked to see, he saw something entirely different. He saw, of all things, a Lamb. What a strange contrast: the Lion and the Lamb! But they are one and the same! Both are blended into one personality. Notice verse 6: "Then I saw a Lamb, looking as if it had been slain, standing in the center of the throne, encircled by the four living creatures and the elders." And not only did he see a Lamb standing, but he says it was a Lamb "looking as if it had been slain." What a strange contrast to the Lion of the tribe of Judah when he looks and sees a Lamb that appeared to have been slain!

But notice also, this is a Lamb that "had seven horns." The horns were a symbol of power and strength often associated with the horns of the ox that would push and gore people, as in Deuteronomy 33:17 and 1 Kings 22:11. The horns are used symbolically of power and strength. This is an unusual Lamb. It had the appearance of having been slain for the simple reason that, as we learn in verse 9, it *had* been slain. This was "the Lamb of God, who takes away the sin of the world," as announced to the world by John the Baptist. This is the Lamb of God, the one who did go as a Lamb to the slaughter, who allowed the Roman soldiers to take him into their possession and nail him to the cross and place him between heaven and earth for men to look at and ridicule. But the Lamb is now seen standing!

This is not a Lamb whose having been slain was a permanent thing. Now John sees a Lamb that has returned to life, and the Lamb is standing. The Lamb is a Lamb that has seven horns. This is a powerful Lamb, and it has seven eyes. The seven eyes "are the seven spirits of God sent out into all the earth." Now we have seen that expression, "the seven spirits of God," earlier in Revelation. The number "seven" is used fifty-four times in Revelation and is a number of completeness or fullness, and to say "the seven spirits of God," is a symbolic way of referring to the Holy Spirit of God. So, here we see Jesus sending the Holy Spirit into all the earth.

The Lamb has power, but not power to be used to mobilize an army to drive out the armies of Rome. Instead, the power of the Lamb has overcome death. He is a conqueror, one who does rule with an iron scepter, but he rules spiritually. He rules in the hearts of men. He has sent his Spirit into the hearts of all those who submit to his reign and his lordship and his kingship.

Jesus himself, when he rose from the dead, just before he ascended into heaven, announced that all power, all authority, had been given to him in heaven and on earth (Matthew 28:18). Revelation 5:7, speaking of the scroll which would reveal the exercise of that power, says: "He came and took the scroll from the right hand of him who sat on the throne." Here we see the Lamb coming to the throne of God.

When did that happen? Well, back in Daniel 7:13-14 we are told that "one like a son of man...approached the Ancient of Days" and was given a kingdom. When Jesus ascended to heaven and came to the Ancient of Days, to the Father, he was given "authority, glory and sovereign power." And I am convinced that what we have seen in Revelation chapter 5 is John observing that very moment when the Son of God ascended, as a Lamb having been slain, to the throne, when he began to exercise power and to reveal the future and to show how he was going to carry out the purpose and plan of God for the destiny of the universe.

Now we are told in verse 8: "And when he had taken it [the scroll], the four living creatures and the twenty-four elders fell down before the Lamb. Each one had a harp and they were holding golden bowls full of incense, which are the prayers of the saints." The bowls of incense are identified for us as the prayers of the saints. The harps seem to be symbolic of the praises of God's people, just as the bowls of incense are the prayers of God's people.

So here we see the living creatures and the elders, who represent the redeemed of all the earth, who are now bringing praises and prayers to the Lamb. In chapter 4 we had seen God receiving the glory, and the honor, and the worship of the four living creatures and all the elders, and now that very same glory and honor and praise and worship and prayers are directed to the Lamb.

Now what does that say about the Lamb? It says he properly can be regarded as God. Jesus was God in the flesh. John said in the beginning of his gospel, in John 1:1: "In the beginning was the Word, and the Word was with God, and the Word was God." Then John explained in verse 14 who this Word was: "The Word became flesh and lived for a while among us. We have seen his glory, the glory of the one and only Son, who came from the Father, full of grace and truth." Here is the Word of God who became flesh, who was God.

Remember, in Matthew 4:8-10 the devil told Jesus to fall down and worship him and he would give him all the kingdoms of the world. But Jesus said: "Worship the Lord your God, and serve him only." God is the only one worthy of man's worship. Later in Revelation 19:10 when John fell down before an angel, the angel refused to accept his worship, because God alone is to be worshiped. In Acts 10:26 when Cornelius fell down before Peter and worshiped him, Peter said, "Stand up,...I am only a man myself." Only God deserves worship.

What are we seeing here? We are seeing Jesus Christ, the Lamb of God, who is now receiving the worship that has been given to God. Jesus was God in the flesh. Jesus is one worthy of worship. We worship him, showing him the honor and the glory which we see being given him by the heavenly beings here in Revelation chapter 5.

Now verses 9-10 say,

And they sang a new song:

"You are worthy to take the scroll

and to open its seals,

because you were slain,

and with your blood you purchased men for God

from every tribe and language and people and nation.

You have made them to be a kingdom and priests to

serve our God,

and they will reign on the earth."

Here is Jesus Christ who purchased with his blood men from every tribe and language and nation. It reminds us of what Paul said to the Ephesian elders in Acts 20:28 when he spoke of "the church of God, which he bought with his own blood." This is the church. The church has been purchased by the blood of Jesus Christ and the church reigns! God's people reign on earth now, today.

You say, "It doesn't look like it." So what? It doesn't even look like Jesus is reigning today from all the evil that we see in this world. It doesn't even look like God is reigning today. Appearances are deceiving, aren't they? We think and act like this world is going to be here forever. It's not. From all appearances it will be, but we know that it's not. It's going to be burned up (2 Peter 3:10).

That which is eternal is God and his people. We may look about us and see persecution, hardship, and struggles, but we need to see God, and we need to lift our eyes to see the Lamb of God who takes away the sins of the world. Then we can have hope and courage and live and reign and have dominion over our spirits. We can actually overcome the power of Satan himself. We can reign now because God made it possible for us through the power of his Spirit in our inner being. God "is able to do immeasurably more than all we ask or imagine," Paul said in Ephesians 3:20. God is able to do it.

We come now to verses 11 through 14:

Then I looked and heard the voice of many angels, numbering thousands upon thousands, and ten thousand times ten thousand.

They encircled the throne and the living creatures and the elders. In a loud voice they sang:

> "Worthy is the Lamb, who was slain,
>
> to receive power and wealth and wisdom and strength
>
> and honor and glory and praise!"

Then I heard every creature in heaven and on earth and under the earth and on the sea, and all that is in them, singing:

> "To him who sits on the throne and to the Lamb
>
> be praise and honor and glory and power,
>
> for ever and ever!"

The four living creatures said, "Amen," and the elders fell down and worshiped.

The Lamb, Jesus Christ, is presented to us now as the one who sits at the right hand of God, who reigns and intercedes for us. He is the one who has been slain, and yet we see him risen, even ascending to the throne of God. What then have we to fear if we should be persecuted, if we should be oppressed, if we should be slain? For what has happened to him will happen to his people. "Behold," he says, "I have overcome!"

In John 16:33, Jesus said, "In this world you will have trouble. But take heart! I have overcome the world." Jesus did, and he ascended to the right hand of the throne of God. Now he awaits you, and he wants you to be his child, to enter his kingdom, to allow him to become the king of your life. He wants to be the Lord of your life and to have you to live and reign with him until that time when, finally, he will receive you to himself. God has great plans for you. He has a purpose for your life.

We are going to see unfolded, as we look into the chapters that are before us in the Revelation, a cosmic and awesome picture that is almost beyond comprehension of the triumph and victory of God over Satan and of God's people over the Satanic forces that seek to destroy us. But we want you to see at the very beginning of the Revelation that God is showing us that we need never despair. God is on his throne, the Lamb is on the throne, and all will be well with God's people because he reigns and he is in charge. Satan can only go so far, and you cannot be destroyed by him if you stay in the hand of God.

Why not come to Jesus and give your life to him. He wants you, he pleads for you. If you believe in Jesus and will repent of your sins and confess your faith in Jesus, we urge you to come and make your request known. You can be baptized into Jesus Christ to live a new life that ends in the resurrection and a home with God.

REVELATION 6:
The Four Horsemen of the Apocalypse

A number of years ago Hollywood produced a movie called *The Four Horsemen of the Apocalypse*. At any rate, that's what we are looking at as we study from the 6th chapter of the Revelation. Let us back up briefly to get the setting, and then we will get a running start into Revelation 6.

We have seen John on the isle of Patmos being shown visions of heaven. We looked at the seven churches of Asia and saw the letters that Jesus wrote to them. We saw their struggles and the tribulations and difficulties which confronted them—which really are typical of the problems and struggles of the church in all the ages.

Then, in chapter 4, a door opens in heaven and John is permitted to see the throne of God, and we see that awesome description of the glory of God on his throne. We are reminded and made aware that God is on his throne, that he rules in the kingdoms of men, that God is very much in charge of our universe, even though it may not seem like it at times.

As we come to chapter 5, we see the Lamb of God coming to the very throne of God and joining God at the throne. To the Lamb a kingdom was given, and he made us to be a kingdom and priests. And those whom Jesus purchased from every tribe and language and people and nation he caused to reign on the earth. Then there is the great exclamation in heaven:

"Worthy is the Lamb, who was slain,

to receive power and wealth and wisdom and strength

and honor and glory and praise!"

We saw in chapter 5 that the one who sat on the throne had in his hand a scroll that was sealed. Then John wept because no one in heaven or on earth was able to open the seals of the scroll which would reveal the future and would also make possible the carrying out of the affairs of the future. Finally, the Lamb appeared, and he was the one who was worthy to open the scroll. As the scroll is opened seal by seal, we are permitted to see what is going to happen in the future.

As we come, then, to chapter 6 of Revelation, we read, beginning with verse 1: "I watched as the Lamb opened the first of the seven seals. Then I heard one of the four living creatures say in a voice like thunder, 'Come!' I looked, and there before me was a white horse! Its rider held a bow, and he was given a crown, and he rode out as a conqueror bent on conquest." It is extremely important to us as we move through Revelation that we understand what these symbols represent. Through the many centuries since this book was written, there have developed all kinds of bizarre notions and interpretations of what the various symbols of the Revelation mean. It is going to be our attempt, as nearly as possible, to allow the Bible to interpret itself as we work our way through this book.

As we come, then, to the first of the seals of the scroll that is opened, we have a scene of a horseman and a horse. It was a white horse, and the rider who sat on it had a bow. He was given a crown, and he rode out as a conqueror bent on conquest. I don't know what is the first impression that comes to your mind as you try to determine what that represents. But I think that what would come to your mind is Jesus Christ. Yet there have been those who have interpreted this as being the anti-Christ! The premillennialists, those who believe that someday in the future God is going to set up a kingdom here on earth and reign a thousand years, have been known to interpret it in that way. But I am convinced, beyond any shadow of a doubt, that this passage has reference to Jesus Christ.

Now I want to tell you why, because my opinion is worth nothing unless what I say has scripture behind it. There is only one other time in the book of Revelation when a white horse is mentioned, and in that one other reference there is no question as to who is sitting on it. That is found in Revelation 19:11 which says:

> I saw heaven standing open and there before me was a white horse, whose rider is called Faithful and True. With justice he judges and makes war. His eyes are like blazing fire, and on his head are many crowns. He has a name written on him that no one but he himself knows. He is dressed in a robe dipped in blood, and his name is the Word of God.

Well, we know who that is. It is Jesus Christ. The Word became flesh.

Now there is more in the passage to identify the rider of the white horse as Jesus. In fact, I know of no commentator who denies that this is Jesus who is being described here in Revelation 19:11. There is no question about who this is. It seems reasonable to conclude that the rider on a white horse in Revelation 19:11 is the same rider on a white horse here in Revelation 6:2.

We do have here a white horse and "…its rider held a bow, and he was given a crown, and he rode out as a conqueror bent on conquest." This expression, "conquer,"—some translations use the term "overcome" or "triumph"—is found throughout the book of Revelation and, with a couple of exceptions, it always, including the two nearest references to it in Revelation 3:21 and Revelation 5:5, refers to Christ or to his people. The conqueror is Jesus Christ. John only uses that word one time in his gospel. It is found in John 16:33, and there he applies that expression to Jesus Christ.

I would like to read in sequence these four references and see if it doesn't suggest to you clearly that we are seeing Jesus Christ as the one who rides out as a conqueror bent on conquest. First, John 16:33: "I have told you these things, so that in me you may have peace." This is Jesus speaking. "In this world you will have trouble. But take heart! I have **overcome** the world." And that is the same Greek word translated "conquer" in Revelation 6:2. "I have conquered the world." Then we turn to Revelation 3:21, and Jesus is speaking. He is addressing the church at Laodicea, and he says, "To him who overcomes," there's the word again, he who **conquers**, "I will give the right to sit with me on my throne, just as I overcame," or just as I **conquered**, "and sat down with my Father on his throne." And in Revelation 5:5 "Then one of the elders said to me, 'Do not weep! See, the Lion of the tribe of Judah, the Root of David, has triumphed.'" He has **conquered**. "'He is able to open the scroll and its seven seals.'" Then we turn to Revelation 6:2, "…and he rode out as a conqueror bent on conquest."

We saw in chapter 5, the previous chapter, the Lion. The Lion has overcome. How did he overcome? He overcame death itself when he rose from the dead. He is the overcomer and, therefore, he made it possible for all who are willing to follow in his way to overcome and to be conquerors. And, of course, Jesus goes forth to conquer men's minds. He is not going forth into the world to destroy man. He goes forth to conquer, to bring every thought into captivity to himself, to make men bow in allegiance to him. He is the conqueror, and he is the one who wears the crown. In Revelation 14:14 we see Jesus: "I looked, and there before me was a white cloud, and seated on the cloud was one 'like a son of man' with a crown of gold on his head and a sharp sickle in his hand." Here's a description of Jesus returning to bring judgment on the earth. And here, in Revelation 6, he is said to be wearing a crown just as he is described as wearing a gold crown in Revelation 14:14.

Now notice the expression that the conqueror "held a bow." There is a fascinating parallel to this passage in the Old Testament in a messianic Psalm—that is, a Psalm that is a prophecy of the Messiah who was to come. It is in Psalm 45:3-6, and I want you to think about this against the background of the words of Revelation 6:2. It says:

> Gird your sword upon your side, O mighty one;
>
> > clothe yourself with splendor and majesty.
>
> In your majesty ride forth victoriously
>
> > in behalf of truth, humility and righteousness;
>
> > let your right hand display awesome deeds.

> Let your sharp arrows pierce the hearts of the
>
> king's enemies;
>
> let the nations fall beneath your feet.
>
> Your throne, O God, will last for ever and ever;
>
> a scepter of justice will be the scepter of your kingdom.

Here's a description of one who is being addressed as God and who rides forth. We are told in verse 4, "In your majesty ride forth victoriously...." The Septuagint translation of this passage as found in Psalm 45 at that point renders it in this way: "...and in thy majesty ride and bend the bow and prosper and reign...." Jesus and the apostles often quote from that Greek translation of the Old Testament. Hebrews 1:8 shows that Psalm 45 is speaking of Jesus. It says:

> But about the Son he says,
>
> "Your throne, O God, will last for ever and ever,
>
> and righteousness will be the scepter of your kingdom."

So Psalm 45 is presenting a description of Jesus Christ riding forth in majesty and bending the bow for the purpose of reigning and for the purpose of prospering.

Now we see in Revelation 6:2 what seems to be, if we allow the Bible itself to provide for us a context, a clear picture of Jesus Christ riding out as a conqueror bent on conquest. This also reminds one of Romans 8, where we are told, beginning with verse 35, "Who shall separate us from the love of Christ? Shall trouble or hardship or persecution or famine or nakedness or danger or sword?" Then we find the answer in verse 37: "No, in all these things we are more than **conquerors** through him who loved us." The same word is used in Revelation 6:2. And so we have seen Jesus Christ, through whom we are more than conquerors.

So, as we come to chapter 6 of Revelation, we are shown, first of all, that Jesus Christ, who has been slain, who has risen from the dead, and who has ascended to the throne of God, is now going forth to conquer and to reign. We want to see that at the very beginning, because now there are going to come some very terrifying scenes, and we need to know beforehand that Jesus Christ is the victor and that his people, therefore, are going to be able to withstand what is going to be described.

Now, of course, Jesus is not literally riding on a white horse through our land trying to convert people, but he uses his people as the instrument of spreading his gospel. Remember, Jesus said all authority had been given to him in heaven and on earth. "Therefore go and make disciples of all nations...." We are the agents that he uses in the battle to conquer men's minds and bring them into captivity to Christ. So, as his people, we are going to be faced with the onslaught of every kind of Satanic force. But, while we are going to be experiencing various kinds of difficulties, we also are made to understand by Revelation chapter 6 that God still has these things under control. He can use them for the purpose of strengthening his people.

So, what do we see next? We come to verse 3: "When the Lamb opened the second seal, I heard the second living creature say, 'Come!' Then another horse came out, a fiery red one. Its rider was given power to take peace from the earth and to make men slay each other. To him was given a large sword." As we read in Matthew 10:34, Jesus one time said: "Do not suppose that I have come to bring peace to the earth. I did not come to bring peace, but a sword." Then he explained what he meant by that. In essence what he says is, "When men are turned to me, when men commit their lives to me, it is going to create extreme difficulties." It may very well be that a man's own family will turn against him. It may happen that he himself will face the cross, and it may be that he will lose his life. Wherever Jesus rides out as a conqueror bent on conquest, the efforts of Satan to destroy will follow. Consequently, the sword will come wherever the gospel goes.

That is precisely what we are seeing in Revelation 6:2-3. Following the efforts of Christ to permeate the world with the message, we see the efforts of Satan to destroy the people of God. That is what we see as the rider of the red horse is given power "to take peace from the earth and to make men slay each other." What we are seeing here, I believe, is not a general slaughter of mankind, but, rather, it has reference to persecution of God's own people. I believe that, first of all, because, not only in Matthew 10:34, but in other passages, there is the constant assurance of God that when people turn to him they are going to face persecution. "In fact, everyone who wants to live a godly life in Christ Jesus will be persecuted" (2 Tim. 3:12). So, when Jesus goes forth, Satan comes with persecution.

But, in the second place, the expression "slay" that is used in this verse is not the normal word that is used in scripture for killing. It is a word that is used regularly of slaughter of God's people or of Christ himself. Now Revelation 6:9 says: "When he opened the fifth seal, I saw under the altar the souls of those who had been slain because of the word of God...." It's the same word "slain" that is used back up here in verse 3. Those people who had been slain for the sake of the word of God are now seen in the presence of God himself. In other words, Satan was defeated by the very efforts that he made to defeat God's people. It backfired on him. The very effort he made to persecute God's people simply resulted in their release to be in the presence of God. Now, in a moment, we are going to see another word for "kill" which has reference to a general slaughter of mankind, rather than one specifically directed to God's people. But the red horse we are seeing here is religious persecution, the persecution of God's people.

Now we come to verses 5-6:

> When the Lamb opened the third seal, I heard the third living creature say, "Come!" I looked, and there before me was a black horse! Its rider was holding a pair of scales in his hand. Then I heard what sounded like a voice among the four living creatures, saying, "A quart of wheat for a day's wages, and three quarts of barley for a day's wages, and do not damage the oil and the wine!"

You may have a different translation. I am reading from the New International Version. Your translation may use an expression other than "day's wages."

The Greek word is "denarius," and a denarius, as we learn in Matthew 20:2, was a common laborer's daily wage. The amount of wheat that is spoken of here, according to the ancient historian Herodotus, was roughly the equivalent of a quart, which works out to the amount of food that would feed one man for one day. This suggests that what we are seeing is a whole day's wage for a quantity of wheat that would last one person one day. What we're seeing, then, is economic hardship.

It does mention that you could buy three quarts of barley for a day's wage. But barley was not considered as good a substance from which to make bread. However, that would provide a man enough for his family. So, whether or not these figures are precise, we are at least being given a picture of economic hardship. It isn't a case of vast famine that is leaving people starving to death. There is enough food for the daily needs of the people, but not any left over for luxuries.

Now it says the oil and the wine were not to be damaged. This suggests that those who were wealthy would still be able to have their luxuries and go beyond the necessities of life. We are seeing here the equivalent of a very great inflation that was taking place in the economy, a period of severe economic hardship. But the point is that it affects primarily God's people. We are seeing here a problem that is created by injustice, for the one who is on the black horse had a pair of scales in his hand. God's people throughout the ages have suffered, not only from the sword of persecution, but they have suffered also, from time to time, economic hardships because of their commitment to Christ. Those in the early days of the church in the Roman Empire often suffered economically because of their convictions and because they had to withdraw themselves from certain activities of their society in which they could not participate. This deprived them of their livelihood. So, here we see a third horse which suggests economic hardship for the people of God.

We come to verse 7: "When the Lamb opened the fourth seal, I heard the voice of the fourth living creature say, 'Come!'" It seems as though, for the third time, God is having an angel to call out the power of Satan against God's own people. What we are seeing here is much the same kind of thing as we saw in the Old Testament where God would refer to Babylon as his servant, then send Babylon down into Judah to wreak havoc and to take the people out of their land and make slaves and captives of them. God is still sovereign, and God can even take Satanic forces bent on evil and use them ultimately for the strengthening of his own people. We saw in the Old Testament in the story of Joseph how his brothers meant their actions toward Joseph for evil, but God meant them for good. So God is still sovereign, and he will only allow destruction to go so far.

Now, let's look at verses 7-8: "When the Lamb opened the fourth seal, I heard the voice of the fourth living creature say, 'Come!' I looked, and there before me was a pale horse!" Your translation may have a different word for the color of that horse. This one says "pale." The word in Greek is the word from which we get our word "chlorine." It's a sort of yellowish-green, a sickly-looking color suggesting death. "Its rider was named Death, and Hades was following close behind him. They were given power over a fourth of the earth to kill by sword, famine and plague, and by the wild beasts of the earth." I think that what we have seen in the cases of the second and third horsemen are difficulties brought on God's people. But now, in verse 8, we are seeing calamities that come on all the earth which we must suffer with all the rest of mankind. These are the sword and famine and plague and the wild beasts of the earth.

There is a fascinating parallel to this particular passage found in Ezekiel 14. Look at Revelation 6:8, and then think about it as I read Ezekiel 14:21: "For this is what the Sovereign Lord says: How much worse will it be when I send against Jerusalem my four dreadful judgments—sword and famine and wild beasts and plague—to kill its men and their animals!" The same four items referred to here as the four judgments of God are mentioned in Revelation 6:8.

This expression, "plague," is a word than can be translated two or three ways from the Greek: either death or pestilence or plague. In fact, it apparently is a term that had reference to what in modern times we call bubonic plague. At any rate, it is suggesting to us disease and things to which all men are subject: the sword, famine, plague, and the wild beasts of the earth. So Christians may expect to suffer not only religious persecution and economic hardship because of their commitment to Christ, but they will also suffer calamities common to the rest of mankind.

Now, what happens to the Christian in all of this? What happens to God's people? Well, fortunately, we are shown another scene in verse nine as the fifth seal is opened:

> When he opened the fifth seal, I saw under the altar the souls of those who had been slain because of the word of God and the testimony they had maintained. They called out in a loud voice, "How long, Sovereign Lord, holy and true, until you judge the inhabitants of the earth and avenge our blood?" Then each of them was given a white robe, and they were told to wait a little longer, until the number of their fellow servants and brothers who were to be killed as they had been was completed.

We have already suggested, back in verses 3 and 4 where we saw those who were being slain, that these are God's people. But now, in verses 9 and 10, we see them underneath the altar in heaven in the presence of God. In other words, Satan's efforts have failed. They have backfired. He has not succeeded in destroying God's people. He has only released them from this life to enter into the presence of God.

And so it says: "Then each of them was given a white robe…." "White" is a symbol which always in the book of Revelation has a connotation of moral goodness. Incidentally, this is another reason for thinking that the rider on the white horse in verse 2 is not the anti-Christ. Always, white represents moral goodness, moral purity, holiness, and, consequently, victory. Christ is the victor, and here we see that God's people are victorious, they are each given a white robe.

Now, we come to what happens to the rest. What happens to those who have persecuted God's people? In verse 12, we see the sixth seal opened:

> I watched as he opened the sixth seal. There was a great earthquake. The sun turned black like sackcloth made of goat hair, the whole moon turned blood red, and the stars in the sky fell to earth, as late figs drop from a fig tree when shaken by a strong wind. The sky receded like a scroll, rolling up, and every mountain and island was removed from its place.

Then the kings of the earth, the princes, the generals, the rich, the mighty, and every slave and every free man hid in caves and among the rocks of the mountains. They called to the mountains and the rocks, "Fall on us and hide us from the face of him who sits on the throne and from the wrath of the Lamb! For the great day of their wrath has come, and who can stand?"

Imagine, he speaks of the wrath of the Lamb, the gentlest of all God's creatures! The wrath of the Lamb suggests something really terrible, such a gentle creature finally exploding in wrath, anger, and vengeance.

There's the awesome picture of what happens, finally, to those who oppose God and his people. The longsuffering of God finally ends, and quickly and suddenly and unexpectedly wrath strikes mankind, and who can stand? God's opponents can only cry out to the mountains to fall on them because of the terror that has gripped them. Finally, they come to the realization that truly there is a God in heaven who reigns and that truly the Son of God died for them, but they rejected him and turned their backs on his offering of love and mercy.

And, finally, we see the vindication of those souls at the altar who cried out and said: "How long, Sovereign Lord, holy and true, until you judge the inhabitants of the earth and avenge our blood?" Perhaps you say, "How can these people who are with God in heaven have such a spirit of vengeance?" It is not a spirit of personal vengeance. It is true that Jesus said, "Father, forgive them, for they do not know what they are doing," and that Stephen said when he was being stoned, "Lord, do not hold this sin against them." But here the cry is for the vindication of the justice and holiness of God. His justice must be served, and those who reject and rebel against the holy and true and merciful God deserve to receive the wrath of God. Those who have suffered from the attacks and the ridicule of people who reject God deserve finally to see the wrath of God poured down on them, and surely it will happen in the great day of his wrath. Who is able to stand?

We have seen those who are able to one day stand victoriously with the one who rode out as a conqueror bent on conquest. In Revelation 17:14 is the final picture: "They will make war against the Lamb, but the Lamb will overcome them because he is Lord of lords and King of kings—and with him will be his called, chosen and faithful followers." If you are among the called of God, if you have accepted his call, if you have allowed yourself to be among those God has chosen, and if you have been faithful to him, then you are prepared to face a God who is both the God of justice and the God of love, and who showed it when he allowed his Son to die for you.

How will you respond to that expression of love? That is the question that comes to each of us. If you are not one of God's children, we plead with you to allow yourself to begin now to walk in the way of Christ, to be washed in the blood of the Lamb that you might be washed, justified, sanctified, and prepared to one day receive the white robe and to stand with the victorious in the very presence of God.

REVELATION 7:

The 144,000

W e are in the middle of sermons taken from the book of Revelation. We are studying Revelation chapter by chapter, and we have now come to the 7th chapter of the book of Revelation. Let me very briefly give you the background leading up to the 7th chapter, then we will read it and comment on it.

In chapter 1 of Revelation, we see one "like a son of man" walking among the lampstands or the candlesticks. According to Revelation's own interpretation, we are seeing Jesus walking among his churches.

Then, in chapters 2 and 3, we see seven typical churches: seven churches of Asia Minor. These are churches like God's churches have been through the ages. They have had their ups and downs, their joys and sorrows, their tribulations, their triumphs, their victories, their defeats, their difficulties, and hardships. They have suffered persecution, and we see them being urged to be faithful, even to the point of death that they might receive the crown of life. It's very difficult to live that life. We are constantly faced with temptations. There sometimes come persecutions, and the Christian may very well be inclined to say: "What's the use? It looks like Satan is in charge of this world, and we might as well give up."

So, lest the Christian become—and continue to be—discouraged, we come to chapter 4 of Revelation, and we see a door opened in heaven and we see the throne of God and the majesty of that scene. Then we are made to realize that God is, in fact, on his throne, that he is in charge of the world, that he has things under control, and that he knows what he's doing.

In chapter 5 of Revelation, we see that marvelous scene when one who looks like a Lamb that had been slain comes to the throne of the one who sat on it, and he takes a scroll and opens the seals. The seven seals that are on the scroll are opened in order that we might see Jesus bringing about the things that are to come to pass. Jesus is seen having ascended to the Father and having come to the throne where he reigns with the Father. We are told that the heavenly beings fall down and worship him, even as they initially worshiped the one who sat on the throne.

Then, as we see the first seal opened in chapter 6, we see Jesus Christ riding out as a conqueror bent on conquest. I think we should point out that there is no kind of time limit placed on this. We have simply seen that when the seal is opened, Jesus rides out as a conqueror bent on conquest. He will continue to do so until every enemy has been put under his feet—even until the last enemy, death, has been conquered.

So, what we have seen as we see the seals opened is the entire period of history from the time Jesus ascended to the throne to the time when he comes again. We see that during that period of time, as Jesus rides out as a conqueror bent on conquest, there will always be those who oppose Jesus and his people. And so we see religious persecution as we see the second seal opened. Then the third seal is opened, and this reveals economic hardship that comes to God's people through the injustice of the world. When the fourth seal is opened, we see God's people suffering the calamities that befall mankind in general—death caused through famine, sword, and plague, etc. However, when the fifth seal is opened, we see that those who have been slain because of the word of God are in the presence of God, preserved and saved by the power of God.

But then we are taken, finally, to see, as the sixth seal is opened, calamity being brought on the whole world. Apparently, the final judgment of God is coming upon the world. As the terrifying scene is described for us at the end of

Revelation 6:12-17, we see the wicked of the earth crying out for the mountains and the rocks to fall on them to hide them from him who sits on the throne and from the wrath of the Lamb. Then we have, finally, the question asked at the end of chapter 6: "…and who can stand?" When the wrath of God is poured out on our world, who is able to stand? Chapter 7, that we are about to look at, provides the answer to that question.

I would like to read for you now two passages from the prophecy of Ezekiel which serve somewhat as a background to what we have read in Revelation chapter 7, Ezekiel 9:4-6 and Ezekiel 21:2-4. [Please read Ezekiel 9:4-6 and Ezekiel 21:2-4 before continuing.]

As we come to Revelation 7, we see a scene in which four angels are

> …holding back the four winds of the earth to prevent any wind from blowing on the land or on the sea or on any tree. Then I saw another angel coming up from the east, having the seal of the living God. He called out in a loud voice to the four angels who had been given power to harm the land and the sea: "Do not harm the land or the sea or the trees until we put a seal on the foreheads of the servants of our God."

I believe that the only connection we might draw between this passage from Revelation 7 and that in Ezekiel 9 is the basic thought of the significance of marking on the forehead.

In Ezekiel, we are told by God that one was to "…put a mark on the foreheads of those who grieve and lament over all the detestable things that are done in it…" (in Jerusalem). Eventually, he said that others were to slaughter all the people except those who had received the mark. Those who received the mark were righteous. Yet when we come to the book of Revelation, we see that when the sword actually comes on the land, it slays both the righteous and the unrighteous. One would get the impression that it didn't do any good to put the mark on the forehead of the righteous because they were slain, too.

But I believe that to understand both Ezekiel and Revelation, we must understand that the protection God gives to his people is not necessarily protection against physical harm. We are told continually throughout the scriptures that everyone who wants to live a godly life in Christ Jesus will be persecuted. Jesus said in John 16:33: "In this world you will have trouble. But take heart! I have overcome the world." God does not exempt you from physical harm. That is not his concern. That isn't to say that he doesn't care if you suffer pain, but the point is that God is concerned to make your life holy so that you can enjoy the presence of God eternally.

So, when we see people who are being sealed in Revelation 7, let us not think that it is to indicate God's people are not going to suffer the same kinds of hardships, calamities, and pestilences that the world suffers, because that is part of what we were being shown in Revelation 6, the previous chapter. Believers and unbelievers alike share in many of the misfortunes that occur in our world. And it is for that very reason that the Christian might cry out and say, "Then what advantage does the believer have?"

That is why we have the fifth seal opened, to let us know that those believers who are slain because of the word of God are going to enjoy the presence of God. They are simply going to be relieved of the suffering, the pain, and the sorrow of this life to enjoy life in the presence of God. The same thing happens as we come to Revelation 7. We see a picture of the angels holding back the winds that are to come on the earth and bring destruction to the earth. But, first, there is a pause while they are holding them back so that God can put his seal on the foreheads of the righteous, on the servants of God.

What is the significance of sealing the servants of our God on their foreheads? Well, there are three other references in the book of Revelation that I think shed light on the significance of this. The first is in Revelation 3:12, where Jesus said: "Him who overcomes I will make a pillar in the temple of my God. Never again will he leave it. I will write on him the name of my God and the name of the city of my God, the new Jerusalem, which is coming down out of heaven from my God; and I will also write on him my new name." Jesus said he would write on those who overcome, those who are conquerors with Jesus. He didn't specify, as he did elsewhere, where he would write on them.

As we turn to Revelation 14:1, we are going to see the 144,000 there that we will be looking at in Revelation 7. Revelation 14:1 says: "Then I looked, and there before me was the Lamb, standing on Mount Zion, and with him 144,000 who had his name and his Father's name written on their foreheads."

Now we move to Revelation 22 where we see the final scene of the redeemed in heaven where they will be with God forever and ever, and it says of them, in verses 3 and 4: "No longer will there be any curse. The throne of God and of the Lamb will be in the city, and his servants will serve him. They will see his face, and his name will be on their foreheads."

Having the name of Christ and God on your forehead is a symbolic way of saying that you are owned by God, your mind has been brought into captivity to Christ. In the Old Testament the high priest wore a gold plate on his forehead engraved with the words, "Holy to the Lord," or "Set apart to the Lord." You find that in Exodus 28:36 and following. Just as during the old dispensation the name of the Lord was written on the forehead of the high priest to indicate that he was the specially consecrated servant of the Lord, so believers in our age, who are called priests in the book of Revelation, now have a new name written on their foreheads, the name of Jesus.

A seal certifies and signifies ownership, and it protects. The point is that Christ owns us, having purchased us with his own blood and, having done so, he protects us throughout life. This is not protection against physical harm, but protection against spiritual destruction by Satan. No one can snatch us out of the Father's hand. You are protected by God, and to have a seal placed on your forehead bearing the name of Christ and God is simply a symbolic way of saying that you are owned by him.

We are just like the people who used to be branded by the slave owner. We are servants, and the word that is used in Revelation for servant is the Greek word that literally means a bondservant or a slave. We are slaves of God and of Christ, and we bear the mark of slavery to him. We have the brand of slavery engraved on our forehead saying, in essence, that we are his. We belong to God. That obviously doesn't mean that God is literally going to scrawl his name on your forehead with some kind of pen. This is symbolism, but it is a way of suggesting that we belong to God.

The point is that the calamities, the judgments of God that come on mankind, are not going to do us eternal harm because we have been sealed by him. This thought is suggested in Ephesians 1:13: "And you also were included in Christ when you heard the word of truth, the gospel of your salvation. Having believed, you were marked in him with a seal, the promised Holy Spirit…." You have been sealed, you who are believers, with the promised Holy Spirit.

Why? Because, according to Acts 5:32, God gives his Spirit to all those who obey him. This occurred, according to Acts 2:38, when you believed and repented and were baptized. You received the gift of the Holy Spirit. He is yours. He is sealing you. He is protecting you from Satan so that Satan cannot destroy you as long as you choose to remain faithful to God. So we are seeing a beautiful picture in Revelation 7, the sealing of God's people so that they cannot be overcome by Satan. God's people will be victorious.

Now in Revelation 7:4 and following, John said:

> Then I heard the number of those who were sealed: 144,000 from all the tribes of Israel.
>
> From the tribe of Judah 12,000 were sealed,
>
> from the tribe of Reuben 12,000….

What is the significance of that 144,000? Who are they? Well, in Revelation 4 something similar was seen. Around the throne in heaven there were twenty-four elders. This naturally suggests the twelve sons of Israel added to the twelve apostles of Christ whose names are on the gates and the foundations of the new Jerusalem which is in heaven (Revelation 21:10-14). These were representatives of the redeemed of all the ages.

So what better way would there be to symbolically present not merely their representatives, but all of God's people, than by multiplying the twelve by twelve and then multiplying that by one thousand, a symbol of completeness and fullness, thus giving us 144,000. Notice that the wall of the new Jerusalem, the city of all God's people described in Revelation 21:17, was 144 cubits. This number is clearly associated with the redeemed of all the ages. These then are those who dwell with God forever and ever, the righteous, those who have been saved.

Now we come to this expression, "…sealed…from all the tribes of Israel." The tribes of literal Israel are symbolic here of spiritual Israel. There are some who think that the writer of Revelation is referring just to the Jews, that is, just to the fleshly descendants of Abraham, Isaac, and Jacob, whose name was Israel. But he is not speaking here about fleshly Israel. He is using Israel as a symbol because, at one time in a special sense, Israel represented the people of God. But now, in Revelation, Israel represents not the Jewish nation, the Hebrew nation, but it is representing those who are the true Israel.

I want to give you ten reasons why I am convinced that that is the case. I want to take time to give you ten reasons, because I think it is extremely important for you to understand that you're one of the 144,000, because there are people who try to convince you that you can't be among this 144,000. Some say that's a very special, exclusive group that has already been picked out, and you can't be part of it. That is not the case.

Reason number one: That spiritual Israel is meant is implied by the strange arrangement of the twelve tribes. Reuben would normally be listed first, as he is in Genesis 49, because Reuben was the firstborn of the sons of Israel. But here Judah is first in the list. That is undoubtedly because, as we have already seen in chapter 5 of Revelation, Jesus is the Lion of the tribe of Judah. So Judah now takes preeminence, because Judah is the tribe that produced our Lord. Therefore, Judah comes before even Reuben, the firstborn of fleshly Israel.

Now if this were referring to literal Israel, one would expect to see the tribes of Ephraim and Dan listed here, but they are missing. You look at that list again and you may be surprised, because, if you were in Sunday school as a child, you were taught the twelve tribes of Israel and you learned about Ephraim and Dan, but they're not mentioned here. Dan is missing, and Joseph is substituted for Ephraim. Manasseh is included, but Ephraim and Manasseh were the two sons of Joseph who took the place of Joseph in the previous listings of the tribes. But here you have a strange arrangement. It seems that God is wanting us to see that this Israel is not to be identified as the fleshly Israel of the Old Testament.

The second reason I believe this is referring to spiritual Israel is the fact that exactly 12,000 from each tribe are listed. Wouldn't it be strange that there would be exactly 12,000 saved from the tribe of Manasseh, exactly 12,000 from the tribe of Simeon, exactly 12,000 from Issachar, and so forth, although these tribes were greatly disparate in their populations? And wouldn't it be stranger yet that not one person from the tribes of Dan and Ephraim would be saved? I think it obvious that here we have a symbolic number. He is not talking about exactly 11,999 plus 1 in each of these tribes. So even the very nature of the listing of these tribes is suggestive of the fact that we are not looking now at fleshly Israel, at the physical descendants of Abraham, but we are looking at spiritual Israel, that is, God's true Israel.

Now let us look at a third reason. In Revelation 14:3, where we have the second discussion of the 144,000, they are said to have been "…redeemed from the earth." Well, this is an expression for God's people found in the new covenant, not in the old covenant. In Acts 20:28, Paul said to the Ephesian elders, "Guard yourselves and all the flock of which the Holy Spirit has made you overseers. Be shepherds of the church of God, which he bought with his own blood." In 1 Corinthians 6:20 Paul said, in speaking of Christians, "…you were bought at a price. Therefore honor God with your body." You were bought. Those who are in the church have been bought—redeemed—from all the earth.

In the fourth place, I believe that this 144,000 included Christians, not just fleshly Israel, because those who were sealed with the name of God on their foreheads in Revelation 22:1-4 are spoken of as servants of God and the Lamb, and the Lamb is Jesus Christ. We are looking at those who are servants of Jesus Christ when we see those who have the seal on their foreheads, the name written on their foreheads. So this has to include more than just those of fleshly Israel.

My fifth reason for believing this is that the New Testament refers to the church as the true Israel of God. For example, in Romans 2:28-29 Paul said:

"A man is not a Jew if he is only one outwardly, nor is circumcision merely outward and physical. No, a man is a Jew if he is one inwardly; and circumcision is circumcision of the heart, by the Spirit, not by the written code. Such a man's praise is not from men, but from God." Throughout the New Testament, we are taught repeatedly that those who are the true Jews are not those who are the fleshly descendants of Abraham.

Even during Jesus' earthly ministry, when the Jews spoke up and said they were descendants of Abraham, Jesus said in essence, "So what?" "...out of these stones God can raise up children for Abraham" (Luke 3:8). In other words, their fleshly descent from Abraham gave them no merit in the sight of God. And here in Romans 2, Paul, who himself was a fleshly descendant of Abraham, had the courage to say, "A man is not a Jew if he is only one outwardly." What is in the heart determines whether or not you are a Jew and truly of Israel. Then in Galatians 3:29 Paul said: "If you belong to Christ, then you are Abraham's seed, and heirs according to the promise." If you are Christ's, then you are of the Israel of God. In Galatians 6:16 Paul said to the church: "Peace and mercy to all who follow this rule, even to the Israel of God." The church is the Israel of God. In Philippians 3:3 Paul said, in speaking of Christians: "For it is we who are the circumcision, we who worship by the Spirit of God, who glory in Christ Jesus, and who put no confidence in the flesh...." Fleshly Israel doesn't mean a thing anymore to God. The question is, "Are you one of the servants of Jesus Christ?" If you are, then you are the circumcision. "Circumcision" was a common term to refer to Jews, as opposed to Christians. And Paul said, "You are the true circumcision if you belong to and glory in Christ Jesus." In James 1:1, James, who is writing a letter to Christians, addresses them in this way:

> James, a servant of God and of the Lord Jesus Christ,
>
> To the twelve tribes scattered among the nations:
>
> Greetings.

He addresses Christians as the twelve tribes. It is not unreasonable, then, to regard the listing of the tribes of Israel in Revelation 7 as a reference to Christians. Further confirmation of this is found in 1 Peter 2:9 where Peter said

Christians "…are a chosen people, a royal priesthood, a holy nation, a people belonging to God…." Palestine is no longer in God's purpose. The Hebrew race has given way to a new, elect race. The Jewish nation has given way to a new, holy nation. In verse 10, Peter refers to this new nation as those who once "… were not a people…." These were the Gentiles. To the Jew, the Gentiles were nothing; Israel was God's chosen people. But Peter goes on to say of those who once were not a people, "…but now you are the people of God; once you had not received mercy, but now you have received mercy." It is reasonable to believe that Revelation invests "Israel" with the new meaning suggested throughout the New Testament.

The sixth reason I believe Revelation 7 refers to spiritual Israel, rather than fleshly Israel, is that the expression, "servants of our God," which is the expression used of those who were sealed, is the term describing those to whom the book of Revelation was written. Revelation was written to Christians who are referred to in Revelation 1:1 as God's servants. Christians, then, are the ones who were sealed in Revelation 7, and those who were sealed were the 144,000.

The seventh reason: The sealing of God is in contrast to the mark of the beast. We are going to talk about the mark of the beast when we get to chapter 13, but I will just anticipate a bit and say that the sealing of those on the forehead with the name of Christ applies to all God's people, and those who have the mark of the beast represent all those who have refused to submit their lives to Jesus Christ.

The eighth reason: In Revelation 14:4, where there is a further description of the 144,000, they are identified as virgins, and there is not a commentator on the face of this earth who believes that the 144,000 were all literally virgins. It is no more reasonable nor necessary to believe they are literally fleshly Israel. This is a symbol. "Undefiled" is symbolic of a people who are pure, a people who have not committed spiritual adultery by forsaking their allegiance to Christ.

In the ninth place, when the 144,000 are referred to in Revelation 14:4, they are spoken of as "firstfruits to God and the Lamb." But James 1:18 speaks of Christians as being the firstfruits of all God created.

In the tenth place, in Revelation 14:5 where the 144,000 are mentioned, they are described as "blameless." That is the term Paul uses of Christians in Ephesians 1:3-4 and 5:24-27. What we have said, in summary, is that the 144,000 who are mentioned in Revelation 7 are all of God's people.

Now we come to Revelation 7:9-10:

> After this I looked and there before me was a great multitude that no one could count, from every nation, tribe, people and language, standing before the throne and in front of the Lamb. They were wearing white robes and were holding palm branches in their hands. And they cried out in a loud voice:
>
> "Salvation belongs to our God,
>
> who sits on the throne,
>
> and to the Lamb."

Who is this great multitude? I am convinced that the great multitude is exactly the same group of people that we mentioned when we spoke about the 144,000. That's a great multitude! You get 144,000 people together and you've got yourself a great multitude. John said he merely heard the number of the 144,000. But what he saw when he looked at them was a great multitude.

I am convinced they are the same people, because if you look very carefully at the description given of the great multitude and then look at the description of the 144,000, particularly as it is elaborated in Revelation 14, the description is the same. I believe there is general agreement among commentators that the great multitude refers to the church, Christians, God's people. And we have already demonstrated that the 144,000 represents the same people. Both are before the throne of God, and the same expressions are used throughout Revelation 7 and 14 to refer to both of these.

What is John trying to tell us about this great multitude? The point is that we have seen them sealed, and now we have seen them in the very presence of God. In other words, the judgment of God is not against these people. The judgment and wrath of God is poured out against those who have rebelled against God and who refuse to submit themselves to the reign of God and the Lamb. It answers the question, "Who is able to stand?" It is those who are in the church, those who are Christians, those who are God's people. And what a scene of rejoicing there is when, finally, after all the tribulations and turmoil, we see God's people victorious at the throne.

The scene continues with verse 11:

> All the angels were standing around the throne and around the elders and the four living creatures. They fell down on their faces before the throne and worshiped God, saying:
>
>> "Amen!
>>
>> Praise and glory
>>
>> and wisdom and thanks and honor
>>
>> and power and strength
>>
>> be to our God for ever and ever.
>>
>> Amen!"
>
> Then one of the elders asked me, "These in white robes—who are they, and where did they come from?"

Elsewhere in Revelation, people in white robes are God's redeemed.

> I answered, "Sir, you know."
>
> And he said, "These are they who have come out of the great tribulation…."

What's the great tribulation? Jesus told us in John 16:33: "In this world you will have trouble. But take heart! I have overcome the world." In Acts 14:22 we are told, "We must go through many hardships to enter the kingdom of God." God's people always suffered tribulation. The tribulation can properly be called "great" because its duration is from the time Jesus rode out as a conqueror bent on conquest until the end of time. But these are people who come out of the great tribulation. They are conquerors. They are the overcomers. They are the victors. We see them at the throne of God. John continues:

...they have washed their robes and made them white in the blood of the Lamb. Therefore,

> "they are before the throne of God,
>
>> and serve him day and night in his temple;
>
>> and he who sits on the throne will spread his tent
>
>>> over them.
>
> Never again will they hunger;
>
>> never again will they thirst.
>
> The sun will not beat upon them,
>
>> nor any scorching heat.
>
> For the Lamb at the center of the throne will be
>
>> their shepherd;
>
> he will lead them to springs of living water.
>
> And God will wipe away every tear from their eyes."

It's the same kind of description we find in Revelation 22, at the end of time, with the redeemed at the throne of God. These are the servants of God, sealed on their foreheads with the name of God and of the Lamb, because they have washed their robes in the blood of the Lamb.

You can be washed in the blood of the Lamb and have the cleansing of your sins, if you will only respond to the invitation of our God. What are you waiting for? Get up, be baptized and wash your sins away, calling on his name.

REVELATION 8:

The Power of Prayer

N ow we come to the 8th chapter of the book of Revelation. I believe we have seen now the completion of the second major section of the book, chapters 4 through 7. Let us back up just a bit and review, so that we have a background for where we are in Revelation.

The first major scene of Revelation is chapters 1 through 3, where we see Jesus Christ walking among the churches. We see this symbolically portrayed in the 1st chapter, and we see concrete illustrations of it in the seven churches of Asia Minor in chapters 2 and 3. We see the harsh realities of the Christian experience in a sinful world.

Then chapter 4 begins a scene where we are taken into the very presence of God, to the throne in heaven. There we see the majesty of God and are assured that he is in charge of our universe, that he controls things, and that we need not fear that things are out of hand.

When we come to chapter 5, we see the Lamb of God who has been slain for the sins of the world and has ascended to the throne of God. He was given a scroll and found worthy of breaking the seals and opening the scroll, so the destiny of the universe might be revealed and carried out.

Then, in chapter 6, we see the seals beginning to be opened one by one, and scenes are unveiled before our eyes. We see, first of all, Jesus Christ, now that he has risen from the dead and ascended to the throne, riding out as a conqueror bent on conquest. As we see seal after seal opened, we see the efforts of Satan to fight against the conquering power of Christ. But we see that the power of Satan is exercised under the limitations that God has imposed on him. We see him inflicting economic hardship, and we see the injustices that he brings about in our world. We see death being the lot of Christians as well as of non-Christians. But we see that those who have been faithful to the word of God are found, when the fifth seal is opened, in the very presence of God and enjoying freedom from this earthly life. Finally we see, as the sixth seal is opened, the wrath of God being poured out on the world.

But we see, in chapter 7, God's redeemed being preserved and protected from that final judgment that is coming on the wicked. In fact, as we come to the close of chapter 7, it says,

> For the Lamb at the center of the throne will be
>
> their shepherd;
>
> he will lead them to springs of living water.
>
> And God will wipe away every tear from their eyes.

It sounds so very much like what we find at the end of the book, Revelation 22:5, where it says, "There will be no more night. They will not need the light of a lamp or the light of the sun, for the Lord God will give them light. And they will reign for ever and ever." Now we have seen God's people finally coming into the very presence of God where they are free from the suffering and the sorrow of this life. I believe at this point we come to the end of a scene, one look at God's dealings with mankind. It begins at the throne of God and culminates with God's people present, with him, at the throne.

Now as we begin chapter 8, we read: "When he opened the seventh seal, there was silence in heaven for about half an hour." There is a period of silence. It's just as though John has to catch his breath. He has seen such awesome things. He has seen one complete scene of the activity of God in our world from the time of the ascension of the Lamb to the throne to the time when his people join him at the throne. It's just as though, after all the tumult and confusion that is seen as God brings wrath on the earth and redeems his people, there has to be a moment of silence to reflect on all this.

But that silence also seems to prepare us for the next scene in Revelation. I believe that what happens now is not something that continues from that point forward in some chronological sense, but rather, we go back to the beginning again. We go back to the throne of God, and now we are going to look at God's activity in our world from another point of view.

Verse 2 says: "And I saw the seven angels who stand before God, and to them were given seven trumpets." These trumpets, as we will see, are trumpets of judgment, trumpets of warning. God always tries to warn mankind of impending judgment before he finally brings it. And what we will be seeing, as we look at the seven angels sounding their trumpets, are warnings—temporary and temporal judgments of God—being brought against sinful men.

In the previous section, as we were looking at the seals being opened, we were seeing the seals of persecution. We were seeing God's people being oppressed. What we see now is a different aspect of the whole picture brought into sharper focus: the fact that the seals of persecution give rise to the trumpets of warning, so that those who would oppress God's people must realize that God will take vengeance. Back in the 6th chapter, when the fifth seal was opened, we saw beneath the altar "…the souls of those who had been slain because of the word of God and the testimony they had maintained. They called out in a loud voice, 'How long, Sovereign Lord, holy and true, until you judge the inhabitants of the earth and avenge our blood?'" As we come to chapter 8 we are seeing the answer to that question being given. God does avenge his people.

Now let's look at verses 3-4: "Another angel, who had a golden censer, came and stood at the altar. He was given much incense to offer, with the prayers of all the saints, on the golden altar before the throne. The smoke of the incense, together with the prayers of the saints, went up before God from the angel's hand." Here we are seeing the prayers of a persecuted people, the prayers of the saints of God, going up to God. But there is something added to the prayers of the saints. (Now, of course, the word "saint," as used in the New Testament, always means God's people. If you are a Christian, you are a saint.)

What we see in Revelation 8:3-4 are the prayers of all the saints going up before God and being received by God. None of us is left out. Our prayers reach the presence of God. But it is not because we are worthy to make our requests known to God. It is because the Lamb of God is worthy. Because we belong to the Lamb, God is willing to hear, and he is ready and anxious to hear our prayers. I believe that is the significance of the statement in verse 3 where it says, "He was given much incense to offer, with the prayers of all the saints, on the golden altar before the throne." I believe what we are seeing here is Jesus Christ adding to our prayers before the throne of God his words of intercession on our behalf.

We see that this is a function and role which Jesus does play for his people. In Luke 22:31-32 Jesus was speaking to Simon Peter and said: "Simon, Simon, Satan has asked to sift you as wheat. But I have prayed for you, Simon, that your faith may not fail. And when you have turned back, strengthen your brothers." Jesus Christ intercedes for his people.

In 1 John 2:1 John said: "My dear children, I write this to you so that you will not sin. But if anybody does sin, we have one who speaks to the Father in our defense—Jesus Christ, the Righteous One." We don't have to go to God the Father alone, but Jesus Christ accompanies us there, and Jesus Christ is our advocate. He pleads our case and our cause. It is because he does so that our prayers can go into the presence of God, and we have the assurance that God will hear and that God will answer.

In Romans 8:34 Paul said: "Who is he that condemns? Christ Jesus, who died—more than that, who was raised to life—is at the right hand of God and is also interceding for us." If you are one of God's people, what a thrilling thing to know that Jesus Christ is interceding for you! His work on your behalf did not end when he died on the cross. He continues to make intercession for you. Jesus is vitally interested in you, each one of you. And Jesus Christ does not have human limitations. Let us never think of Jesus as too small to accomplish tasks which we are describing. Jesus knows you by name, and Jesus Christ continues to intercede on your behalf. His blood continues to cleanse you from all sins.

But that is not all he does. In Hebrews 7:25 the writer of the Hebrew letter told us more about the interceding work of Jesus Christ when he said: "Therefore he is able to save completely those who come to God through him, because he always lives to intercede for them." Jesus Christ always lives to intercede for you. Some of these passages are so personal they almost overwhelm us. To think that Jesus continues to be constantly aware of your needs, your activities, and of your prayers that go up before the Father!

Now what happens when our prayers go before the throne of God? Does God have his hands tied behind his back? Is God looking the other way, totally uninterested in our affairs? Absolutely not! Our God is alert. His eyes search over the earth seeking those whom he may help, those who are willing to serve him, and here we see, in verse 5, the response of God to the prayers of his people. "Then the angel took the censer, filled it with fire from the altar, and hurled it on the earth; and there came peals of thunder, rumblings, flashes of lightning and an earthquake."

What we have seen is God's response to your prayers. He hurls fire on the earth. He does avenge God's elect. It's not that God's people are a vengeful people trying to encourage the retaliation of God, but they are people who recognize the holiness and the righteousness and the justice of God and realize that rebellion against God demands satisfaction. When God's people are being oppressed, God does take action, and God does respond to the prayers of his people who cry out. Now we don't always know how God will accomplish it, and we see the response of God described here in Revelation 8 only in highly symbolic ways.

Let us not get carried away and over-literalize the things that are said here. Rather, let us understand that the kind of language used here is the kind of language that was used by the prophets of the Old Testament. So often they used physical terms to describe the spiritual realities of God's activity. For example, consider the matter of God sending fire on the earth.

I would like for you to look, for just a moment, at Luke 12:49-53. Jesus said, "I have come to bring fire on the earth, and how I wish it were already kindled!" Let's pause there a moment. Jesus said, "I have come to bring fire on the earth." Now we can take that literally, if we want to. We can see Jesus getting a bowl of fire and just throwing it out on the earth. But that's not the way this kind of language is employed in scripture. That's not the significance of it. Let's let Jesus tell us what he meant by that statement. If we understand that, we can begin to understand the significance of what is said in Revelation 8 about the angel taking the censer and hurling fire on the earth. What does it mean? That's the symbol, but what's the meaning of the symbol?

Jesus said: "I have come to bring fire on the earth, and how I wish it were already kindled! But I have a baptism to undergo, and how distressed I am until it is completed! Do you think I came to bring peace on earth? No, I tell you, but division." In the idea of hurling fire there is something destructive involved. Hurling fire is the symbol, but causing division is the significance. Jesus elaborates: "From now on there will be five in one family divided against each other, three against two and two against three. They will be divided, father against son and son against father, mother against daughter and daughter against mother, mother-in-law against daughter-in-law and daughter-in-law against mother-in-law."

In other words, when Jesus rides out as a conqueror bent on conquest, Satan is going to do everything in his power to fight against those who will follow Jesus Christ. He will enter their homes and try to cause strife and stress and friction. When one turns to Jesus and the other does not, there will be conflict. It's painful. It's as though Jesus has brought fire on the earth. So here's an illustration from Jesus of the kind of expression that is found in Revelation 8.

No, we are not seeing Jesus literally sending fire on the earth in Revelation 8, but we are seeing the response of God to the prayers of his people. We are seeing judgment brought. We are seeing that when we cry out to God, he hears and he answers. He responds to our prayers. And then, as we read the rest of chapter 8, we see an elaboration on the idea. Beginning at verse 6 we read:

Then the seven angels who had the seven trumpets prepared to sound them.

The first angel sounded his trumpet, and there came hail and fire mixed with blood, and it was hurled down upon the earth. A third of the earth was burned up, a third of the trees were burned up, and all the green grass was burned up.

The second angel sounded his trumpet, and something like a huge mountain, all ablaze, was thrown into the sea. A third of the sea turned into blood, a third of the living creatures in the sea died, and a third of the ships were destroyed.

We are seeing God bringing his judgments on the people. People are being warned by the calamities and catastrophes that happen on the earth. There are some who do repent, but there are others who—even in spite of God's activities and the calamities that are brought on the earth—see the awesome power of God and still refuse to turn to God.

Now we look at the third angel in verse 10: "The third angel sounded his trumpet, and a great star, blazing like a torch, fell from the sky on a third of the rivers and on the springs of water—the name of the star is Wormwood. A third of the waters turned bitter, and many people died from the waters that had become bitter." What's happening now? There is no escape for those who are under the wrath of God. The earth is being struck. The sea is being struck. The inland waters are being hurt.

Then we come to verse 12: "The fourth angel sounded his trumpet, and a third of the sun was struck, a third of the moon, and a third of the stars, so that a third of them turned dark. A third of the day was without light, and also a third of the night." What is the significance of the third, the third, the third? All it means is that this is not the final judgment of God that we are seeing here. These are only the kinds of judgments that God brings all along the way on the people of the world to try to get them to see that God is active in his world, that God is the God who responds to his people, that the calamities of the world should cause us to turn to God, that there is no escaping from God.

It reminds me in sort of a reverse way of what we find in Psalm 139:7-10:

> Where can I go from your Spirit?
>
> Where can I flee from your presence?
>
> If I go up to the heavens, you are there;
>
> if I make my bed in the depths, you are there.
>
> If I rise on the wings of the dawn,
>
> if I settle on the far side of the sea,
>
> even there your hand will guide me,
>
> your right hand will hold me fast.

If I go up to the heavens, if I descend into the earth, if I go across the sea, wherever I go, God is present. And that is reassuring to his people because there is no way that God is ever going to abandon us or leave us.

But for the world, it ought to be a terrifying thought that there is no escape from God. That's why in Revelation 6 we saw that people who opposed God cried out and said "…to the mountains and the rocks, 'Fall on us and hide us from the face of him who sits on the throne and from the wrath of the Lamb! For the great day of their wrath has come, and who can stand?'" There is no escaping from the presence of God. But here, in Revelation 8, we are not seeing the final judgment of God on the world. We're seeing the continuing activity of God in bringing his judgments on the earth, and his warnings by calamities on the earth, to try to cause people to respond to him and to come back to him.

Can God respond today? We often say that God is not doing today the miracles he did in previous times. There are people who get all upset when you make that kind of statement, and they say, "Isn't God the same yesterday, and today, and forever?" He is. But God chooses to act in different ways and operates in different ways from time to time. God places on himself his own limitations, if he so chooses. But while God may not be operating today with the kinds of miracles that were done through Jesus Christ, God is still as active as he ever was in our world, and he still can accomplish his purposes without ever doing the kinds of things that were seen under the leadership of Moses or of Christ.

You know, even in the Old Testament, God often, without miracles, operated dramatically and powerfully in response to his people. He used the miracles of Moses in order to bring his people out of Egyptian bondage. He used absolutely no miracles and accomplished just as great a thing when he freed his people from Babylonian captivity and allowed them to come back to the land of Palestine to rebuild Jerusalem and the temple. There were no miracles involved there. There was simply an idea planted in the mind of Cyrus. Even before that, God used the armies of Babylon to destroy his people and lead them into captivity. That was God's judgment being brought because of sinful people.

And yet, as the people finally responded to the message of the prophets and cried out to him, God was willing to let them come back. God can operate powerfully in our world. He planted a thought in the mind of Caesar Augustus that a census should be taken of the entire Roman world so that Jesus could fulfill a prophecy of the Old Testament by being born in Bethlehem, although he grew up in Nazareth. God is still able to operate dramatically.

Some think that God is bound in our world today by all the laws of nature. That's not true. Our universe does not operate according to law; it operates according to God. God is the one who controls our universe, not laws, unless they be laws that God has devised—which are not necessarily the same things that we have crystallized into the so-called laws of nature. God still has a free hand to operate in our world. I think we need to gain the conception of the relationship of God to our universe that the ancient psalmist had in Psalm 65. We seem to think that somehow, due to the laws of nature, God is trapped and unable to operate. But God controls all of this. He can do whatever he wants to, whenever he wants to. He does not have to obey any laws that men have crystallized. Look at Psalm 65. I would like you to read the entire 13 verses so you may gain an appreciation of how God relates to our universe. [Please read Psalm 65 before continuing.]

God is doing all of this. God is the one who brings the Spring to us. God is the one who showers the earth with water, who blankets it with a soft layer of snow. God is doing these things. It's not mother nature. It's not some law that is foreordained that causes this. Almighty God is blessing us with rain; he causes the rain to fall on the righteous and the unrighteous. It's no accident. It's not just by some foreordained meteorological phenomenon that rain and showers and hail come. God brings them; God does it. God is active in our world. He is active for the benefit of his people.

We are not a people who are incapable of effecting any change in our world. When we pray to God that kingdoms may fall, God answers. When we pray for people who are sick, God answers. God can operate in our world today, and he does operate. Let us never think that we have a God who does not care what is happening to his people. Here in Revelation we see the prayers of all the saints going up before the throne of God, and we see the response of fire hurled on the earth. God responds to the prayers, the cries, of his people even today, and let us never forget it. So we come to Revelation chapter 8, and we see the judgments of God being brought on those who oppress God's people, and we see God's efforts to warn people, by judgments all along the way, of the impending final judgment that is to come.

Unfortunately, many people expect a literal fulfillment of these prophecies. They expect some day in the future to look into the heavens and see some strange astronomical phenomena in the sky. Well, Revelation isn't talking about that. They expect that a third of all the grass on the earth is literally going to burn up, and there will be two-thirds left. These are ideas completely foreign to the whole nature of prophecy.

Let's go back a minute to Isaiah. Let me show you how the Bible speaks about God's activity in this world. In Isaiah chapter 13, for example, God is talking about the destruction that is coming upon Babylon. In Isaiah 13, beginning with verse 10, there is this description of what happens when Babylon is destroyed:

> The stars of heaven and their constellations
>> will not show their light.
> The rising sun will be darkened
>> and the moon will not give its light.

Then let us come down to verse 13:

> Therefore I will make the heavens tremble;
>
> and the earth will shake from its place
>
> at the wrath of the Lord Almighty,
>
> in the day of his burning anger.

Well, that never happened literally. Babylon was destroyed. It still lies in ruins. God, however, brought his judgment on the world, and the prophets described it in these terms.

Let's look at another illustration, in Isaiah 34. This time we see Edom, a very insignificant little nation, but one that had enough power to be a thorn in the side of other nations and a nation that thought she could never be destroyed. Now here are the words of the prophet Isaiah concerning the destruction coming on Edom. Isaiah 34:4-5:

> All the stars of the heavens will be dissolved
>
> and the sky rolled up like a scroll;
>
> all the starry host will fall
>
> like withered leaves from the vine,
>
> like shriveled figs from the fig tree.
>
> My sword has drunk its fill in the heavens;
>
> see, it descends in judgment on Edom,
>
> the people I have totally destroyed.

Well, no literal sword came shooting down from heaven on Edom. The sky was not rolled up literally. The stars were not dissolved literally. But God's judgment described in these symbols came to Edom, so there is not an Edomite on the face of the earth anymore. That nation has long since been lost in antiquity. God brings his wrath on people. He brings his warnings and his judgments on people, and he responds to the cry of the people of God.

What we have seen in Revelation 8 is one of the greatest passages on the power of prayer. Your prayers count. When you pray, God listens because of

Jesus Christ who intercedes for you. God is continually watching out on your behalf. Jesus continues to care for you. He wants to answer your cries and your pleas. We need to recognize that this is part of what's involved in God's dealing with our world, even in our time.

If you're not a Christian, you have missed out on the most important thing in the world: coming into a new relationship with God so that you are preparing yourself for eternity with God. Don't allow yourself to continue in rebellion and enmity against God, but become a follower of the Lamb who intercedes with God on your behalf. Give your life to the one who is able to bring you into the presence of God.

We sometimes sing that hymn, "When This Passing World Is Done," and there is one phrase in there that says, "When I stand with Christ on high, looking o'er life's history." That's what Revelation is helping us to do. We are standing with Christ on high and looking over life's history to see how God is dealing with man, to see what is significant, and to see the fact that we are dealing with the awesome realities of eternity. Let us get our heads out of the sand, get our minds away from this earthbound existence here, and realize that we are creatures of eternity. God has prepared a destiny for us in his presence where there will be no pain or sorrow anymore, where God himself will wipe every tear from our eyes. That's what God wants for you. Why not give your life to him, be baptized into him, and begin a new life?

REVELATION 9:

God's Warnings to Repent

O ur lesson comes from the 9th chapter of the book of Revelation. For those of you who may be here for the first time and are catching the middle of this series, let me pause for a moment at the beginning to drop back and very briefly try to explain what we understand Revelation to be saying to this point.

Back in the 1st chapter of Revelation, we saw Jesus walking among his churches, and, in chapters 2 and 3, we saw seven typical churches with their problems and their difficulties and their victories. It is obvious that in the world the church struggles against sin and against Satan. And sometimes the struggles become so overwhelming as to cause Christians to almost give up.

So, at that point, we are taken, in chapter 4, into heaven itself, to the throne of God, to be reminded that God is on his throne and God is in charge in our world. His people, therefore, can have hope, and conquer, and, ultimately, they will gain victory.

In chapter 5, we see the beautiful scene where the Lamb of God, slain for the sins of the world, ascends to the very throne of God and joins the Father at the throne. There he receives the same worship as the Father.

Then, in chapter 6, we see the Lamb of God riding out as a conqueror bent on conquest, having been slain—crucified, resurrected, and having ascended to the throne of God. He then, through the means of his people, begins to evangelize and to conquer the minds of men throughout the world. The result of that is that Satan tries to destroy the works of God. As the world is being evangelized, Satan is also doing his best to destroy the people of God. As the second seal is opened, we see religious persecution coming. We see another seal opened, and we see the economic hardship that comes to God's people, especially as they are attempting to serve God and they encounter the injustices of our world. Then we see death, which is the common lot of mankind, believer and unbeliever. Death does not harm God's people, for they are seen next in the very presence of God. And then we see, finally, the destruction God brings on mankind.

But, in chapter 7, we see again that those who are the people of God are sealed and spared from the final destruction that befalls the wicked, and we find the people of God rejoicing at his throne forever and ever.

Then we come to chapter 8 of Revelation, and we see, as the seventh seal is opened, a series of angels bearing trumpets—trumpets of warning to those who would harm God's people, and we see trumpet after trumpet sounding. At the very beginning, we see the prayers of God's people ascending to his throne, and we see God responding to the prayers of his people by hurling fire on the earth. As we look at the series of trumpets of warning that follow the seals of persecution, we are able to see that God is trying to warn the wicked—those who are unbelievers, those who may even have been tormenting and persecuting God's people—to warn them to repent and turn to God.

In the previous section where we saw the seals being opened, we saw God's people and unbelievers alike suffering the hardships and the difficulties of this life. But now, as we see the trumpets of judgment and warning, we are seeing that God does bring specifically on the unbeliever his judgment and his warnings. When we saw the first four trumpets sound in Revelation 8, we saw the natural calamities of the world that come on mankind which should serve as warnings from God. They should cause men to consider the fact that life is very fragile, that death is something that is the lot of all mankind, and that, therefore, we need to think beyond death, beyond this life, to realize that God is one before whom we will give account of our lives.

Now, as we come to the 9th chapter of the book of Revelation, we read: "The fifth angel sounded his trumpet, and I saw a star that had fallen from the sky to the earth. The star was given the key to the shaft of the Abyss." Now, what is that "star that had fallen from the sky to the earth"? Well, we would initially, of course, think in terms of a heavenly body. But the next verse speaks of the star as "he." So the star is merely a symbol, and John is speaking about a person to whom was given the key to the shaft of the Abyss. It was given to him. It was not something that he rightfully had, nor something whose authority was of himself, but, at least for a limited time, he was given certain power.

Who was this person? I believe it has reference to Satan. In Luke 10:18, Jesus Christ said, "I saw Satan fall like lightning from heaven." Satan is the one who has fallen like "lightning from heaven." Here we see the star that had fallen from the sky—from heaven, and he was given the key of the Abyss. And then, when we see the horrible things that come out of the Abyss, we surely see satanic powers and influences at work. Revelation 12:9 says: "The great dragon was hurled down—that ancient serpent called the devil or Satan, who leads the whole world astray. He was hurled to the earth, and his angels with him." So, if we allow the Bible to interpret itself, I believe we must understand the fallen star as being Satan. "The star was *given* the key to the shaft of the Abyss." We need to understand that Satan's power is limited, that he is checked, that he can only go so far, that whatever power he has is permitted him by God.

Now verse 2 says: "When he opened the Abyss, smoke rose from it like the smoke from a gigantic furnace. The sun and sky were darkened by the smoke from the Abyss." What is the significance of the darkening of the sun and the sky? I believe it is a symbol of the deception and spiritual blindness Satan inflicts on men. Let us allow the scriptures to provide the clues for understanding. We go back to 2 Corinthians 4:3-4. Paul said: "And even if our gospel is veiled, it is veiled to those who are perishing. The god of this age has blinded the minds of unbelievers, so that they cannot see the light of the gospel of the glory of Christ, who is the image of God."

Satan is one who causes spiritual blindness so that the gospel of Christ might not penetrate the hearts of men. I believe Romans 1 provides the closest thing to a parallel to what we have seen in Revelation 9. In verse 21 Paul spoke of those who had rejected what knowledge of God had been provided them, "For although they knew God, they neither glorified him as God nor gave thanks to him, but their thinking became futile and their foolish hearts were darkened." Satan deludes and deceives mankind, and he darkens the souls of those who reject the knowledge of God.

Now Revelation 9:3-4 says: "And out of the smoke locusts came down upon the earth and were given power like that of scorpions of the earth. They were told not to harm the grass of the earth or any plant or tree, but only those people who did not have the seal of God on their foreheads." Here we see locusts coming out of the Abyss, but these are most unusual locusts. We are not speaking now about a literal plague of locusts.

That this is a symbol is clearly indicated by the further description that is given of these locusts. Nine times language is employed that shows that John is speaking symbolically. Notice that while these were locusts, their torment, according to verse 5, was like the torment of scorpions. Then, according to verses 7-10, they were like horses.

> On their heads they wore something like crowns of gold, and
> their faces resembled human faces. Their hair was like women's
> hair, and their teeth were like lions' teeth. They had breastplates
> like breastplates of iron, and the sound of their wings was like the
> thundering of many horses and chariots rushing into battle. They
> had tails and stings like scorpions….

These are not real locusts. This is a symbol. But what is the symbol trying to say to us?

Well, these locusts are unlike literal locusts. Literal locusts eat grass and eat all the green vegetation of the earth, but these locusts were not to harm the vegetation of the earth; they were not to hurt the grass, and they were not to hurt the trees. The only thing these locusts are permitted to harm is men. The point is that here is something that affects men. In what way does it affect men? Well, in verse 5 we are told: "They were not given power to kill them, but only to torture them for five months. And the agony they suffered was like that of the sting of a scorpion when it strikes a man." These locusts were to bring torture to mankind. What kind of torture? I believe the kind of torture that is spoken of here is the agony that comes into the lives of men who have allowed themselves to be dominated by sin.

Let's go back to the prophecy of Joel. In the 1st chapter of Joel there is a description of a plague of locusts. It's a very graphic description of how the locusts come and strip the land. The plague of locusts was one of the terrors of that ancient world, and even today in some parts of the world there is hardly anything as devastating and as terrifying as a plague of locusts. In Joel 1 we see a description of the judgment of God being brought in the form of a plague of locusts. As we come to verse 12 of chapter 1, after the description of what the locusts did, notice the conclusion and the significance of it all. He shows the aftermath of the plague:

> The vine is dried up
>
> and the fig tree is withered;
>
> the pomegranate, the palm and the apple tree—
>
> all the trees of the field—are dried up.
>
> Surely the joy of people
>
> is withered away.

Here, ultimately, is the significance of what is taking place. Joy is withered away from people. Here we see the anguish of spirit of men who have been rebellious toward God.

Now, as we look at Revelation 9, notice that the people who are being harmed by the locusts here are not God's people. His people are spared completely. They're not going to be tortured. Why? Because God's people have the joy of God residing in them. They have peace of mind, the peace that passes all understanding. Notice, in verse 4, John said: "They were told not to harm the grass of the earth or any plant or tree, but only those people who did not have the seal of God on their foreheads." Earlier in Revelation we saw that this seal of God identifies God's people, those that belong to Christ. So, the plague of locusts is going to hurt all except God's people.

In 2 Timothy 2:19 we are told: "Nevertheless, God's solid foundation stands firm, sealed with this inscription: 'The Lord knows those who are his.'" God knows his people. He is not going to allow your heart to be overwhelmed so that it is totally crushed. That is not to say there will never be sorrow in our lives. It's not to say there will never be anguish in our lives, but it is to say that God is going to bring to your lives a satisfaction, and he is going to fill the needs of your lives in a way that those who have refused any relationship to Christ can never know.

God's people are in a unique position. In 2 Peter 2:9, Peter said: "…the Lord knows how to rescue godly men from trials and to hold the unrighteous for the day of judgment.…" God knows how to deliver the godly from trials. He is going to spare you the anguish, the terror, that so often afflicts the hearts of those who know they are not right with God. What we are seeing here—in terms of one of the most terrifying things that bothered the people of that time, a plague of locusts—is the terrifying description of the awfulness of sin.

The description of these grotesque creatures ends with these words in verse 10: "They had tails and stings like scorpions, and in their tails they had power to torment people for five months." What's the significance of the five months? Verse 5 had already said that, "They were not given power to kill them, but only to torture them for five months." I think it is simply a way of saying two things.

First, this is not the final torment of the wicked being described here in Revelation 9. This is not the eternal torment of the fire of hell. What we are seeing here is something that is limited, it is just for "five months;" it is not the eternal punishment of the wicked. We are seeing here that in this lifetime the wicked experience an anguish of soul that eats away at them and never gives them complete satisfaction. There is always the gnawing suspicion that something is wrong. There is a terrifying realization of alienation from God.

But, second, I believe the "five months" is simply to say that God is the one who determines how long and how intense the anguish of spirit is going to be within man. God has set boundaries, and God knows what man can endure and what he needs to endure for the purpose of trying to bring him to his senses. God permits such spiritual torment not to destroy man, but to try to warn man. These are trumpets of warning that the angels are sounding to try to cause men to realize the awfulness of the condition they are in.

But what's the significance of "five"? I don't think there is any particular significance to that at all except just to suggest the two points that we have already made. It's like asking of the parable of five wise and foolish virgins, "Why five?" I don't know. I don't think it is particularly significant. He had to choose a number. Consider the parable of the man who had five talents. Why five? Why not twelve? Why not sixty-three? I don't know. He just chose five. Let us not press details of the picture so that we distort the picture. Some will take the description of the locust and try to give some explanation of the meaning of the teeth on the locust, the meaning of the sting on the tail, the meaning of the long hair like a woman, and things like that. But I believe there is not necessarily any particular significance to all the details except as they contribute to the picture of the grotesqueness and the awfulness and the ugliness of the forces of Satan.

Now verse 11 says: "They had as king over them the angel of the Abyss, whose name in Hebrew is Abaddon, and in Greek, Apollyon." These names mean "destruction" and "destroyer." This is a perfect description of Satan. He is the one who wants to destroy man. He is not out to serve you. He is out to deceive you and delude you and to get you to think that his pleasures are the things that bring real satisfaction in life. Yet in the living of life it becomes so apparent that there comes a void and an emptiness that can never be satisfied by the kinds of deceitful pleasures that Satan sets before us. Let us seek to find our joy in those delights that God has provided for man's well-being and man's happiness. So, I believe, as we look at the fifth angel and the trumpet sounding, that we are seeing that God is permitting anguish of spirit in the hearts of unbelievers for the purpose of warning them and trying to make them see in their very misery their need for God and to cause them to repent and turn to him.

Verse 12 says: "The first woe is past; two other woes are yet to come." Now we look at one of those two woes. Beginning at verse 13 we read:

> The sixth angel blew his trumpet, and I heard a voice coming from the horns of the golden altar that is before God. It said to the sixth angel who had the trumpet, "Release the four angels who are bound at the great river Euphrates." And the four angels who had been kept ready for this very hour and day and month and year were released to kill a third of mankind. The number of the mounted troops was two hundred million. I heard their number.
>
> The horses and riders I saw in my vision looked like this: Their breastplates were fiery red, dark blue, and yellow as sulfur. The heads of the horses resembled the heads of lions, and out of their mouths came fire, smoke and sulfur. A third of mankind was killed by the three plagues of fire, smoke and sulfur that came out of their mouths. The power of the horses was in their mouths and in their tails; for their tails were like snakes, having heads with which they inflict injury.

But then I want you to remember that the ones who are going to be harmed here are not God's people. The ones who are going to be hurt are the unbelievers, those who are opposed to and even persecuting God's people.

Remember, the first five trumpets of warning in chapter 8 were the direct consequence of the prayers of God's people going before his throne. Fire was hurled on the earth against those who had been tormenting and persecuting God's people. And what we are seeing here in chapter 9 is a continuation of the same idea. In verse 13, when the sixth angel sounded the trumpet, we were taken back to the altar at the throne of God. There a voice was heard ordering the four angels to be released who had been bound at the great river Euphrates. Again, God was the one permitting this to be done. They have been bound, and in God's good time and his appointed hour he permits Satan to bring devastation to men who are in rebellion against God and who have opposed and persecuted God's people.

I believe what we see here when the sixth trumpet sounds is the warfare that occurs in our world, which, in the most vivid and graphic way, serves as a warning to the world, "Your ways are perverted ways. Your ways are corrupt ways that can only bring destruction." War certainly shows man at his ugliest, man at his worst, and it is as though man ought to see in the wars that take place on earth that men need to turn to God. Now we see a third of mankind killed. As we saw in the case of the first four trumpets, we see the use of the "third," which is simply to indicate that this not the final judgment of God on mankind, but only a portion of humanity is affected here. This represents the warning judgments of God that come to our earth as war after war after war affect and plague humanity.

But notice what happens in verses 20-21: "The rest of mankind that were not killed by these plagues still did not repent of the work of their hands; they did not stop worshiping demons, and idols of gold, silver, bronze, stone and of wood—idols that cannot see or hear or walk. Nor did they repent of their murders, their magic arts, their sexual immorality or their thefts." Notice, they did not repent, they did not repent. What's the significance? All of this is to bring mankind to its senses and say, "Give yourself to God. He loves you; he cares for you." These were judgments of warning on men in the hope of causing them, by the awfulness of these things, to repent, to turn to God. Yet we see the hardness and callousness of the hearts of men, that they would not repent. They would not turn to God. We also see the patience and the longsuffering of God, that he continues to warn while there is yet time and say, "Repent." Yet, man says, "I will not repent."

But what would you say right now to God, to a God who has tried in every way to warn you of the wrath that is to come by the temporary troubles that befall us in this life? Would you reject God and his love, or would you allow the things that you see in this life to warn you and to bring you to a realization of the fact that God really is on his throne, that there is no joy in following the ways of Satan, that they only bring destruction, that true joys and true peace of mind are to be found in that relationship with God who cares for you, who has tried his best to show you the way, and who has loved you so much that he let Jesus die for you? What will you do about all that? Won't you give your life to Jesus, believe in him, trust him, repent of your sins, confess your faith in him who loved you and gave himself up for you, be baptized into him, and begin to walk with him?

REVELATION 10:

Delay No Longer

W e have come to the 10th chapter of Revelation. I would like to give you the background to what is found in this chapter, so you can see the chapter in its context. Without knowing the context, this chapter cannot be understood.

At the very beginning, in chapter 1, we see Jesus walking among his churches.

In chapters 2 and 3 we see the churches experiencing hardship and difficulties and probably wondering why it must be so: "Is God really on our side? Is he really there to help us?"

So, in chapter 4 we see a door standing open in heaven. There we see the throne of God and we see that God is really in charge of his universe.

In chapter 5 we see Jesus, the Lamb slain, coming to the throne of God and joining the Father. We see glory and honor ascribed to the Lamb of God who takes away the sins of the world. In chapter 5 we see a book that was sealed, and only the Lamb was worthy to open the seals.

Now in chapter 6, as he opens the seals one by one, we see the future opened up, and we see what is to happen between the time when Jesus came till the time when he will come again. When the first seal is opened, we see Jesus riding out to conquer. When the second seal is opened, we see the persecution that follows in the wake of the proclamation of the gospel of Christ, and we see how God's people suffer. As other seals are opened, we see them suffer from economic hardship caused by injustice and from the natural calamities that occur in our world. But we see that those who die and are faithful, even to the point of death, are found in the very presence of God. God protects them. And finally, we see the destruction of the wicked.

In chapter 7 we see that the righteous have been saved.

Then we come to a series of trumpets that are blown by seven angels. These are revealed to us as the seventh seal is opened. They represent the warning judgments of God that come on the wicked in the world in response to the prayers of the righteous that go up before the throne of God.

So in chapters 8 and 9, as we see six trumpets sound in response to the prayers of the saints of God, we see God bringing judgment on rebellious humanity. Yet, in Revelation 9:20-21, we see that after all these warning judgments inflicted on those who oppose God's people:

> The rest of mankind that were not killed by these plagues still did not repent of the work of their hands; they did not stop worshiping demons, and idols of gold, silver, bronze, stone and wood—idols that cannot see or hear or walk. Nor did they repent of their murders, their magic arts, their sexual immorality or their thefts.

All through this period from chapters 8 through 9, we have been looking at the judgments on the unrighteous and the ungodly in our world.

Now from chapter 10:1 right through chapter 11:14 we see a parenthesis as John is shown a vision of that which is going to happen for the benefit of God's own people. We have seen the judgment of God being poured out on the wicked in chapters 8 and 9. But before we hear the last trumpet blown, God wants us to see that we are going to be preserved, that, finally, we will be presented before the throne of God and, ultimately, we will be victorious.

We are ready now to look at chapter 10, and we begin at verse 1:

> Then I saw another mighty angel coming down from heaven. He was robed in a cloud, with a rainbow above his head; his face was like the sun, and his legs were like fiery pillars. He was holding a little scroll, which lay open in his hand. He planted his right foot on the sea and his left foot on the land, and he gave a loud shout like the roar of a lion. When he shouted, the voices of the seven thunders spoke.

It's an awesome spectacle that John beholds as he sees this gigantic angel who plants one foot on the land and one on the sea and roars with a great voice.

And we wonder, "What is this angel doing here anyway? What is his purpose, and how does he fit into the picture of what we have seen in Revelation?" Some have misunderstood the angel as being Jesus Christ himself. In scripture, Jesus Christ is never spoken of as an angel. In fact, in the book of Hebrews, in chapter 1, Jesus is placed in direct contrast to the angels. He is not an angel. He is the Son of God. He is superior to the angels, according to Hebrews 1. So, we're not seeing Jesus in Revelation 10:1-3. We are seeing an angel who comes from the throne of God.

Now it is true that the symbolism that surrounds this angel—his being robed in a cloud, a rainbow above his head, his face like the sun, and his legs like fiery pillars—are symbols associated with the throne of God and with Jesus Christ, as we have seen in Revelation 1 and 4. But the point is, we are being shown that this angel is not an evil angel, but an angel who comes from the throne of God himself. He is surrounded by the symbols associated with the Father and the Son. So, the angel is a representative of Jesus Christ, and he plants one foot on the land and one on the sea and he begins to roar like a lion. And when he shouts, the seven thunders speak.

There is a fascinating passage in the 29th Psalm which reminds us of what we find here in the seven thunders speaking. I don't believe that the seven thunders that speak in Revelation 10 are saying the things that are found in the 29th Psalm. Yet in the 29th Psalm you find the voice of the Lord spoken of seven times, and the voice of the Lord thunders. And I believe that as we read the 29th Psalm, we can get a feel for what must be taking place here. I want to simply read to you at this point the 29th Psalm:

> Ascribe to the Lord, O mighty ones,
>
> > ascribe to the Lord glory and strength.
>
> Ascribe to the Lord the glory due his name;
>
> > worship the Lord in the splendor of his holiness.
>
> The voice of the Lord is over the waters;
>
> > the God of glory thunders,
> >
> > the Lord thunders over the mighty waters.
>
> The voice of the Lord is powerful;
>
> > the voice of the Lord is majestic.
>
> The voice of the Lord breaks the cedars;
>
> > the Lord breaks in pieces the cedars of Lebanon.
>
> He makes Lebanon skip like a calf,
>
> > Sirion like a young wild ox.
>
> The voice of the Lord strikes
>
> > with flashes of lightning.
>
> The voice of the Lord shakes the desert;
>
> > the Lord shakes the Desert of Kadesh.
>
> The voice of the Lord twists the oaks
>
> > and strips the forests bare.
>
> And in his temple all cry, "Glory!"
>
> The Lord sits enthroned over the flood;
>
> > the Lord is enthroned as King forever.
>
> The Lord gives strength to his people;
>
> > the Lord blesses his people with peace.

What we have seen in Revelation 8 and 9 are the judgments of God against nations. And in the middle of all this, one might wonder what is happening to the people of God. What is their destiny? What is their fate in the middle of all that is happening? What we are seeing is that, while the voice thunders, it is for the preservation and protection of God's people, for the Lord will bless his people with peace. And it is to say that, even in the middle of our world where the judgments of God are continually poured out on the wicked, God's people are able to experience peace in their hearts, and they will find strength to bear up under the burdens that may come on them as well. So, we are hearing the voice of the Lord thundering through the means of an angel.

Elsewhere in the Old Testament we have the suggestion that the roaring of the voice of God is really something that is associated with peace for the people of God. Let's look for a moment at Hosea 11:10-11:

"They will follow the Lord;

he will roar like a lion.

When he roars,

his children will come trembling from the west.

They will come trembling

like birds from Egypt,

like doves from Assyria.

I will settle them in their homes,"

declares the Lord.

In other words, here is a roaring of the Lord for the purpose of the preservation of his people whom he will preserve in their homes.

Then we turn to the next such prophecy of the Old Testament. Joel 3:16 says:

The Lord will roar from Zion

and thunder from Jerusalem;

the earth and the sky will tremble.

But the Lord will be a refuge for his people,

a stronghold for the people of Israel.

The roaring of the Lord may be terrifying to the hearts of the ungodly, but to the people of God it is reassuring that God is the awesome ruler of our universe, and that the power that men possess in our world is nothing compared to the power of God. So, as we see the angel of God who plants a foot on the sea and plants a foot on the land and towers above the earth, we realize we need not fear what is happening to righteous men on the earth, because God is going to protect his people.

Now we continue in verse 4: "And when the seven thunders spoke, I was about to write; but I heard a voice from heaven say, 'Seal up what the seven thunders have said and do not write it down.'" Well, John had been seeing revelations, and as he was seeing them he was writing down the things that he saw. Now he hears the seven thunders speak, and he is about to write down what they say when a voice says, "Don't write. Seal these things up." And you say, "What is the significance of that?" I believe the significance is that God is saying to us, "Now look, I am not revealing everything to you of my purposes and how I am going to deal with our world. There are some things that still cannot be revealed, that you cannot bear, that you cannot understand." It reminds me of the passage back in Deuteronomy 29:29 which says: "The secret things belong to the Lord our God, but the things revealed belong to us and to our children forever, that we may follow all the words of this law."

In our time, we hear preachers on the radio speaking to the American people about the book of Revelation. It distresses me that so often they pick details out of context and say they refer to what is happening today in Lebanon, Afghanistan, or some such place, when really they don't have any idea what they are talking about. They are trying to see and hear things God never intended to reveal in the first place. They are trying to draw back the veil on the future and see things about which God is not intending to speak. As we study Revelation, we must allow the Bible to interpret itself, and we must not try to read into these symbols and these passages our own wishes and desires of how we think things ought to be or may be in the future. There are some things that belong to God, and God simply has not chosen to reveal to us everything we would like to know about what is going to happen. We must content ourselves with the things that have been revealed.

So often people spend their lives caught up in speculations about the future and trying to see things that God never wanted to reveal, rather than devoting their lives to faithful obedience to the things that God has clearly revealed that we must do. God has shown us so clearly in scripture how we ought to live our lives, how we ought to treat each other, what God expects us to do with reference to the poor, with those who are in need, and the way we should treat our husbands and wives and children and how we should treat the people where we work. The Bible is so clear about the way we are to live our lives and how we are to be pleasing to God. Yet so many overlook the obvious things just as the hypocrites in Jesus' day overlooked the more important things, being obsessed with their irrelevant traditions. It's amazing how many commentators try their best to suggest what was being said when the seven thunders spoke, though the voice from heaven told John to seal it up, that this is not for the world to know.

I believe we are being told that God has purposes and plans and capacities that are beyond our ability to understand. But he has chosen to reveal to us enough that we can take courage, because that is the reason Revelation was written: to provide comfort and assurance to the people of God, so they will realize that God is in charge and his people are going to be victorious. So, what he is saying to us in chapter 10 is, "Don't worry about the awesome calamities that befall our world. Don't worry about the wars and the chaos and the confusion of our times. Just realize and remember that you, as God's people, are going to be preserved. You will be protected, and you will be brought ultimately into the very presence of God, if you continue faithfully, even to the point of death."

Now we come to verses 5-6: "Then the angel I had seen standing on the sea and on the land raised his right hand to heaven. And he swore by him who lives for ever and ever, who created the heavens and all that is in them, the earth and all that is in it, and the sea and all that is in it, and said, 'There will be no more delay!'" The King James version says that there should be "time" no longer. But it means essentially the same thing, there will be "delay" no longer. That's the real meaning of this expression. When the King James says "there should be time no longer," that means God is going to act suddenly and quickly, and there will be no more delays. In other words, when God, in his good time, decides he is going to act, he is going to act suddenly and quickly, and it is going to be all over.

But what we have seen is God's patience continually extended. We have seen God time and again sending his judgments on the earth to try to warn the hardening hearts of men of the fact that one day they are going to stand in the presence of God. Yet we are told they "did not repent of the work of their hands," and again, "Nor did they repent," but finally the time is going to come when God says, "No more. There will be no more delay!" Then the seventh angel will sound the trumpet, Jesus will come again, and then we will all finally stand before the throne of God in judgment and be told our final destiny. There will come a time when the patience of God is going to end, when there will be no more delay, and he will come.

Now notice the end of verse 6 through verse 7: "'There will be no more delay! But in the days when the seventh angel is about to sound his trumpet, the mystery of God will be accomplished, just as he announced to his servants the prophets.'" That time when the seventh angel sounds his trumpet will be a time of good news for the people of God. It is a tragedy that so many Christians find a bit of terror in the thought of Jesus coming again. Yet, as we come to the very end of Revelation, there is great anticipation of the time. "Come, Lord Jesus" is the final prayer of the Bible. What a great day it's going to be when the Lord returns and takes his people into eternal bliss! What are those strange attractions of this world that make us want to live here longer anyway? Aren't they the deceitful delusions of Satan? Surely, we ought to look forward with anticipation to that time when the seventh angel sounds his trumpet, when the delay of God's bringing the end of this world will finally cease, and when God will bring salvation to all who are faithful to Christ.

We continue at verse 8:

Then the voice that I had heard from heaven spoke to me once more: "Go, take the scroll that lies open in the hand of the angel who is standing on the sea and on the land."

So I went to the angel and asked him to give me the little scroll. He said to me, "Take it and eat it. It will turn your stomach sour, but in your mouth it will be as sweet as honey." I took the little scroll from the angel's hand and ate it. It tasted as sweet as honey in my mouth, but when I had eaten it, my stomach turned sour.

In the Old Testament, there is, in the prophecy of Ezekiel, a parallel to what we have seen here. The same kind of thing happened in the experience of Ezekiel, and we turn back to Ezekiel 2:9 and read through Ezekiel 3:3:

Then I looked, and I saw a hand stretched out to me. In it was a scroll, which he unrolled before me. On both sides of it were written words of lament and mourning and woe.

And he said to me, "Son of man, eat what is before you, eat this scroll; then go and speak to the house of Israel." So I opened my mouth, and he gave me the scroll to eat.

Then he said to me, "Son of man, eat this scroll I am giving you and fill your stomach with it." So I ate it, and it tasted as sweet as honey in my mouth.

And now notice verse 14: "The Spirit then lifted me up and took me away, and I went in bitterness and in the anger of my spirit, with the strong hand of the Lord upon me." I believe what happened to Ezekiel helps us understand a little better what's happening here in Revelation. Ezekiel, in the vision, was given a scroll to eat. It was sweet in his mouth, and later he went in bitterness.

What is this all about? Well, let's look at Psalm 119:103:

How sweet are your promises to my taste,

sweeter than honey to my mouth!

Now look at Jeremiah 15:16-18:

When your words came, I ate them;

they were my joy and my heart's delight,

for I bear your name,

O Lord God Almighty.

I never sat in the company of revelers,

never made merry with them;

I sat alone because your hand was on me

and you had filled me with indignation.

Why is my pain unending

and my wound grievous and incurable?

Will you be to me like a deceptive brook,

like a spring that fails?

The experience of receiving the word of God—and, of course, the idea of eating the scroll—is the idea of absorbing the word of God, taking it into your very heart and letting it lodge there and become a part of you.

John does this, and the reaction is that it was sweet as he took it, because the word of God is precious, and it is sweeter than honey. But following that there came a certain bitterness which may be explained in one of two ways. One is that the message of God cuts two ways. The sweet message of God is good news to the righteous, but it is a terrifying and bitter message to those who are disobedient and who reject the word of God. So, the message of God that was presented to John in the little scroll was both sweet and bitter.

The second—and, I believe, more likely—possibility is that whenever the sweet word of God is proclaimed, God's people in turn experience the bitter reaction of the wicked and impenitent to the presentation of the word. At least that is what we see in the very next chapter of Revelation: when the word of God is proclaimed, the messengers of the word of God are slain. That is the thing we saw back in Revelation 6 as well. When the word of God went forth, the next thing we saw was the persecution of the people of God.

So, the gospel is a message which brings to its messengers sweetness as well as the bitterness of the persecution which comes. But for those who faithfully proclaim the message of God, there is that unspeakable joy and that final exultation which comes when we hear at the end of it all, "Well done, good and faithful servant!...Come and share your master's happiness!" And that's what God's people look forward to, the final reward which comes to those who are righteous and who live for God faithfully, even to the point of death.

The final statement that we find in Revelation chapter 10 apparently has something to do with God's message pertaining to his people. We see in Revelation 10:11: "Then I was told, 'You must prophesy again about many peoples, nations, languages and kings.'" When the revelation of God has come to his servants, the servants of God are always ordered to take that message and proclaim it. And John, in the remaining portion of the book of Revelation, is doing that very thing. He is giving his prophecy concerning many peoples, nations, languages, and kings. As we continue through the book of Revelation, we are going to see more of what God has said through John, his servant, pertaining to the destiny of nations, peoples, languages, and kings.

In the next message, in Revelation 11, we are going to see one of the most joyous and terrifying visions yet. But what we have seen here is God pausing for a moment to say, "I am going to preserve my people. I have warned the wicked to turn from their ways, but they did not repent. I have brought calamities on the wicked, but as far as my own people are concerned, I am going to turn the calamities and judgments to the glorifying of my own people and to the preservation of my own people and to their ultimate salvation." Right now we need to realize that God's patience does ultimately wear thin, that there is going to come that occasion, and we don't know when it will be, when God will say that "There will be no more delay!" There will be no more delay when the seventh angel sounds his trumpet. The earth will be destroyed, and Jesus will come again to bring his people to the very throne of God.

Don't you want to be among that number? Don't you want to live your life in such a way that you have no fear of that impending judgment, but rather can look forward with anticipation to the coming of Jesus Christ and be able to express fervently from your heart the prayer, "Come, Lord Jesus"? If you have not been living faithfully for Christ, won't you open the door of your heart and let him back into your life? And if you have never given your life to Jesus, why not believe in him, repent of your sins, confess your faith in Christ, and, right now, be baptized into him? You can have your sins washed away and have the assurance that you are now God's child, having been born of water and spirit. Then you can finally breathe a sigh of relief knowing that Jesus has borne your sins and your iniquities and that he is now confessing your name before the Father so that when he comes again, he can introduce you to the Father and say, "This is my child. I want you to receive him to be with us forever." What a great day that will be!

REVELATION 11:

The Two Witnesses

I have been preaching through the New Testament chapter by chapter for the past six years, and we are now in the book of Revelation. Now we have come to the 11th chapter, which some have called the most difficult chapter of the most difficult book of the Bible. My task is simply to try to make this chapter easy to understand and to help you to see what God is saying to us through the chapter. I believe that if I am able to do that, even in a small way, that you will be thrilled and inspired and encouraged.

You have heard the reading of the chapter already, but I want, before we get into the chapter itself this evening, to drop back and, very quickly, review the book of Revelation to this point to give you the background against which we enter this chapter, because the book of Revelation is a marvelous unity. It is not simply a hodgepodge of various odd symbols thrown together in some way to confuse you, but if Revelation is carefully and thoughtfully studied, it will be seen to be a book of beautiful unity.

In chapter 1 of Revelation, we see Jesus in the middle of his churches, reminding us of his promise, "…surely I will be with you always, to the very end of the age."

In chapters 2 and 3, we see the church struggling, suffering, seduced, and some of its soldiers slain, and we sense the church that has been urged to be faithful even to the point of death wondering if it is really worth it. Is Satan winning the battle?

Chapter 4 of Revelation answers with a resounding, "No!" We see a door open in heaven and one sitting on the throne, and we are made to realize that God is in charge of his creation, he rules and reigns.

In chapter 5, we see the book of human destiny sealed, but the Lamb of God, who has been slain, ascends to the throne and is found worthy to open the seals and to reveal and carry out God's purposes. He begins to reign.

In chapter 6, as the first seal is opened, we see him riding out as a conqueror bent on conquest which, according to 2 Corinthians 10:3-5, is accomplished through the agency of God's people. Through their warfare, they are taking captive every thought to make it obedient to Christ. But where the gospel goes, persecution follows. So the next three seals, when they are opened, reveal Christians suffering persecution, economic hardship, and even death. But, lest this discourage the soldiers of the cross, we see, when the fifth seal is opened, the souls of those who have been slain because of the word of God living in his very presence. Having been reassured that death cannot destroy God's people, the sixth seal is opened, the final wrath of God is seen poured out on a rebellious world, and the question is asked, "Who is able to stand?"

Chapter 7 answers, "The servants of our God." They are preserved, protected, and seen standing before the throne and before the Lamb. We are told that God will wipe away every tear from their eyes. But what about God's people while they are on the earth? Doesn't God hear the cries, the prayers, of his persecuted people?

He does. Chapters 8 and 9 show, in God's warning trumpets, judgment being sounded against those who persecute God's people, demonstrating that he does hear their prayers. His people pray, and God hurls fire on the earth. The first four trumpets sound, and we see God sending natural calamities on the world. The fifth trumpet sounds, and we see the wicked experiencing the spiritual agonies that accompany their sinful manner of life. The sixth trumpet sounds, and we see the wicked afflicted with the agony of warfare. All these judgments are designed to turn men back to God. But we are told at the end of the 9th chapter that the rest of mankind who were not killed with these plagues did not repent, and the statement is repeated for emphasis, "Nor did they repent." All that remains now is the return of Christ and the final destruction of the wicked.

But, in the meantime, what is happening to God's people while these judgments are being brought against the wicked? Chapter 10:1 through chapter 11:14 forms a parenthesis to explain to us what happens to God's people during all this. Chapter 10 introduces and, now, chapter 11 describes it.

We begin the study of the 11th chapter of Revelation with verse 1: "I was given a reed like a measuring rod and was told, 'Go and measure the temple of God and the altar, and count the worshipers there.'" There was a long time when I was totally baffled by that verse. I couldn't understand what could possibly be meant by the suggestion of measuring the temple of God and counting the people and measuring the altar, etc. But, finally, it was called to my attention that the Bible talks about measuring things elsewhere, in other prophetic literature of the Bible. I believe that we should allow the Bible to interpret itself as far as possible, and I believe that we can find something of the significance of the measuring if we drop back into two or three Old Testament records.

Concerning the temple of God, Ezekiel 42:20 says: "So he measured the area on all four sides. It had a wall around it, five hundred cubits long and five hundred cubits wide, to separate the holy from the common." Here, we see the temple of God being measured, and it is being measured to make a separation between the holy and the common.

Now, let's turn to chapter 22 of the same book of Ezekiel and verse 26, and we will see another passage referring to this measuring process and its significance. There it says: "Her priests do violence to my law and profane my holy things; they do not distinguish between the holy and the common; they teach that there is no difference between the unclean and the clean; and they shut their eyes to the keeping of my Sabbaths, so that I am profaned among them." Here, we see that there needs to be a distinction made between the holy and the unclean, between that which is God's and that which is not God's. The measuring that we saw in chapter 42 is for the purpose of making that kind of distinction.

Ezekiel 48:35, the last verse of Ezekiel, says:

"The distance all around will be 18,000 cubits.

"And the name of the city from that time on will be:

THE LORD IS THERE."

The temple is measured. It is measured, and determined as being holy, and the presence of God is there.

Now, we turn to one other prophecy of the Old Testament, a passage that actually has more direct bearing on what we are seeing in Revelation, which should help us to get the background and meaning of the concept of measuring. This is Zechariah 2:1-5 which says:

Then I looked up—and there before me was a man with a measuring line in his hand! I asked, "Where are you going?"

He answered me, "To measure Jerusalem, to find out how wide and how long it is."

Then the angel who was speaking to me left, and another angel came to meet him and said to him: "Run, tell that young man, 'Jerusalem will be a city without walls because of the great number of men and livestock in it. And I myself will be a wall of fire around it,' declares the Lord, 'and I will be its glory within.'"

Actually, there are two ideas suggested in the measuring process: one is the idea of separation and distinguishing that which is holy, and the other is the idea of protection.

Let us see how these ideas apply to Revelation 11. The temple is to be measured. Actually, the word "temple" would better be translated "sanctuary," because it does not have reference to the whole temple complex. There are two Greek words translated "temple," but the word here is one that has reference to the holy place and the holy of holies, the inner sanctuary of the temple. John is to measure the temple of God and the altar and count those who worship in it.

The measuring here is to distinguish a holy people, a people separated for God, a people protected by God, because the presence of God is here. The point is that although the saints will suffer, they will not perish. That is made clear in verse 2: "But exclude the outer court; do not measure it, because it has been given to the Gentiles. They will trample on the holy city for 42 months." Now the temple is mentioned again. This does not have reference to the literal temple that was in the city of Jerusalem. To treat it so is to do violence to the way in which the book of Revelation and the New Testament deal with the concept of the temple.

The temple of God is spoken of in the New Testament as being the church of God. For example, in 1 Corinthians 3:16-17, Paul said: "Don't you know that you yourselves are God's temple and that God's Spirit lives in you? If anyone destroys God's temple, God will destroy him; for God's temple is sacred, and you are that temple." "You" is plural, and has reference to all the Christians together, the whole church. In the Old Testament, God had ordered the people of Israel to build a house where he might dwell, where his presence might be. When we come to the New Testament, there is a transformation of the concept, because now the church becomes the temple of God where the Spirit of God dwells. He dwells in us individually, as Paul mentions in 1 Corinthians 6:19-20, and he dwells in the church as a whole. We are the temple of God.

Again, in 2 Corinthians 6:16-17 Paul said:

> What agreement is there between the temple of God and idols? For we are the temple of the living God. As God has said: "I will live with them and walk among them, and I will be their God, and they will be my people."
>
> "Therefore come out from them
>
> and be separate,
>
> says the Lord.

Touch no unclean thing,

and I will receive you."

"I will be a Father to you,

and you will be my sons and daughters,

says the Lord Almighty."

Chapter 7, verse 1, continues: "Since we have these promises, dear friends, let us purify ourselves from everything that contaminates body and spirit, perfecting holiness out of reverence for God." The writer of 2 Corinthians, the apostle Paul, says that we are a temple of the living God and, consequently, we ought to come out of the world. We ought to be a separated people. We ought to be a people no longer living in the contaminations of body and spirit.

So, just as the measuring of the temple was suggestive of the idea of making a distinction and separation between the holy and the unclean, so God's people, the church, are to be a people who are a holy people, a people set apart, sanctified and protected by God. That's the picture we are seeing in Revelation 11:2. We need to remember that Revelation is written in the context of the new covenant, where Christians are identified as the true Jews. Notice Romans 2:28-29; Galatians 3:29; Galatians 6:16; Philippians 3:3; James 1:1, and 1 Peter 2:9-10. These are some references showing that, under the new covenant, Christians are regarded as the true Israel, the Israel of God, those who are Jews indeed, the true circumcision. And, just as individual Christians are the true Jews, so collectively, Christians who form the church comprise the temple of God. That is what we are seeing in Revelation 11:1-2. We are seeing the church of the living God measured, separated, and protected because the Lord is there. His presence is with his people.

But while God preserves and protects his people, the fact remains that his people will still suffer. In verse 2 he says, "But exclude the outer court; do not measure it, because it has been given to the Gentiles. They will trample on the holy city for 42 months." The temple, the court, the holy city, all of these refer to God's people. Remember, the court was also a part of the temple of God. The holy city, here, does not have reference to literal Jerusalem. The holy city is the expression of the new Jerusalem that is spoken of in Hebrews 12:22-23 where the writer says: "But you have come to Mount Zion, to the heavenly Jerusalem, the city of the living God. You have come to thousands upon thousands of angels in joyful assembly, to the church of the firstborn, whose names are written in heaven. You have come to God, the judge of all men...." So, the holy city represents God's church. What we are seeing here are terms referring to the church.

In this composite symbol, we see the church, on the one hand, protected because God is there, but, on the other hand, exposed to the world so that the church continues to suffer persecution. Now, the court, the holy city, and the temple represent the church of Christ. Both aspects of the experience of God's people are seen, both protection and persecution. In Luke 12:4-5, you recall Jesus said: "I tell you, my friends, do not be afraid of those who kill the body.... Fear him who, after the killing of the body, has power to throw you into hell." This has always been the experience of God's people. There has never been a need to fear those who can kill the body. Yet God's people have always been exposed to the persecution of those who oppose God and his cause and his people. But, at the same time, God's people have always been protected, preserved, so that they cannot be thrown into hell. As long as we are faithful to God, as long as we remain his people, we are protected, though we may be persecuted.

Homer Hailey wrote on this passage, "The measured temple symbolizes the inner or spiritual life of the true worshippers which neither Satan nor his instruments of persecution can reach; this is measured and protected by God. But He has not promised to protect the physical life of the body of Christians from being sacrificed and trampled under foot...." As Jim McGuiggan put it, "He permits the suffering but will not permit the annihilation—the inner sanctuary is kept by him."

This harmonizes with what follows in this chapter, what is taught throughout the book of Revelation, and what is taught throughout the New Testament. Jesus said to his disciples: "In this world you will have trouble...." (John 16:33). God's people will be a persecuted people. Remember, the scripture says, "...

everyone who wants to live a godly life in Christ Jesus will be persecuted." The point is, God's people need to understand that in this life there will be suffering, there will be hardships, there will be persecution, there will be every effort on the part of Satan to seduce, to allure into his way of life; and, in this world, we endure all of this. But, the point also is that Satan cannot destroy, that he is not able to snatch anyone out of the Lord's hand. We can leave God, but as long as we stay with God, Satan cannot overcome us. So what we are seeing, I believe, in the composite picture of Revelation 11:1-2 is the church, persecuted and protected.

Now we need to deal with the number given in Revelation 11:2. What is the "42 months"? I believe that when we understand the significance of the 42 months, we will understand even better that these verses are speaking about God's people, his church. Forty-two months is the same thing as three and a half years and, on the Jewish calendar of 360 days in a year, that equals 1,260 days. That also is the same thing as the expression of Revelation 12:14, "a time, times and half a time,"—"time" being a year, "times" being two years, and "half a time" being half a year—which add up to three and a half years. We have three and a half years expressed in four different ways.

I want you to see how these terms are used elsewhere in the book of Revelation, so that you will begin to understand what is meant by that 42 months period of time. First, here in Revelation 11:2, we have seen the holy city being trampled underfoot for 42 months. In the next verse, the church is proclaiming the gospel to the world on a day-by-day basis for 1,260 days, which is the same period of time. The church is being persecuted, but protected from the full wrath of Satan during this period of three and a half years in Revelation 12:6 and 12:14. Satan is trying to deceive God's people during this period which is spoken of as 42 months in Revelation 13:5.

Now what do we see here? We are seeing the same period of time spoken of in terms of days, months, years, and even "a time, times, and half a time." It is a period when the church is being persecuted, a period when the church is proclaiming the gospel to the world, a time when Satan is trying to deceive the people of God. This expression, "a time, times and half a time" is also used in Daniel 12:7. Let me read that to you, also, because I want you to get the full picture, and this will complete the references found in the Bible to this period of time. Daniel 12:7 says this: "The man clothed in linen, who was above the waters of the river, lifted his right hand and his left hand toward heaven, and I heard him swear by him who lives forever, saying, 'It will be for a time, times and half a time. When the power of the holy people has been finally broken, all these things will be completed.'"

Even in Revelation where that expression is used, it has reference to the time when the holy people are being broken in pieces, a time of persecution of God's people. Now, we ask a simple question. What is the period of time during which the church suffers persecution, during which the church is trying to proclaim the gospel to the world, the time during which the world is being seduced by Satan? It is the period from the time the church began on the day of Pentecost to the time that Jesus comes again. The church has been preaching the gospel. The church, consequently, is suffering persecution, and Satan is trying his best to seduce the people of God. This expression, then, has reference to the entire Christian age, and that is important for us to understand.

We're learning now in chapter 11 about the condition of the people of God. In chapters 8 and 9, we've been seeing what's been happening to the world. Now, we are going to learn about God's people during the time when all the calamities, spiritual agonies, and warfare are affecting the people of the world. Here's what's happening to the people of God: they are preaching the word, they are being persecuted, they are suffering—but they are being protected by God so that they cannot be destroyed. The gates of Hades will not prevail against the church, and God's people will ultimately be triumphant. That is the message we are seeing. Don't you remember that Jesus said: "Blessed are you when people insult you, persecute you and falsely say all kinds of evil against you because of me"? That's how it will always be with God's people. We are not, in this life, going to have a bed of roses. But we will have the continual presence and protection and preservation of the power of God working among us.

You might say, "Why would Revelation use a symbol of three and a half years to speak of the entire Christian age? Does that make sense?" Well, superficially, it may not. But I believe we must let the Bible interpret the Bible, as far as possible. So does the Bible have anything else to say about a three and a half year period from which Revelation might have drawn such a symbol for a period of the proclamation of God's message and the persecution of the people of God? It does.

All we have to do is drop back to James 5:17. There, you recall that James said: "Elijah was a man just like us. He prayed earnestly that it would not rain, and it did not rain on the land for three and a half years." There's the figure that we are seeing over and over again in Revelation. Now you might say, "What is the possible connection, if there is any, between what happened in the case of Elijah for three and a half years and the use of such a symbol in Revelation?" Well, that three and a half year period just happened to be in the days of Elijah and Ahab when God's message was being proclaimed and his people were being oppressed.

Let's go back and look at that in 1 Kings 17:1, and I want to show you several references in 1 Kings related to it. It says: "Now Elijah the Tishbite, from Tishbe in Gilead, said to Ahab, 'As the Lord, the God of Israel, lives, whom I serve, there will be neither dew nor rain in the next few years except at my word.'" Now, look at chapter 18:10: "As surely as the Lord your God lives, there is not a nation or kingdom where my master has not sent someone to look for you. And whenever a nation or kingdom claimed you were not there, he made them swear they could not find you." Now, notice verse 13: "Haven't you heard, my lord, what I did while Jezebel was killing the prophets of the Lord? I hid a hundred of the Lord's prophets in two caves, fifty in each, and supplied them with food and water." Here is a period of the prophets' proclamation of God's word when the prophets had to be hidden in a cave because of the persecution that was brought against them. While this was a period of proclamation of God's message and the persecution of God's people, it was also a time of the protection of God's people so they could not be destroyed.

1 Kings 18:4 says: "While Jezebel was killing off the Lord's prophets, Obadiah had taken a hundred prophets and hidden them in two caves, fifty in each, and had supplied them with food and water." God's people were oppressed. Many were killed. But God preserved his people. Later, when Elijah was in a condition of despair and saying, "I am the only one left," God said, "Elijah, there are seven thousand who have not yet bowed their knees to Baal." Chapter 19, verse 18 says, "Yet I reserve seven thousand in Israel—all whose knees have not bowed down to Baal and all whose mouths have not kissed him."

We need to realize that we are not alone in the world. We are not fighting our battles alone. There are people elsewhere in this world who are trying to please God, to serve God, and we know that God is on the throne, and that he is in charge, and his people will be triumphant. Let us not be like little children who come and say, "Well, everybody else is doing it." We ought to grow up and realize that's a lie of Satan. Everybody else isn't doing it. There are still people who are serving God, who are committed to him, and who have not bowed their knees to Baal.

We need to realize that and understand that here was a period in history, a three and a half year period of the proclamation of the message of God, the persecution of God's people, but the preservation of God's people. That the speaker in Revelation had the three and a half year period of Elijah's day in mind is indicated by the statement in Revelation 11:6, "These men have power to shut up the sky so that it will not rain during the time they are prophesying...." That's a perfect statement of what happened in the days of Elijah. The heavens were shut, and it did not rain for three and a half years.

Now, we move to verse 3: "And I will give power to my two witnesses, and they will prophesy for 1,260 days, clothed in sackcloth." Now who are the two witnesses? In verse 4, he says: "These are the two olive trees and the two lampstands that stand before the Lord of the earth." Then, we are told in verse 10 that, "...these two prophets had tormented those who live on the earth." So the two witnesses are called two olive trees, two lampstands, two prophets. To what can this possibly refer? Well, let's think about it a minute. There is only one other time in scripture where two olive trees are associated with lampstands. Again, it is an Old Testament reference which, I believe, gives us the background to what we are seeing here.

So we drop back to Zechariah 4:1-6:

> Then the angel who talked with me returned and wakened me, as a man is wakened from his sleep. He asked me, "What do you see?"
>
> I answered, "I see a solid gold lampstand with a bowl at the top and seven lights on it, with seven channels to the lights. Also there are two olive trees by it, one on the right of the bowl and the other on its left."
>
> I asked the angel who talked with me, "What are these, my lord?"
>
> He answered, "Do you not know what these are?"
>
> "No, my lord," I replied.
>
> So he said to me, "This is the word of the Lord to Zerubbabel: 'Not by might nor by power, but by my Spirit,' says the Lord Almighty."

Now, we have two olive trees which represent the word of the Lord. What are the two olive trees doing? They are standing there on either side of the lampstands furnishing the olive oil to provide the light from the lampstands. So we have seen in the scripture where the lampstands and the olive trees are tied together. When we return to the more immediate context of Revelation, we see, in the last verse of the first chapter, that the lampstands represent the churches.

Well, what was the purpose of the church as it went out into the world? It served as a witness to the whole world. It was carrying the message of the prophets into the whole world. Now there is one other thing that we need to know in connection with all this. According to Revelation 11:7, these two prophets are going to be killed: "Now when they have finished their testimony, the beast that comes up from the Abyss will attack them, and overpower and kill them."

Revelation tells us who the beast makes war against, elsewhere, in chapter 13 and verse 7. It says: "He was given power to make war against the saints...." The beast makes war against the saints. That's God's people, the church.

So who are the two witnesses, the two lampstands, the two olive trees, the two prophets? It is the gospel-proclaiming church. Why is it spoken of as two? There may be several reasons. One is suggested in a principle established in Deuteronomy and repeated in 2 Corinthians 13:1: "Every matter must be established by the testimony of two or three witnesses." The point is that the church serves as an adequate witness to the world.

It may also be that the two witnesses represent two things: the word of God, as suggested by the olive trees in Zechariah 4, and God's people, because the word of God is what God's people carry into the world. But what happens? Well, Revelation 11:4-5 says: "These are the two olive trees and the two lampstands that stand before the Lord of the earth. If anyone tries to harm them, fire comes from their mouths and devours their enemies. This is how anyone who wants to harm them must die."

You may say, "That doesn't sound like the church to me. How is fire coming out of the mouth of the church? That doesn't make sense." Let's go back to Jeremiah. Jeremiah 5:14 says:

Therefore this is what the Lord God Almighty says:

"Because the people have spoken these words,

I will make my words in your mouth a fire

and these people the wood it consumes."

As the church goes forth presenting the word of God, it converts many, but it is like a fire consuming those who reject it.

Then again, it says in verse 6: "These men have power to shut up the sky so that it will not rain during the time they are prophesying; and they have power to turn the waters into blood and to strike the earth with every kind of plague as often as they want." You say, "Can the church do that?" We have already read Revelation 8 that says, "Yes, the church can do that." The prayers of the saints are sent to the throne of God, and God hurls fire down on the earth. God hears the prayers of his persecuted people. Yes, the prayers of the church have power to change the world, to affect the world, to affect the governments of the world. When we say, "Pray for the kings of the earth," we're meaning it. It makes a difference. God hears our prayers and his suffering and persecuted people will be avenged by the wrath of God. That's what Revelation 8 is telling us. The church is not some kind of insignificant, trivial little institution on the face of the earth. It's God's powerful people proclaiming his message and powerfully affecting the course of the world.

Now, notice verses 8-10:

> Their bodies will lie in the street of the great city, which is figuratively called Sodom and Egypt, where also their Lord was crucified. For three and a half days men from every people, tribe, language and nation will gaze on their bodies and refuse them burial. The inhabitants of the earth will gloat over them and will celebrate by sending each other gifts, because these two prophets had tormented those who live on the earth.

The two prophets tormented them, not in the sense that the church was trying to be mean to the world, but in the sense that Elijah was called by the wicked Ahab, "you troubler of Israel." That's how the world sees the church, as the source of its troubles. From God's point of view, it was Ahab who was the troubler of Israel.

But the point of the whole passage seems to be that, at the end of time when the period of the proclamation of the church is about to come to an end, the power of the church to proclaim the message throughout the world is going to be curtailed to such an extent that the church is no longer able to carry on. It appears that the church has been killed. It reminds us of what Jesus said in Luke 18:8: "…when the Son of Man comes, will he find faith on the earth?" We do know there will be some because, when he comes again, one will be taken and the other left. But there will be a brief time at the end where it will seem as though the gates of Hades have prevailed against the church. This three and a half years of evangelization by the church includes a brief period at the very end when it looks like Satan has won. Then what happens?

Then we come to an exciting climax, which is found here in the middle of the book of Revelation in chapter 11, beginning at verse 11:

> But after the three and a half days a breath of life from God entered them, and they stood on their feet, and terror struck those who saw them. Then they heard a loud voice from heaven saying to them, "Come up here." And they went up to heaven in a cloud, while their enemies looked on.
>
> At that very hour there was a severe earthquake and a tenth of the city collapsed. Seven thousand people were killed in the earthquake, and the survivors were terrified and gave glory to the God of heaven.

Here we see God's people caught up to heaven. Jesus is coming again. The wicked are being destroyed. We don't have the full description here because, all of a sudden, it is cut off with the words in verse 14: "The second woe has passed; the third woe is coming soon."

Now the seventh angel finally sounds, and there is finished the mystery of God that is spoken of in chapter 10:

> The seventh angel sounded his trumpet, and there were loud voices in heaven, which said:
>
> > "The kingdom of the world has become the kingdom of
> >
> > our Lord and of his Christ,
> >
> > and he will reign for ever and ever."

God is triumphant. His people have gone to be with him. They have been caught up to meet the Lord in the air, and so they will be with the Lord forever, because

> > "The kingdom of the world has become the kingdom of
> >
> > our Lord and of his Christ,

and he will reign for ever and ever."

And the twenty-four elders, who were seated on their thrones before God, fell on their faces and worshiped God, saying:

"We give thanks to you, Lord God Almighty,

who is and who was,

because you have taken your great power

and have begun to reign."

Note what was said, back in Revelation 4:8, when we came for the first time to the throne of God to see God sitting on his throne. Angels were falling down before him and saying:

"Holy, holy, holy

is the Lord God Almighty,

who was, and is, and is to come."

Now he is spoken of as simply one who "is and who was." It doesn't say, "and is to come," because now he *has* come! Jesus has come, and he has delivered his people at the very time that Satan had, apparently, gained a victory. God's people are triumphant! They are preserved, they are protected, they are saved to reign with him forever and ever.

Then, we are told:

"The nations were angry;

and your wrath has come.

The time has come for judging the dead,

and for rewarding your servants the prophets

and your saints and those who reverence your name,

both small and great—

and for destroying those who destroy the earth."

Then God's temple in heaven was opened, and within his temple was seen the ark of his covenant. And there came flashes of lightning, rumblings, peals of thunder, an earthquake and a great hailstorm.

Notice that now, finally, God's people have gone to meet him, and the temple of God is opened, the sanctuary, where the ark of the covenant was, and where only one man could go one time in a year into the holy of holies. But when Jesus shed his blood on the cross of Calvary, the veil was ripped from top to bottom, the holy place was opened, and now it is open for all who accept the message of Jesus Christ.

I believe the greatest commentary on this is found in Hebrews 10:19-25:

> Therefore, brothers, since we have confidence to enter the Most Holy Place by the blood of Jesus, by a new and living way opened for us through the curtain, that is, his body, and since we have a great priest over the house of God, let us draw near to God with a sincere heart in full assurance of faith, having our hearts sprinkled to cleanse us from a guilty conscience and having our bodies washed with pure water. Let us hold unswervingly to the hope we profess, for he who promised is faithful. And let us consider how we may spur one another on toward love and good deeds. Let us not give up meeting together, as some are in the habit of doing, but let us encourage one another—and all the more as you see the Day approaching.

The sanctuary of God is open in heaven where the ark rests and where the presence of God is, and we have direct access to him who had been veiled for so long. So let us draw near with full assurance of faith, having our bodies washed with pure water, having our hearts sprinkled to cleanse us from a guilty conscience.

Finally, in Revelation 11, we see the same scene that was seen the first time we saw God on his throne in Revelation 4. We are told that there came flashes of lightning, rumblings, peals of thunder, and God in all of his awesome glory is there awaiting us.

Will you come to him now, give your heart to him, and begin to walk in his way? If you believe in Jesus, repent of your sins, confess your faith, and have your body washed with pure water. Your heart will be sprinkled to cleanse you from a guilty conscience—sprinkled by the blood of Jesus Christ, shed on the cross. He split the curtain, and opened the way to the presence of God.

REVELATION 12:

The Dragon and the Woman

We are considering "The Dragon and the Woman," taken from Revelation 12. We have been studying through Revelation, and by the time we came to the end of the 11th chapter, we came to the end of the world. We came to the time when Jesus had already come again, yet we have eleven more chapters in Revelation. What happens? Well, we're dropping back to the beginning again.

In the first eleven chapters, we have seen the conflict between the church and those who are persecuting and opposing it. Now, as we come to chapter 12, we're going into the background of all this. We are looking at what's behind all this. There is a greater struggle taking place behind the scenes that accounts for the troubles that the church has in the world. So we're dropping back to the time when Jesus came into our world the first time, and we're eventually going to see Jesus coming again. In Revelation we see a recapitulation. We see God dealing with his people—from Christ's first coming to his second coming—seen from several perspectives as we work our way through the book of Revelation.

There are many diverse interpretations and radically different views of what Revelation is all about, largely due to a misunderstanding of the basic nature of the book. There are those who hold to a continuous historical interpretation of Revelation in which they assume that Revelation is a prophecy of that which was to occur in sequence from the time John wrote this until the end of time.

By the time they are in the 11th chapter of Revelation, they have moved historically up to about the time of Constantine, or into the fourth or fifth centuries. But then they have a horrible time dealing with chapter 12 because, very clearly, chapter 12 is telling us about the birth of Jesus and about his ascension into heaven. Historically that just doesn't fit after chapter 11. So Revelation is forced into an unnatural structure. I believe that we must allow Revelation to interpret itself, to form its own framework for interpretation.

There are those who say that all of Revelation has already been fulfilled. These, who take the preterist view of Revelation, believe that Revelation was written for its own time, for the first century or, at best, the first two, three, or four centuries. They believe it is dealing in a historical way with events taking place in the first century, or the first few centuries after Christ. Some say that everything in the book of Revelation, from chapter 1 through 22, has already, centuries ago, been fulfilled, and there is nothing of the future to be found in Revelation. They say that Revelation isn't even talking anywhere about the second coming of Christ, that it does not anywhere talk about the eternal reward of the righteous. It was all fulfilled and came to a climax when the pagan Roman Empire fell. Those who hold that view do so largely because in the first and last chapters of Revelation there are statements that this book is telling us about things which "must soon take place." There is almost an obsession with the word "soon" or "shortly," as though everything in the book has got to take place in a very, very brief period of time.

Yet in the chapter we are studying tonight, Revelation 12:12 says:

> "Therefore rejoice, you heavens
>
> and you who dwell in them!
>
> But woe to the earth and the sea,
>
> because the devil has gone down to you!
>
> He is filled with fury,
>
> because he knows that his time is short."

The same word is used here. The devil has a "short" time, and yet he has been at work here for 2,000 years or more already since Jesus came the first time.

But, to get around that problem, one writer who takes this view said in his commentary that, actually, none of the symbols of Revelation have anything to do with time! The 1,260 days, three and a half years, 42 months, the time, times and half a time have, really, nothing to do with time. Yet, after having said that, it is argued that "shortly" means just a very limited number of years. There is a strange inconsistency in all of this, and I think many have forced Revelation into a very strange shape by demanding, on the basis of a word here or there, or a preconception about what the book is supposed to do, how it should be interpreted.

I haven't really spent much time presenting alternative interpretations. I have just presented what I believe Revelation is actually saying. As we go along, I believe other points of view can be seen against the background of this as being inadequate and really not providing us with the great encouragement and inspiration that the book of Revelation is designed to give our lives. Certainly, it is designed to bring comfort to the people of God, as all interpreters agree. It says to God's people that if you are faithful, even to the point of death, you will be victorious. Therefore, let us be faithful, and let us endure.

We come now to the 12th chapter of Revelation, and I believe this marks a major division in the book. Chapters 1 through 11 are one section, and chapters 12 through 22 form the second major section of the book.

We start now in Revelation 12:1-2: "A great and wondrous sign appeared in heaven: a woman clothed with the sun, with the moon under her feet and a crown of twelve stars on her head. She was pregnant and cried out in pain as she was about to give birth." Now, verse 5 says: "She gave birth to a son, a male child, who will rule all the nations with an iron scepter. And her child was snatched up to God and to his throne." If we just look at those two verses, we might be inclined to think of this, as the Roman Catholic Church has more traditionally interpreted it, as referring to Mary, because it does clearly speak of the birth of Jesus Christ and, obviously, the woman who gave birth to Jesus Christ was Mary.

So one might conclude at once that we are seeing here a mention of Mary, under the term of a woman. But as we read all this chapter has to say about this woman, Mary simply cannot fit. This woman is described as accomplishing far more things than could be explained in terms of Mary. If we will allow the Bible to explain itself, I believe we will come to an understanding of what this woman is, and we must understand what the woman is, or we miss the entire point of this chapter.

So, who is the woman? She is "...clothed with the sun, with the moon under her feet and a crown of twelve stars on her head." Now there is one place in the Bible which I think serves as the background for this particular symbol. Genesis 37:9-10 speaks of Joseph and says:

> Then he had another dream, and he told it to his brothers. "Listen," he said, "I had another dream, and this time the sun and moon and eleven stars were bowing down to me."
>
> When he told his father as well as his brothers, his father rebuked him and said, "What is this dream you had? Will your mother and I and your brothers actually come and bow down to the ground before you?"

Let us pause and think about this for a moment. Here's Joseph. He has a dream. He dreams about the sun and the moon and eleven stars bowing down before him. Joseph's father was Jacob. Remember, Jacob was the one whose name was changed to Israel, and Israel is the one who has the twelve sons. Eleven are mentioned here as stars. Joseph is the twelfth. And Jacob understands what is being implied by the dream. He, Israel, is represented by the sun, and his wife, and the eleven sons of Israel are represented by the moon and eleven stars in the dream. So what do we have here? We have the sun and the moon and the stars as a beautiful representation of the people of Israel.

What we are seeing, I believe, in the symbol that is used in Revelation chapter 12:1-2 where we see a woman clothed with the sun, with the moon under her feet and a crown of twelve stars on her head, is simply a rearranging of the symbolism that is found in Joseph's dream. I wonder what better symbolism you could use to represent Israel than a woman surrounded by these objects. In much of the art that is associated with the Roman Catholic Church, you will see pictures of Mary clothed with the sun, with the moon under her feet and wearing a crown with twelve stars. This perpetuates the notion that Mary is referred to here. But, in reality, what we are seeing is the people of God spoken of in terms of a woman, specifically a woman who "…cried out in pain as she was about to give birth."

I want you to understand that, in addition to this, the Old Testament frequently portrays Israel as a woman who is about to give birth. This provides additional reason for believing that the symbolism in Revelation pertaining to the woman giving birth has reference to Israel. Now, let me show you just three examples out of several that could be given in the Old Testament. Let's go to Isaiah 26:17:

> As a woman with child and about to give birth
>
> writhes and cries out in her pain,
>
> so were we in your presence, O Lord.

Now let's turn to Isaiah 66:7-8:

> "Before she goes into labor,
>
> she gives birth;
>
> before the pains come upon her,
>
> she delivers a son.
>
> Who has ever heard of such a thing?
>
> Who has ever seen such things?
>
> Can a country be born in a day
>
> or a nation be brought forth in a moment?
>
> Yet no sooner is Zion in labor
>
> than she gives birth to her children."

We turn again to Micah 5:2:

> "But you, Bethlehem Ephrathah,
>
>> though you are small among the clans of Judah,
>
> out of you will come for me
>
> one who will be ruler over Israel,
>
> whose origins are from of old,
>
> from ancient times."

Here, in very specific and pointed terms, Micah refers to the birth of Jesus Christ. Matthew 2:4-6 shows this prophecy of Micah refers to the birth of Jesus in Bethlehem. It is the fulfillment of the prophecy of Micah. Out of Judah one is being born. Israel is giving birth to a child. And that is precisely what we are seeing in Revelation, chapter 12. The nation of Israel is that which eventually brought forth the Messiah, the Christ, into the world.

Now, however, there is an interesting transformation that occurs in the symbolism of the woman in Revelation 12. It refers to more than simply the Israel of the old covenant. It comes to take on the larger significance, as Israel continually does in the book of Revelation, not only of the people of the old covenant, but of God's people in the new covenant.

At the end of the book of Galatians, Paul speaks of Christians as the Israel of God. And throughout the New Testament, God's people who are Christians, followers of Christ, are spoken of over and over again as the true circumcision, the seed of Abraham. Abraham was the one who not only was the father of fleshly Israel, but was the father of spiritual Israel—which includes all those who are faithful to God and, now, to Jesus Christ his son. So, initially, we see the woman in Revelation as giving birth to the Christ, and then we see, later on, the woman representing those who follow Christ. The woman is a symbol for all of God's people, both under the old covenant and under the new.

Let's continue with Revelation 12:3: "Then another sign appeared in heaven: an enormous red dragon with seven heads and ten horns and seven crowns on his heads." Later, the Lord willing, we'll discuss the significance of the seven heads and the ten horns and the seven crowns, or diadems, on the heads, because in the next chapter we're going to see a beast coming up out of the sea that has these things in common with the dragon. It will be easier at that time to explain the significance of the seven heads and the ten horns and the seven crowns.

Continuing with verse 4: "His tail swept a third of the stars out of the sky and flung them to the earth. The dragon stood in front of the woman who was about to give birth, so that he might devour her child the moment it was born." Now, who is the dragon? Revelation 12 explains itself in unmistakable terms as to who the dragon is, because verse 9 says: "The great dragon was hurled down— that ancient serpent called the devil or Satan, who leads the whole world astray. He was hurled to the earth, and his angels with him." Then, in the latter part of verse 10, he is described as

...the accuser of our brothers,

who accuses them before our God day and night.

So the dragon is the devil, Satan.

Well, what is Satan doing? Satan is shown in verse 4 as standing in front of the woman who was about to give birth, so that he might devour her child the moment it was born. This is precisely what Satan did when Jesus came into the world and was born in Bethlehem. Satan did all he could to try to see that Jesus was destroyed. He had all the male babies killed by Herod, hoping that that would get rid of Christ. But that didn't work, because Jesus was taken down into Egypt. Satan made the effort at the very beginning, at least, to destroy the Christ.

Verse 5 says: "She gave birth to a son, a male child, who will rule all the nations with an iron scepter. And her child was snatched up to God and to his throne." Virtually all commentators on Revelation agree the child is Jesus Christ, but there are a few here and there who have tried to explain that in some other way. The picture is so clear that it hardly needs explanation. But let me, for the record, show you why we know for certain that when we look at the child we are seeing Jesus Christ.

We go back to the Old Testament background again, back to Psalm 2:7-9, which says:

> I will proclaim the decree of the Lord:
>
> > He said to me, "You are my Son;
>
> today I have become your Father.
>
> Ask of me,
>
> > and I will make the nations your inheritance,
> >
> > the ends of the earth your possession.
>
> You will rule them with an iron scepter,
>
> > you will dash them to pieces like pottery."

This is a Messianic Psalm, that is, a Psalm prophesying concerning the Christ. We know that because, in Hebrews 1:5, the writer quotes from that particular Psalm, the part that we have read in verses 7-9, and applies it to Jesus. He says:

> For to which of the angels did God ever say,
>
> > "You are my Son;
> >
> > today I have become your Father"?
>
> Or again,
>
> > "I will be his Father,
> >
> > and he will be my Son"?

So here we are seeing Jesus Christ clearly revealed to us.

We can see that also because in Revelation 12:10, when finally Jesus is caught up to heaven, to the throne, John said:

> Then I heard a loud voice in heaven say:
>
> > "Now have come the salvation and the power and the
> >
> > kingdom of our God,
> >
> > and the authority of his Christ.

> For the accuser of our brothers,
>
> > who accuses them before our God day and night,
>
> has been hurled down."

Jesus has ascended into heaven, and he has ascended with all authority.

In Revelation 19:13-15, also, we see the connection made as we see the concept of his ruling with a rod of iron presented:

> He is dressed in a robe dipped in blood, and his name is the
> Word of God. The armies of heaven were following him, riding
> on white horses and dressed in fine linen, white and clean. Out
> of his mouth comes a sharp sword with which to strike down the
> nations. "He will rule them with an iron scepter."

Surely, that's unmistakably referring to Jesus. Recall John 1:1 and 14: "In the beginning was the Word, and the Word was with God, and the Word was God....The Word became flesh and lived for a while among us. We have seen his glory, the glory of the one and only Son, who came from the Father, full of grace and truth."

Now, back to Revelation 19:14-15: "The armies of heaven were following him, riding on white horses and dressed in fine linen, white and clean. Out of his mouth comes a sharp sword with which to strike down the nations. 'He will rule them with an iron scepter.' He treads the winepress of the fury of the wrath of God Almighty."

So Jesus Christ is seen in Revelation 12:4-5, and verse 5 says: "She gave birth to a son, a male child, who will rule all the nations with an iron scepter. And her child was snatched up to God and to his throne." Back in Revelation chapter 5, we saw the Lamb who had been slain coming to the throne, and there he is spoken of as having received power and wealth and wisdom and strength and honor and glory and praise. He was given a kingdom, and people in the kingdom reigned with him on earth. Here, also, we see Christ having been caught up to the throne.

Earlier, as I was preparing some of my thoughts, Jehovah's Witnesses came by the house, and I thought, "Well, this will be an interesting opportunity to try out some of this." So I invited them in, and they came in and they began, of course, as they always do, talking about the kingdom. I told them, "You know, that's just what I am studying about here in Revelation 12." They were trying to say that the kingdom has not come yet, that we are looking forward to the kingdom. "Well," I said, "that's where we disagree, because as I understand the scripture, Paul said, in Colossians 1:13, '…he has rescued us from the dominion of darkness, and brought us into the kingdom of the Son he loves.' Paul says we are already in the kingdom. We're citizens of the kingdom of God." Well, they said, "We believe that Jesus is the king, but he doesn't have a kingdom yet."

They wanted to go back to Daniel 2, so we went back to Daniel 2:44 where it speaks of the fact that in the days of the kings of the fourth kingdom, which is the Roman empire, God would set up a kingdom which will never be destroyed. They tried to say that's something yet to come. But the fourth kingdom, as we pointed out, was the Roman empire.

Then I suggested we go to Daniel 7:13-14, because there we can see not only that Jesus is now king, but that he also has a kingdom. So we turned there and read: "In my vision at night I looked, and there before me was one like a son of man, coming with the clouds of heaven." And I said, "Now, isn't the son of man Jesus?" They said, "Yes." I continued reading, "He approached the Ancient of Days," and I said, "Is that God, the father?" They said, "Yes." I continued, "…and was led into his presence." I asked, "When did Jesus ascend with the clouds to the Ancient of Days?" They acknowledged that was his ascension to heaven, which the Bible records in Acts 1.

All right, "What happened when he ascended to heaven? Notice Daniel 7:14: 'He was given authority, glory and sovereign power; all peoples, nations and men of every language worshiped him. His dominion is an everlasting dominion that will not pass away, and his kingdom is one that will never be destroyed.'" I said, "Doesn't it say here that he was given a kingdom when he ascended to heaven? Didn't that happen a long time ago?" They replied, "Yes, but we believe that Jesus is going to yet come and set up a kingdom." I said, "Wait a minute now. I know that is what you believe, but now what did the Bible say here? Didn't it say what I was saying, that he set up a kingdom?" They said, "Well, yes." So, we moved on to another point. That is what Revelation is saying to us here, that Jesus ascended to the throne of God, he was given authority, and the kingdom of our God has come. It is now here.

Now we move along to Revelation 12, verse 6: "The woman fled into the desert to a place prepared for her by God, where she might be taken care of for 1,260 days." We haven't time to go back and explain all over again what we went through last Sunday evening, but this period of 1,260 days refers to that period from the time when the church began until right at the time when Jesus is going to come again.

That wouldn't apply to Mary then. This woman is not Mary. Mary is not still living here through this entire period, but the church is. That's the whole point. The woman represents the people of God, and throughout scripture the church and the people of God are spoken of in terms of a woman. Remember, the bride of Christ. You have a great chapter, Ephesians 5, where you have a discussion of the husband and wife, which is really speaking of Christ and his church, the church being the bride of Christ. We have here the church under the figure of a woman who fled into the desert where she has a place prepared by God. We are going to see more about the desert in a little bit.

There is a pause now in verses 7-9:

> And there was war in heaven. Michael and his angels fought against the dragon, and the dragon and his angels fought back. But he was not strong enough, and they lost their place in heaven. The great dragon was hurled down—that ancient serpent called the devil or Satan, who leads the whole world astray. He was hurled to the earth, and his angels with him.

As we go back to the gospel account, Jesus speaks of Satan being driven out. I believe that if we will look at these references and also at what is said in Revelation, we will see a consistent picture presented to us.

First, we go to Luke 10. Remember, Jesus had sent out the seventy-two two by two to begin to preach the gospel of the kingdom. They went out, and they came back excited because demons had been driven out in the name of Christ. Notice Luke 10:17-20:

> The seventy-two returned with joy and said, "Lord, even the demons submit to us in your name."
>
> He replied, "I saw Satan fall like lightning from heaven. I have given you authority to trample on snakes and scorpions, and to overcome all the power of the enemy; nothing will harm you. However, do not rejoice that the spirits submit to you, but rejoice that your names are written in heaven."

Jesus says, in response to the missionary activity of the seventy-two, their proclamation of the gospel message, the good news of the kingdom of God, that "I saw Satan fall like lightning from heaven," and I think he saw that in the same way as the prophets of old saw the coming of the Christ. They would often speak in the past tense of something that was yet to occur. And I think that Jesus here is speaking in anticipation of something, because, as we turn now to John 12:31-33, Jesus says, "'Now is the time for judgment on this world; now the prince of this world will be driven out. But I, when I am lifted up from the earth, will draw all men to myself.' He said this to show the kind of death he was going to die." Jesus speaks of his death and, in connection with his death, he speaks of Satan being driven out.

Move on to Matthew 12:28-29. There Jesus speaks of tying up the strong man. He is referring to Satan, because there has been the driving out of demons, and the Pharisees had accused Jesus of driving out demons by the power of Beelzebub. So, in verses 28-29, Jesus said,

> But if I drive out demons by the Spirit of God, then the kingdom of God has come upon you.
>
> Or again, how can anyone enter a strong man's house and carry off his possessions unless he first ties up the strong man? Then he can rob his house.

When Jesus died on the cross and rose from the dead and ascended into heaven, he, once and for all, conquered the power of Satan. It was as good as done from the foundation of the world, but, in reality and actuality, the time in which it occurred was at the cross and the resurrection and the ascension into heaven when Jesus finally sat down at the right hand of God and began to rule and reign. That is when Satan was driven out, and that is the picture we are seeing in Revelation 12.

Let me give you some more references to solidify the point and make it clear. In 1 Peter 3:21-22, Peter said, "…and this water symbolizes baptism that now saves you also—not the removal of dirt from the body but the pledge of a good conscience toward God. It saves you by the resurrection of Jesus Christ, who has gone into heaven and is at God's right hand—with angels, authorities and powers in submission to him." The submission of the authorities and powers and angels is in connection with his going into heaven. And now, notice in Ephesians 6:12 the task that is before each of us as Christians, followers of Christ, "For our struggle is not against flesh and blood, but against the rulers, against the authorities, against the powers of this dark world and against the spiritual forces of evil in the heavenly realms."

Let's turn to Colossians 2:13-15. Paul says,

> When you were dead in your sins and in the uncircumcision of your sinful nature, God made you alive with Christ. He forgave us all our sins, having canceled the written code, with its regulations, that was against us and that stood opposed to us; he took it away, nailing it to the cross. And having disarmed the powers and authorities, he made a public spectacle of them, triumphing over them by the cross.

Our struggle is against powers and authorities, but when Jesus died on the cross, he triumphed over them. He ascended to heaven, and Satan was driven out, which means the victory is ours. Our struggle is not against flesh and blood, it is against the authorities and powers that Jesus has triumphed over. We, as his people, then, are victors. The battle has been won through the death, burial, and resurrection of Jesus Christ.

Now we come to the magnificent passage in Hebrews 2:14-15 that pulls all this together: "Since the children have flesh and blood, he too shared in their humanity so that by his death he might destroy him who holds the power of death—that is, the devil—and free those who all their lives were held in slavery by their fear of death." As children of God, we are no longer in slavery. Satan does not have us bound. Christ has bound Satan, and we are now able to overcome the rulers, the authorities, the powers of this dark world, because of the death of Jesus through which he brought the power of Satan to nothing. There is a beautiful message in all this for God's people which says victory is ours because Jesus, through his death, his burial, his resurrection, and his ascension into heaven, has overcome Satan. Satan is hurled out, he's bound, and when we get to Revelation 20 we will see more about that. Satan can no longer keep you in slavery because his power has been broken.

Let's go back to Revelation 12:10:

Then I heard a loud voice in heaven say:

"Now have come the salvation and the power and the

kingdom of our God,

and the authority of his Christ.

For the accuser of our brothers,

who accuses them before our God day and night,

has been hurled down."

Remember, when Jesus rose from the dead he said, "All authority in heaven and on earth has been given to me." So now, when he is called up to the throne of God, the voice says, "Now have come the salvation and the power and the kingdom of our God, and the authority of his Christ." We're in the kingdom now. It began when Jesus sat down at the right hand of God and began to reign and to rule when he ascended to heaven. He will reign and rule until all his enemies are put under his feet, and then, according to 1 Corinthians 15:24, he will hand over the kingdom to the Father.

Jesus will protect you who have confessed his name. He'll confess you before the Father who is in heaven. Victory is ours, for, as Revelation 12:10 continues:

> "For the accuser of our brothers,
>
> who accuses them before our God day and night,
>
> has been hurled down."

Satan has no way in which he can defend his accusations against you. Who will bring any charge against those whom God has chosen? Paul said in Romans 8:31: "If God is for us, who can be against us?" Certainly not Satan.

Notice Revelation 12:11:

> "They overcame him
>
> by the blood of the Lamb
>
> and by the word of their testimony;
>
> they did not love their lives so much
>
> as to shrink from death."

We overcome. Why? Because of the blood of the Lamb—because Jesus Christ shed his blood on Calvary, because of "the word of their testimony," because we carry forth the message of salvation, and because "they did not love their lives so much as to shrink from death."

We simply count our lives as nothing. Paul says in Romans 12:1: "…offer your bodies as living sacrifices, holy and pleasing to God—which is your spiritual worship." We are saved by the blood of Jesus Christ. It is not because of our own merits, but because of the merit of Jesus Christ who loved us and gave himself up for us.

Now we continue in Revelation 12:12:

> "Therefore rejoice, you heavens
>
> and you who dwell in them!

> But woe to the earth and the sea,
>
> > because the devil has gone down to you!
>
> He is filled with fury,
>
> > because he knows that his time is short."

His time is limited. God is one day going to hurl Satan into the lake of burning sulfur.

We continue:

> When the dragon saw that he had been hurled to the earth, he pursued the woman who had given birth to the male child. The woman was given the two wings of a great eagle, so that she might fly to the place prepared for her in the desert, where she would be taken care of for a time, times and half a time, out of the serpent's reach.

What a beautiful picture is given to us there of the woman who is brought into the desert and taken care of. It reminds us of that great passage in Exodus 19:4 where God said of Israel: "You yourselves have seen what I did to Egypt, and how I carried you on eagles' wings and brought you to myself." Jesus is shown here in Revelation giving the church eagles' wings, so the church will be protected from the harm that Satan wants to bring. Yes, there is persecution, but there is protection, the same thing that we saw in chapter 11.

Revelation 12 continues: "Then from his mouth the serpent spewed water like a river, to overtake the woman and sweep her away with the torrent. But the earth helped the woman by opening its mouth and swallowing the river that the dragon had spewed out of his mouth." We have no exact parallel anywhere else in scripture, but the figure seems to me rather clear, because here the dragon is spouting water out of his mouth to destroy. What is it that can come out of the mouth of Satan to destroy the people of God?

Well, Satan has three major weapons that are revealed to us in Revelation. There is persecution, there is seduction, and there is deception. What comes out of the mouth? Deception. And the stream that comes out of the mouth of

Satan is a stream of lies and falsehood that only the people of the earth—that is, worldly people who are bound to this earth—swallow down whole. The acceptance of these falsehoods and delusions of Satan makes a clear distinction between the people of God and the people of the world.

The chapter concludes: "Then the dragon was enraged at the woman and went off to make war against the rest of her offspring—" Who's that? "...those who obey God's commandments and hold to the testimony of Jesus." Yes, Satan is going to fight you. He couldn't destroy the Christ. He couldn't destroy the church. He's trying to destroy you, but the message of Revelation 12 is that Satan is a loser. Satan tried to defeat Jesus on earth, and he failed. Satan tried to defeat Jesus in heaven, and he failed. He has tried to defeat the whole church, and he has failed. The gates of Hades will not overcome the church. Finally, he tries to destroy you, and the message of Revelation is that if you are faithful to Jesus, he can't do it. Victory is yours! What a tremendous scene is painted for us by God through John in the Revelation: Victory for the people of God!

Why not become one of the victors, one of the winners, one of God's people? Believe in Jesus, trust him. Repent of your sins. Confess your faith in him. Allow his precious blood to cleanse you from your sins as you are buried with him in the water of baptism, that you may rise into new life, having had the bondage of sin broken and having the opportunity of living eternally with God. We invite you to him.

REVELATION 13:
The Mark of the Beast

W e are studying our way through the book of Revelation chapter by chapter, and we have come to Revelation 13, "The Mark of the Beast."

In Revelation 12, we saw the dragon, Satan, persecuting the church, and we find that Satan employs various means to accomplish his designs of destroying the church. Chapter 13:1 says: "And the dragon stood on the shore of the sea." The King James Version says, "And I stood on the sand of the sea." The ancient Greek texts generally have "he," and I think it fits better in the context. The dragon comes down to the sea and stands on the seashore.

Next, we see him finding a helper in his efforts to destroy God's people. Verse 1 continues: "And I saw a beast coming out of the sea. He had ten horns and seven heads, with ten crowns on his horns, and on each head a blasphemous name." We see a beast coming out of the sea. What is the significance of the sea? Perhaps it has no particular significance; but, if it does have any significance—and I am inclined to think that it does—it has reference, apparently, to the nations. Notice Isaiah 17:12:

> Oh, the raging of many nations—
>
> > they rage like the raging sea!
>
> Oh, the uproar of the peoples—
>
> > they roar like the roaring of great waters!

So, here, the nations are spoken of under the figure of the raging sea. Even in the book of Revelation itself, in 17:15, we read: "Then the angel said to me, 'The waters you saw, where the prostitute sits, are peoples, multitudes, nations and languages.'"

We see a beast coming from the sea, a beast emerging from the nations, from the peoples. Notice that all of these are plural: peoples, multitudes, nations, and languages. This beast does not emerge out of a single nation, out of a single people, at some particular point in human history. This is a beast that emerges from the peoples, the languages, the nations. This beast is something that is in existence over a vast period of time—the persecuting power of human governments.

I believe that is borne out as we look at a further description of the beast in verse 2: "The beast I saw resembled a leopard, but had feet like those of a bear and a mouth like that of a lion. The dragon gave the beast his power and his throne and great authority." Again, we must allow the Bible to be its own interpreter. If we do that, there is one passage in prophecy in the Old Testament that serves as the perfect setting and background for what we see in Revelation 13. That is found in Daniel 7:2-8. There, we are given a description of four beasts that came out of the sea:

> Daniel said: "In my vision at night I looked, and there before me were the four winds of heaven churning up the great sea. Four great beasts, each different from the others, came up out of the sea.
>
> "The first was like a lion, and it had the wings of an eagle. I watched until its wings were torn off and it was lifted from the ground so that it stood on two feet like a man, and the heart of a man was given to it.
>
> "And there before me was a second beast, which looked like a bear. It was raised up on one of its sides, and it had three ribs in its mouth between its teeth. It was told, 'Get up and eat your fill of flesh!'

"After that, I looked, and there before me was another beast, one that looked like a leopard. And on its back it had four wings like those of a bird. This beast had four heads, and it was given authority to rule.

"After that, in my vision at night I looked, and there before me was a fourth beast—terrifying and frightening and very powerful. It had large iron teeth; it crushed and devoured its victims and trampled underfoot whatever was left. It was different from all the former beasts, and it had ten horns.

"While I was thinking about the horns, there before me was another horn, a little one, which came up among them; and three of the first horns were uprooted before it. This horn had eyes like the eyes of a man and a mouth that spoke boastfully."

Now if we go back to Revelation 13 again, we will see that this single beast that rises out of the sea is a perfect composite picture of four separate, distinct beasts that are found in Daniel 7. You find the same three animals—the leopard, the bear, and the lion—and you notice in Daniel that the fourth beast is not identified with any animal. In Revelation 13, the beast is a composite of the three animals, and it also incorporates the fourth beast of Daniel because that beast has ten horns. So, when you put the four beasts of Daniel 7 together, you have a beast that has seven heads (because the third beast in Daniel had four heads and there were three other beasts—a leopard, a lion, and a bear—making seven heads) and ten horns.

What is the significance of all this? In Daniel, from which this is drawn, the four separate beasts represented successive kingdoms: the Babylonian, the Persian, the Greek, and the Roman. If you compare Revelation 13 with Daniel 2, it becomes crystal clear. What do we have? What would be a better way to represent the governments of the world than a composite of the four beasts, representing four successive, great world empires?

Put them all together into one, and you have a beast that represents human governmental powers that persecute God's people. The Babylonians, the Persians, the Greeks, and the Romans all were persecutors of the people of God. Consequently, I think the imagery that is drawn from Daniel helps us to see that we are looking, in Revelation 13, at an instrument of Satan that kills God's people. That specific instrument, represented by the beast, is persecuting human governments.

If we drop back again to verse 1, I believe there is further confirmation of that. In describing the beast, it says that the beast had "…ten horns and seven heads, with ten crowns on his horns." What we are seeing here is that the human governments take on themselves the characteristics of the one who has given them their power, Satan himself. Satan is the one who is represented as the dragon with the seven heads, ten horns, and ten crowns. The beast has ten horns, and "horns" throughout the Bible are used as suggestive of destructive power.

The beast has seven heads. "Seven" is a symbol of completeness. A "head" is a symbol of authority. Here is a symbol of complete authority. Does this mean Satan has complete authority? It is complete in the sense that it affects all human governments throughout the whole earth. It's true, of course, that whatever authority Satan has is under the ultimate authority of Jesus Christ who has all authority on earth and in heaven. It is true, also, that governments, as individuals, yield in differing degrees to the power Satan exercises. But his power is world-wide.

Paul said, in Ephesians 2:2: "…in which you used to live when you followed the ways of this world and of the ruler of the kingdom of the air, the spirit who is now at work in those who are disobedient." In Ephesians 6:12, Paul said, "For our struggle is not against flesh and blood, but against the rulers, against the authorities, against the powers of this dark world and against the spiritual forces of evil in the heavenly realms."

The powers of this dark world are headed by a single world ruler, that prince of this world whom Jesus said he would hurl down, Satan, the dragon. We are seeing in Revelation 13 human, persecuting governments that simply reflect the characteristics of Satan himself. Satan had seven crowns on his heads, indicating his authority to rule. But it is an arrogated authority, it's an authority that he has taken on himself. It is not a legitimate, rightful authority. It is an authority that is under the dominion of God himself.

There is a slight distinction though in the descriptions of the dragon and of the beast which I think is somewhat significant. On the sea beast in chapter 13, verse 1, we find the crowns sitting, not on the heads, but on the horns. Here is a picture, perhaps, of crowned cruelty in the persecuting power of human governments. Authority was given to them by Satan and used by Satan for his purposes. We see a good description of what's taking place here back in Luke 4, verses 5 and 6, when Satan confronted Jesus. Remember, it says: "The devil led him up to a high place and showed him in an instant all the kingdoms of the world. And he said to him, 'I will give you all their authority and splendor, for it has been given to me, and I can give it to anyone I want to.'" But Satan was not able to give it to Jesus. Jesus refused to have that kind of authority at that time. But, in Revelation 13, John sees the dragon giving authority to these world rulers to persecute the people of God.

Now that we have seen what this sea beast is all about, we continue in verse 3:

> One of the heads of the beast seemed to have had a fatal wound, but the fatal wound had been healed. The whole world was astonished and followed the beast. Men worshiped the dragon because he had given authority to the beast, and they also worshiped the beast and asked, "Who is like the beast? Who can make war against him?"

What is the picture here? Here the beast has seven heads and now one of the heads is wounded in such a way that the beast appears to die. But then, to the surprise of everybody, it seems to revive and come back and exercise its power again so that the world marvels and wonders and says, "Who is like the beast? Who can make war against him?"

If we get the picture of what the beast is, I think we can begin to understand. The beast seems to be killed, but he revives. That was to convince the world of the futility of resisting the beast. In other words, you have tried to kill this horrible, ugly, monstrous creature, and it has been unsuccessful. So, you're likely to say, "What's the use of trying to fight?"

The history of the world shows that when evil governments are seemingly destroyed, evil governments rise again. That seems to be the pattern of world history: an evil, corrupt, oppressive government is destroyed, and there's great rejoicing. Then, to the dismay of the world, here comes another human government just as bad as that one, or maybe worse. Then men gather together and put that one down, and there's great rejoicing, and here it comes again. It seems to mirror the picture we are getting here. Here's the persecuting human government, the instrument and agent of Satan, seemingly being destroyed—killed, and here comes another just as bad as the first, or this one seems to regain its strength to come back again. Finally, it gets to the point where men will tend to be astonished and say, "It's no use. We might as well give up." And once God's people give in, there is no hope.

As you look back in Old Testament history, you see this time and again. What did Nebuchadnezzar in the Babylonian empire do? He erected an image and required all the people to bow down and worship it. What is he saying? He is saying: "Who is like Nebuchadnezzar?" and he is requiring the people to say, "Who is like Nebuchadnezzar?"

What happened in the Assyrian empire? Sennacherib came down into Judah with the most massive army the world had ever seen. Sennacherib brought that army down and surrounded the city of Jerusalem, and the people in Jerusalem were terrified. Hezekiah tried to calm the people by saying, "We have God to help us." But, in 2 Chronicles 32:14-15, Sennacherib said:

> Who of all the gods of these nations that my fathers destroyed has been able to save his people from me? How then can your god deliver you from my hand? Now do not let Hezekiah deceive you and mislead you like this. Do not believe him, for no god of any nation or kingdom has been able to deliver his people from my hand or the hand of my fathers. How much less will your god deliver you from my hand!

What did Sennacherib say? He said, "Who is like Sennacherib? Your God is nothing. I have wiped out the gods of surrounding nations; who's your God anyway?"

Of course, we know the end of that story. Sennacherib turned back, an angel of the Lord killed 185,000 of his soldiers, and it was clear who really is in charge. God takes that kind of abuse only so long. It may seem that Assyria has fallen, and there is rejoicing, but Babylon arises, and Babylon falls. Persia arises, and Persia falls, and the Greek empire arises, and so it goes. The Roman empire arises, and Caesar demands of the people that they bow down and say, "Caesar is Lord." We see repeated, again and again, the question, "Who is like the beast?" And the answer the Christian gives is, "Our God is the one who has the power in heaven and on earth!"

Notice Revelation 13:5 says: "The beast *was given* a mouth to utter proud words and blasphemies and to exercise his authority for forty-two months. He opened his mouth to blaspheme God, and to slander his name and his dwelling place and those who live in heaven." And, notice in verse 7: "He *was given* power to make war against the saints and to conquer them. And he *was given* authority over every tribe, people, language and nation." The beast has no authority in and of himself. It was given to him. God has given to him and has permitted him to exercise certain authority in our world, but God is saying, "You can go this far and no farther."

The authority that the beast has is a limited authority, and it is limited not only by extent of power, but it is limited by extent of time. It says in verse 5: "The beast was given…to exercise his authority for forty-two months." God has ordained that that will continue only so long and no longer, and there is nothing Satan can do to change it. God has ordained the powers that exist and how long they can operate. So, the power of the beast, the power of persecuting human government, is limited, and it can only go so far.

We come to verse 7: "He was given power to make war against the saints and to conquer them. And he was given authority over every tribe, people, language and nation." This is one of only two times in Revelation where that term "conquer" is used of anything other than God, Christ, and God's people. There comes a time, which we learn in Revelation is at the very end of time, when it is going to seem as though Satan and his forces are victorious. And here, it seems that the people of God have been overcome.

This is a perfect parallel of what's found in chapter 11, verse 7. Just remember 13:7 and 11:7, and study them together in their contexts. Revelation 11:7 says: "Now when they have finished their testimony, the beast that comes up from the Abyss will attack them, and overpower and kill them." That's God's people. But then, as you read the rest of chapter 11, that doesn't last for very long. It's a very brief period, three and a half days, then God's people are caught up to meet the Lord in the air and so we will be with the Lord forever. And so it is in Revelation 13, the conquering is temporary, it's limited, it's only for a time.

Now we come to verses 8 through 10:

All inhabitants of the earth will worship the beast—all whose names have not been written in the book of life belonging to the Lamb that was slain from the creation of the world.

He who has an ear, let him hear.

If anyone is to go into captivity,

into captivity he will go.

If anyone is to be killed with the sword,

with the sword he will be killed.

This calls for patient endurance and faithfulness on the part of the saints.

The point is, the saints of God know God will avenge his people, that God will be triumphant, that those whose names are written in the Lamb's book of life will not finally be destroyed. Rather, God will resurrect them, they will be saved, and they will enjoy the presence of God forever. So the message of this part of Revelation is: Don't worry about oppressive, persecuting, human governments. God in his good time is going to take care of that, and he is going to preserve you. That is the patience and the faith of the saints, that God does come out victorious, and so do his people.

But now, Satan is not finished. That's one instrument he uses in his warfare, persecuting human governments. But there comes another as we come to verse 11: "Then I saw another beast, coming out of the earth. He had two horns like a lamb, but he spoke like a dragon." What's this beast? This beast had two horns like a lamb, and he spoke like a dragon. What we are seeing in this beast is also described to us in Revelation 16:13: "Then I saw three evil spirits that looked like frogs; they came out of the mouth of the dragon, out of the mouth of the beast and out of the mouth of the false prophet." In Revelation 12 and 13, we are introduced to the dragon, the sea beast, and the earth beast, in that order.

In Revelation 16, when they are described, they are described in terms of the dragon, the sea beast, and the false prophet. The false prophet is in the same position as the earth beast. In case that's not obvious, then go to Revelation 19:20, and there it becomes clear: "But the beast was captured, and with him the false prophet who had performed the miraculous signs on his behalf. With these signs he had deluded those who had received the mark of the beast and worshiped his image. The two of them were thrown alive into the fiery lake of burning sulfur." Now we have the false prophet identified as the one who deluded those who had received the mark of the beast. We have, then, the earth beast identified elsewhere as the false prophet, and that's exactly what the earth beast is doing, he is deceiving the nations. He spiritually deceives and misguides.

I believe that is why he is described in terms of a lamb that speaks like a dragon, because the lamb is the symbol that is continually used throughout Revelation in reference to the Lamb of God who takes away the sin of the world, Jesus Christ. Here we see this seemingly innocent, harmless creature that comes out of the earth described as a lamb. But it is really, so to speak, a dragon in lamb's clothing, because it speaks with the voice of the dragon, but has the appearance of a lamb. It's deceptive, you see. It's the perfect picture of false religion that deceives, that creates an illusion of innocence, like a lamb.

But the message is a message that destroys, it's the message of the dragon, of Satan. I believe that's what we're seeing.

We see it described in 2 Corinthians 11:14: "And no wonder, for Satan himself masquerades as an angel of light." What does that mean? The next verse says: "It is not surprising, then, if his servants masquerade as servants of righteousness. Their end will be what their actions deserve." Satan has his servants, too. They appear as servants of righteousness, but they speak with the voice of the dragon. They say what Satan wants them to say.

We see the same thing spoken of by Jesus in another figure of speech in Matthew 7:15: "Watch out for false prophets. They come to you in sheep's clothing, but inwardly they are ferocious wolves." Here is a picture of wolves in sheep's clothing, but in Revelation, it's the dragon in lamb's clothing. But what happens to them? Jesus tells us in Matthew 7:22-23: "Many will say to me on that day, 'Lord, Lord, did we not prophesy in your name, and in your name drive out demons and perform many miracles?' Then I will tell them plainly, 'I never knew you. Away from me, you evildoers!'" Here were men who had deluded themselves into thinking they were prophets of God, exorcists, and faith-healers, or something similar, but the verdict of Jesus was that they were evildoers and he never knew them. What were they? Wolves in sheep's clothing. They were dragons in lamb's clothing. What we're seeing when we see this beast that comes out of the earth is false religion which has much to gain from governments that persecute those who are truly God's people.

Notice Revelation 13:12: "He exercised all the authority of the first beast on his behalf, and made the earth and its inhabitants worship the first beast, whose fatal wound had been healed." Anti-Christian government and anti-Christian religion have always worked hand in hand. You can trace it right down through history, and you see the priest who is promoting the proconsul. You see, in nation after nation, persecuting governments being promoted and supported by a religious establishment.

Notice verse 13: "And he performed great and miraculous signs, even causing fire to come down from heaven to earth in full view of men." Notice, false religions are capable of producing great signs. But are they genuine miracles? Look at the next verse: "Because of the signs he was given power to do on behalf of the first beast, he deceived the inhabitants of the earth. He ordered them to set up an image in honor of the beast who was wounded by the sword and yet lived." No, they're not genuine miracles; they deceive. Paul said in 2 Thessalonians chapter 2 that the lawless one would do counterfeit miracles.

Now we turn to Revelation 13:15: "He was given power to give breath to the image of the first beast, so that it could speak and cause all who refused to worship the image to be killed." Again, it *was given* to him. God permits it. He's given this power. It is not something he has within himself, and it is under the limit and control of God so that he can only go so far.

Now, in verse 16: "He also forced everyone, small and great, rich and poor, free and slave, to receive a mark on his right hand or on his forehead...." What is the mark that is given? Verse 17 continues: "...so that no one could buy or sell unless he had the mark, which is the name of the beast or the number of his name." Earlier in Revelation, we saw that the followers of the Lamb were sealed on their foreheads. As we saw earlier, that simply was a way of saying that they were under the protection of God, and they belong to the Lamb of God. When it spoke of them being sealed on the forehead, it didn't mean that there was literally some kind of stamp placed on their foreheads as a visible sign. It simply means there are those who have been marked out as followers of the Lamb.

What are we seeing when we come to this passage? To receive a mark of someone was simply to belong to someone, or to serve or worship someone. Slaves were branded or marked to show that they belonged to a certain individual. Having the mark of the beast simply means nothing more than that these are people who bear in their lives those characteristics that mark them as being followers of Satan, rather than being followers of God.

How do I know that? Because Revelation spells it out for us. For example, Revelation 14:9:

> A third angel followed them and said in a loud voice: "If anyone worships the beast and his image and receives his mark

on the forehead or on the hand, he, too, will drink of the wine of God's fury, which has been poured full strength into the cup of his wrath."

The idea of receiving the mark is the idea of being one who worships the beast. The same thing is in verse 11: "And the smoke of their torment rises for ever and ever. There is no rest day or night for those who worship the beast and his image, or for anyone who receives the mark of his name."

Notice also Revelation 20:4:

I saw thrones on which were seated those who had been given authority to judge. And I saw the souls of those who had been beheaded because of their testimony for Jesus and because of the word of God. They had not worshiped the beast or his image and had not received his mark on their foreheads or their hands. They came to life and reigned with Christ a thousand years.

Those who do not receive the mark of the beast are simply those people who don't worship the beast, those who simply are followers of Jesus, followers of the Lamb.

Those who have the seal on their foreheads were identified in Revelation 7:3 as God's people. But that is not like some kind of little chain you hang around your neck; that's not what makes you a Christian. The mark of the Christian is the evidence of love and peace and joy, the fruit of the Spirit in the life of the Christian (Galatians 5:22). So it is with those who have the mark of the beast. You can mark them, mark them out by their lives, by whom they are worshiping, whom they are honoring with their lives.

We come to the statement concerning "a mark on his right hand or on his forehead." We have already seen, in the case of those who were sealed on the forehead who were followers of the Lamb, that this suggests the disposition of the mind, the thoughts, of those who are so sealed. Their minds are set in the direction of the Lamb of God. In a similar way here, those who have the mark of the beast on their hands or their foreheads have their actions and thoughts directed toward the beast and toward Satan. They show the mark, the evidence, the stamp, of Satan in their manner of life. One who has the mark of the beast is simply one who manifests in what he thinks and does the evidence of the dominion of sin and Satan in his or her life.

Let us notice Revelation 13:17: "…so that no one could buy or sell unless he had the mark, which is the name of the beast or the number of his name." As long as those who are sealed by God are in a minority to those who are marked by Satan, economic hardship is a very possible and very likely companion. Those who bear the mark of the beast, who participate in false religion and who cooperate with persecuting human governments, are likely to cause economic problems for the Christian. In every age this has happened.

As we have seen from the beginning, we are not talking about one point in human history, we are talking about what has happened throughout history and will happen till Jesus comes again. This is a description of the way you can expect things to be. But the beauty of it all is that victory is yours! And how do we know? Because of the last verse in chapter 13: "This calls for wisdom. If anyone has insight, let him calculate the number of the beast, for it is man's number. His number is 666." What does that mean?

It is the number of "man" in the sense of "mankind." The number of the beast is up. His number is the number of man. What is the number of man? Six. Man was created on the sixth day. Man falls short of the perfection of seven. His number is six. Six falls short of seven, it fails. The beast's days are numbered. The number of the beast is the number of man, and that number is six, six, six— that is, failure after failure after failure. The beast glories in man and in human affairs and, consequently, must fail.

It may be significant, incidentally, that the numerical number of Jesus in the Greek language is 888. He exceeds perfection, while man continually falls short. Man's number is 666. Consequently, all that is wrapped up with man, apart from God and Christ, will fail. Persecuting human governments will come to an end, false religion will fail, but Jesus will be triumphant. Victory is through him. We are more than conquerors through him who loved us.

While we may not be experiencing economic hardship today, it is not an unreasonable expectation that in our lifetimes we might so suffer due to our allegiance to Christ and his way. But failure cannot be ours if we place our trust in Jesus. If Jesus enters your life, you will find victory on victory and, finally, eternal life with God and his son, Jesus. It is your choice. Choose this day whom you will serve.

REVELATION 14:
The Final Harvest

W e are studying Revelation chapter 14, The Final Harvest. It may seem strange that in the middle of the book of Revelation we would be speaking of the final judgment. We would be inclined to say, "Well, if we are going to deal with the final judgment in the middle of the book, what's left?" Well, what's left is to look over the Christian era again and see other aspects of the problems, trials, and victories of God's people. I believe part of the difficulty that many have in understanding Revelation comes from an assumption—an unfounded assumption—that Revelation is a continuous chronological narration from the beginning of the Christian era to the end. But, as you read Revelation, it just doesn't work out that way. Instead, we are seeing a series of visions throughout the book looking at the Christian era from various vantage points and calling attention to various aspects.

Now we come to Revelation 14. As a background, in chapter 12 we had that horrible picture of Satan under the figure of a dragon with many horns and heads. In chapter 13, we saw that terrifying picture of the beast coming up out of the sea. Then we saw the beast of the earth coming up, and we saw those who had the mark of the beast and saw some very grim sights presented to us.

All this might strike terror even into the heart of the Christian. So, as happens throughout the book of Revelation, before we go into that final terrifying moment of judgment and the final wrath of God being poured out on the wicked, there is a pause to speak to the heart of the Christian to say, "Don't be afraid, because you will be preserved and you will be protected. The terrifying things that are to come will be for a brief time, but, ultimately, victory will be yours." After seeing the terrifying beasts coming up from the sea and the earth and those bearing the mark of the beast persecuting the people of God in chapter 13, we are again provided reassurance in Revelation 14 that God's people will be preserved and will enjoy the presence of God eternally.

As we begin this chapter, we see the 144,000 who were on the earth (verse 3) and who now are at the throne of God in heaven. They can sing together a new song now because they share, being the redeemed of all the ages, the new experience of the presence of God and of the Lamb. They are together on

…Mount Zion,

which cannot be shaken but endures forever"

(Psalm 125:1).

If we are wondering who these 144,000 are, they are followers of the Lamb who, according to some translations, are called virgins (verse 4) because they did not become unfaithful to Christ. Some mistakenly assume that the writer is speaking here about literal virgins, but that is contrary to the whole idea. It is speaking spiritually. They are the ones who are faithful to Christ. This idea is presented in the same terms by the apostle Paul in 2 Corinthians 11:2 where he said to the church, "I am jealous for you with a godly jealousy. I promised you to one husband, to Christ, so that I might present you as a pure virgin to him." The idea is that the church is to be spiritually faithful and loyal to one husband, to Christ, and, in that sense, they maintain their purity and their virginity. In other words, these are faithful followers of the Lamb of God. These 144,000 were "purchased from among men" (verse 4). Who are they? Let's let the Bible explain to us.

Who are those purchased from among men? In Acts 20:28, the apostle Paul said, "Guard yourselves and all the flock of which the Holy Spirit has made you overseers. Be shepherds of the church of God, which he bought with his own blood." That's what Jesus bought on the cross with his blood, the church of God. So when we see those who have been purchased from among men, the only people that have been purchased by the blood of the Lamb are those who are the church. The 144,000 of Revelation, then, has reference to the church. We see the same idea expressed in 1 Corinthians 6:20, when Paul, in writing to the church, says, "…you were bought at a price," and that price was the precious blood of Jesus Christ.

These 144,000 in Revelation 14 are also described as being "firstfruits to God and the Lamb" (verse 4). What does this mean? The background to the idea of the firstfruits is back in the Old Testament. Exodus 23:19 is perhaps the first clear reference to it. It says, "Bring the best of the firstfruits of your soil to the house of the Lord your God." Many other passages in the law of Moses say that the Israelites, when they made sacrifices to God, were to present the firstfruits of the land. That would be the choicest of the crop and the first to come forth. In Jeremiah 2:3, we see this concept of the firstfruits being used figuratively to refer to the people of God. It says,

> Israel was holy to the Lord,
>
> the firstfruits of his harvest;…

Israel, the people of God, is spoken of as the firstfruits of God's harvest. So the people of God are the firstfruits.

We find the same idea being expressed by James when we come back to the New Testament. James applies it now to the people of God who, in the new dispensation, are Christians, those in the church. James 1:18 says, "He chose to give us birth through the word of truth, that we might be a kind of firstfruits of all he created." Christians are God's firstfruits. Both in the Old and New Testaments, "firstfruits" is a way of referring to the people of God, all the people of God. So, when we come to the book of Revelation and we see the 144,000 being referred to as firstfruits to God and the Lamb, if we allow the Bible to interpret itself, that means the church. Of course, the 144,000 would include the redeemed of all the ages, in the sense of God's people in the Old Testament and God's people under the New Covenant. It is the redeemed of all the ages, those who have been purchased by the blood of the Lamb.

There are those in our time who teach that 144,000 is a special, select group of super-Christians who are going to someday inherit the new heaven, and all the rest of us who weren't quite as good are going to end up on the new earth. That's just totally foreign to what Revelation 14 is saying when it describes to us who the 144,000 are. They are all of God's people. No exceptions. They are the firstfruits. They are those purchased. They are followers of the Lamb. They are spiritually chaste. They have not committed adultery or fornication with the beast, as we saw in the previous chapters. They are the ones who are true and faithful, loyal to Jesus Christ, who is the husband of the church, which is the bride of Christ.

These 144,000 people are those who have the name of the Lamb and of God on their foreheads, in contrast to the rest of mankind—small and great, rich and poor, free and slave—who have the mark of the beast on their foreheads, as seen in Revelation 13:16-17. Those who have the name of God and the Lamb, who are sealed on their foreheads, are those who are redeemed by God, and those who have the mark of the beast on their foreheads are those who are followers of Satan and the beast. Mankind is simply divided into these two: those who have the mark of Satan, those who have the mark of Christ. You are either one, or the other. You are either God's, or you are Satan's. That is the teaching throughout scripture.

No lie is found in the mouths of the 144,000, and they are blameless (verse 5). And you say, "Doesn't that suggest a super group out of the church?" You might say, "Many of us probably told some kind of lie along the way, but these have told no lies." Is that really what is said? Look at it again. It says, actually, that no lie was found in the mouths of the 144,000. Why are they found without a lie? Because those lies have been forgiven by the cleansing blood of the Lamb. That's true of all Christians. When we enter the presence of God, we are found without sin. Why? Because we have never committed any sins? No, but because the blood of the Lamb has kept right on cleansing those who have been followers of the Lamb, those who have been walking in the light.

That seems to be one of the hardest messages, for some reason, for Christians to understand, yet it is so clearly taught to us in 1 John 1:7: "But if we walk in the light, as he is in the light, we have fellowship with one another, and the blood of Jesus, his Son, purifies us from every sin." Yes, you may have told a lie, you may have committed any number of various kinds of sins, because we all sin. John said that. If we say we don't, we are liars, and God's word has no place in our lives. But the blood of Jesus keeps on purifying us as we are really walking in the light and faithfully making that effort to follow our Lord. The blood keeps purifying so that when you arrive, finally, at the judgment seat of God, you are not carrying that great load of guilt of sins with you, because it has been washed clean by the blood of the Lamb. So there are no lies there, because they have all been erased and cleansed. They have been wiped away by the blood of the Lamb. We can come to the judgment joyously, not because we somehow have attained any goodness, but because, in spite of our sins and because of our faith in Jesus, he has promised that he will confess us before the Father.

Just as in Revelation 11:12 we look at heaven and then drop back to look at the situation on the earth before Jesus comes again, so in Revelation 14:1-5 we look at heaven and then, beginning in the next verse, verse 6 of chapter 14, we drop back and look at the situation on the earth before Jesus comes again. One of the things that sometimes creates confusion as people study Revelation is that there is sometimes a flashback as we are reading through the book, and we need to watch and look for those. Here we're clearly seeing a scene in heaven, and the redeemed are there, the church is in heaven. But in the very next verse, we are dropping back in time and looking at the scene here on earth before the judgment, before we find the church and the redeemed in heaven.

We encounter three angels. Actually, we are going to see six, but first we want to look at three. These three are to be seen together because they are bearing the same kind of message. It is the message of warning. Chapter 14 of Revelation divides itself into three sections. Each section begins with the statement, "I looked," or "I saw." The very opening verse of Revelation 14 says, "Then I looked...." Verse 6 begins, "Then I saw...." Verse 14 begins, "I looked...." These form three separate units. The first is showing us the redeemed in heaven, the second is showing us the earth again and the warnings that God tried to give mankind concerning the judgment which is to come, and the final verses, 14 through 20, show us the judgment that is coming.

We come to verses 6 through 13. Here we see three angels, in verses 6, 8, and 9, who belong together because each is warning mankind to turn men to faith in God and to turn them away from sin and from the judgment of sin which is to come. The coming judgment is eternal good news to the people of God because it means their deliverance. Look at verses 6-7:

> Then I saw another angel flying in midair, and he had the
> eternal gospel to proclaim to those who live on the earth—to
> every nation, tribe, language and people. He said in a loud voice,
> "Fear God and give him glory, because the hour of his judgment
> has come. Worship him who made the heavens, the earth, the sea
> and the springs of water."

Here we have the angel bringing the message, the eternal gospel, even though it is a message of judgment. For God's people, the judgment is not something to fear. It's victory day for the people of God. It is the time when, finally, we're delivered from the oppression of persecutors.

This is expressed in the last book of the Old Testament, in the last chapter of the Old Testament, in Malachi chapter 4:1-2, where we see both sides of judgment. It says: "'Surely the day is coming; it will burn like a furnace. All the arrogant and every evildoer will be stubble, and that day that is coming will set them on fire,' says the Lord Almighty. 'Not a root or a branch will be left to them.'" There is the terrifying side. But now, the other side. "'But for you who revere my name, the sun of righteousness will rise with healing in its wings. And you will go out and leap like calves released from the stall.'" The sun of righteousness will rise with healing in its wings. That, too, is a scene of judgment for God's people.

As we look at this particular message of the angel, we are seeing a message of judgment in verse 7, "…because the hour of his judgment has come." Some see here a picture of an angel coming at the very last moment of human history, crying to mankind, and saying, "The hour has come." But this is the message of God throughout the age, because even John himself, in his first letter, in 1 John 2:18, said: "Dear children, this is the last hour...." He was writing that back in the first century. He said this is the last hour. If you follow the usage of John as he employs the word "hour," he doesn't mean that this is the last sixty-minute interval of human history, but, rather, this is the hour of God, this is the time of God. This is the time to turn to God. It is the time of the judgment of God. We always stand in the last hour, so to speak, because for all we know, the Lord could come in this hour. The message of the gospel is continually a message of urgency.

The second angel tells us that Babylon is fallen. It is spoken of as an accomplished fact, a characteristic of Bible prophecy when speaking of the certainty of future fulfillments. In fact, these are the words used by Isaiah, in Isaiah 21:9, in prophesying the fulfillment of the destruction of the city of Babylon. He said, "Babylon has fallen, has fallen!" It was a future event, but he could say it *has* fallen because of the certainty of its accomplishment. Here the angel says, "Fallen! Fallen is Babylon...." You can count on it!

This is the first time Babylon is introduced in Revelation. Often in Revelation a thought is introduced that later is developed more fully. Here is an example of that, because when we get to chapters 17 through 19, we are going to learn a lot more about Babylon. But, for now, it is sufficient to say that Babylon is actually the world's seductive attractions that lead men away from God. We'll develop that thought later, just as John develops the thought later in chapters 17 through 19.

Look again at the statement in Revelation chapter 14:8: "Fallen! Fallen is Babylon the Great, which made all the nations drink the maddening wine of her adulteries." The word "maddening" is the Greek word "humos," which can equally well be translated "passion." If you look at it from that point of view, John is saying that God has made all the nations drink the wine of the passion of Babylon's fornication, her passionate immorality. Incidentally, the NIV incorrectly uses the word "adulteries" here and later in chapters 17 and 18.

There are two separate Greek words for "adulteries" and "fornications." It will later become especially important to notice that John is speaking of the fornication of Babylon, "the great prostitute." She is not an adulteress, but a fornicator.

Here is the third instrument of Satan for the destruction of God's people. We have seen two introduced in chapter 13, namely, the beast that comes out of the sea—representing the oppressive, persecuting, political powers of the earth—and the beast that comes out of the earth, which represents false religion. Now we come to the third instrument of Satan, and that is seduction. This represents the effort to seduce God's people. Satan wants us to believe that the attractions of this earth and those things that are contrary to the will of God provide life, and fulfillment, and excitement. He wants to lead us away from an attachment to God. We see here, however, the warning for our benefit that Babylon is fallen, that those earthly enticements are only for a time. But God's people, those who have seen the true joys and have loved Christ, will enjoy his presence and have joy forever.

The third angel announces that those who are attached to this world will perish with this world. Here, in this life, the wrath of God is mixed with grace. But, eventually, in hell, the wrath will be unmixed, the final and decisive judgment will have been made. This realization, and the certainty that God's people will be avenged by God, should encourage God's people to patiently endure all afflictions and trials.

Let's look at verses 9 through 11. The third angel said:

> If anyone worships the beast and his image and receives his mark on the forehead or on the hand, he, too, will drink of the wine of God's fury, which has been poured full strength into the cup of his wrath. He will be tormented with burning sulfur in the presence of the holy angels and of the Lamb. And the smoke of their torment rises for ever and ever. There is no rest day or night for those who worship the beast and his image, or for anyone who receives the mark of his name.

It's popular these days to try to minimize the wrath and the judgment of God and the reality of hell, but you simply cannot believe the Bible and deny them. You cannot believe Jesus Christ and deny those things because Jesus had more to say about them than even his apostles did in the New Testament writings. Here in Revelation, in no uncertain terms, we are introduced to the thought that the followers of the beast, the followers of Satan and his demons, are going to experience burning sulfur and be tormented in the presence of the holy angels and of the Lamb. The smoke of their torment will go up forever and ever, and they will have no rest day or night. How could you say anything more clearly than that? It is a terrifying thing to enter eternity unprepared to meet God. This is something we must realize.

If we sensed the reality of that fact, perhaps we would be more enthusiastic and diligent in trying our best to turn men to God, to persuade men that God does love them and that he is trying to spare them from eternal punishment. Jesus has done his best to say, "This is the way it is. Don't water it down. I'm telling you the reality of the matter, that there are only two possible destinies: either you spend eternity in my presence, or not in my presence. And, if you are not in my presence, but are simply with Satan and his followers, then what do you have to look forward to?"

However, verse 12 says, "This calls for patient endurance on the part of the saints who obey God's commandments and remain faithful to Jesus." Knowing the alternatives should cause us to steadfastly endure, to continue to follow the commandments of Jesus, and to have faith in him. We have had set before us in crystal-clear terms that there are only two destinies. Jesus said you will either enter in by the narrow way, or you will enter by the broad way—there are only two. We must make men aware of that fact and of the awfulness of failing to choose God's way.

We see that even if the believer experiences death at the hands of those who bear the mark of the beast, eternal blessedness is his. Notice verse 13, one of the most reassuring and comforting verses in all the Bible:

Then I heard a voice from heaven say, "Write: Blessed are the dead who die in the Lord from now on."

"Yes," says the Spirit, "they will rest from their labor, for their deeds will follow them."

We have just seen that the smoke of the torment of the wicked rises forever and ever, and they have no rest day or night. Now we see that the followers of the Lamb are able to rest from their labors.

The final harvest has come. Jesus, the one like a son of man who ascended in the clouds to the Ancient of Days, as described in Daniel 7:13, was prophesied as coming in the same manner as he went, according to Acts 1:9-11. We see in Revelation 14:14 the one like a son of man seated on the cloud as the earth is reaped in judgment. It says: "I looked, and there before me was a white cloud, and seated on the cloud was one 'like a son of man' with a crown of gold on his head and a sharp sickle in his hand." This is in perfect harmony with what John wrote in his gospel in 5:27: "And he has given him authority to judge because he is the Son of Man." Here is the son of man on the cloud who is about to judge all the earth. No longer does he bear the crown of thorns; he wears the crown of victory. He brings a sickle to gather the firstfruits of those who are his.

I believe Joel 3:13 provides a most informative picture of what we are seeing described in Revelation 14. It says:

Swing the sickle,

for the harvest is ripe.

Come, trample the grapes,

for the winepress is full

and the vats overflow—

so great is their wickedness!

Here, Joel combines the two figures we see in the last part of Revelation 14, the sickle put forth to reap the harvest, and the grapes put in the winepress where the wicked are trampled out. We see the two aspects of the final judgment of God, the judgment of the righteous, and of the wicked. They are mentioned separately, but they happen simultaneously.

What we see in Matthew 3:12 is the expression of the whole picture of Revelation 14:14-16. John the Baptist said: "…he will clear his threshing floor, gathering the wheat into his barn and burning up the chaff with unquenchable fire." Jesus is going to gather the righteous. The picture in Revelation has the angels doing the gathering, but that is also in harmony with what has been revealed to us in the gospels. Matthew 13:39 says: "…and the enemy who sows them is the devil. The harvest is the end of the age, and the harvesters are angels." Notice, also, Matthew 24:31: "And he will send his angels with a loud trumpet call, and they will gather his elect from the four winds, from one end of the heavens to the other." We are seeing the elect of God being gathered in Revelation 14.

We come to another aspect. Two angels come bringing judgment on the wicked. Each comes from the very sanctuary of God in heaven where the cries of the persecuted people of God have ascended, as we saw in Revelation 8. God's first response is that the wicked should be thrown into the great winepress of God's wrath. In Isaiah 63:3-4, God said:

> I have trodden the winepress alone;
>
>> from the nations no one was with me.
>
> I trampled them in my anger
>
>> and trod them down in my wrath;
>
> their blood spattered my garments,
>
>> and I stained all my clothing.
>
> For the day of vengeance was in my heart,
>
>> and the year of my redemption has come.

So, in the trampling of the grapes in the winepress of God's wrath, we see the final judgment on the wicked. The result is an awesome scene of blood— 1,600 stadia across, which would be somewhere from 160 to 200 miles. Here was a sea of blood of that dimension up to the bridle of a horse in depth. That suggests that the final judgment of God is thorough, complete, and universal; it encompasses all the wicked.

Why do we have the number 1,600? Perhaps, it is that 1,600 is the square of 40, and 40 is the traditional standard of punishment. The Israelites wandered forty years in the wilderness as the punishment of God. Forty lashes of the whip, save one, was used in the punishment of criminals. The squaring of the 40 would suggest the fullness, the completeness, and the finality of the wrath of God.

This sea of blood is outside the city, away from the presence of God, forever. Perhaps the most complete statement of the message of Revelation 14 is found in Galatians 6:7-8: "Do not be deceived: God cannot be mocked. A man reaps what he sows. The one who sows to please his sinful nature, from that nature will reap destruction; the one who sows to please the Spirit, from the Spirit will reap eternal life." The choice is clearly set before you, and the choice is whether you will serve God, or be a follower of Satan.

If you believe in Jesus, repent of your sins, confess your faith in him, and be baptized into him that you may, one day, when that judgment comes, be found in him, not having a righteousness of your own, but that which is through faith in Christ. If you trust him and believe him, obey him, and act on it now.

REVELATION 15:

The Redeemed and the Wrath

O ur lesson is on "The Redeemed and the Wrath," from Revelation 15. As a background for understanding chapter 15, we want to review, in a general way, what we have seen so far in Revelation.

In chapters 1 through 3 of Revelation, we see the church, under the symbol of seven lampstands, as a light in a world of darkness. Jesus is seen among the lampstands, reminding us of his promise, "…surely I will be with you always, to the end of the age."

In chapters 4 and following, we see the seven seals removed from the book of human destiny to reveal the trials that will afflict the people of God. Yet we see God's people preserved and protected, reminding us of the words of Jesus in John 16:33, "In this world you will have trouble. But take heart! I have overcome the world."

In chapters 8 through 11, we see the seven trumpets sound as God avenges his people with warning judgments against the ungodly, designed to cause them to repent. We are reminded of the words of Jesus in Luke 18:7, "And will not God bring about justice for his chosen ones, who cry out to him day and night? Will he keep putting them off?"

In chapters 12 through 14, we are shown the reason for the conflict God's people experience in this world. It is because of a more profound conflict between Christ and Satan that is taking place behind the scenes. Satan, having failed to destroy Christ, seeks to destroy his people. He employs persecuting governments (represented by the beast of the sea), false religion (represented by the beast from the earth), and the seductions and sensual enticements of this world (represented by Babylon) to lead people away from God.

Those who bear the mark of the beast, those who have given their allegiance to Satan, will ultimately be thrown into the great winepress of God's wrath. But those who are sealed with the name of God on their foreheads, those who are servants of God, will be gathered to God in the final harvest. These great scenes in the various sections of Revelation are not designed to prophesy nor to reveal specific historical events, but to show God's people what they may expect to experience in their life in Christ.

Chapters 1 through 3 say that the church will struggle as a flickering light in a world of darkness, but that those who are faithful, even to the point of death, will receive the crown of life. Chapters 4 through 7 say that the church will experience trials in this life, but that even those who are killed will finally be found in the presence of God. Chapters 8 through 11 inform us that God is not unaware of the trials of his people, but that he does hear our prayers and he does respond with judgment against the wicked. Even in the most desperate hours of the church's existence at the end of time, when it looks like Satan has won, God's people will be caught up to meet the Lord in the air, and so we will be with the Lord forever. Chapters 12 through 14 show that the gates of Hades will not overcome the church, that all the forces of Satan combined cannot destroy God's people. The saying will still be true, "Blessed are the dead who die in the Lord."

As you can see, we are not going to learn about Afghanistan, Iran, Israel, Egypt, the Arabs, the European Union, or war in the Middle East in the book of Revelation. We are going to learn about something far transcending the petty politics of pagan political powers. We are going to learn about victory in Jesus. We're going to gain the courage to stand up and be counted for Jesus. We're going to gain the strength to say, "Out of my sight, Satan!" We are going to find abundant reasons to keep pressing the battle in Jesus' name and to understand that our struggle is not against flesh and blood, but against the rulers, against the authorities, against the powers of this dark world, and against the spiritual forces of evil in the heavenly realms. We are going to be made keenly conscious of the fact that there are spiritual realities and eternal truths that stand behind the transitory and illusory images of the dying and failing world order. With that kind of background, we are ready to begin Revelation 15.

John said, "I saw in heaven another great and marvelous sign: seven angels with the seven last plagues—last, because with them God's wrath is completed." John said, "I saw…another…sign." In Revelation 12:1-2, he saw the sign of the radiant woman and her child, the people of God and Christ. In the second sign, in Revelation 12:3, he saw the enormous red dragon that opposed them, Satan himself. Now he sees another sign that is great and marvelous, because it will reveal the wrath of God poured out on the ungodly, vindicating the redeemed, and showing the ultimate powerlessness of the dragon.

In Revelation 15:2-4, John said,

And I saw what looked like a sea of glass mixed with fire and, standing beside the sea, those who had been victorious over the beast and his image and over the number of his name. They held harps given them by God and sang the song of Moses the servant of God and the song of the Lamb:

"Great and marvelous are your deeds,
Lord God Almighty.
Just and true are your ways,
King of the ages.
Who will not fear you, O Lord,
and bring glory to your name?
For you alone are holy.
All nations will come
and worship before you,

for your righteous acts have been revealed."

Before we see the wrath, we see the redeemed. We see that they are victorious. We see before the throne of God what looked like a sea of glass mixed with fire. Back in Revelation 4, when we saw the first vision of the throne of God, we saw a great sea of glass before the throne, but now we see something added. We see a sea of glass mixed with fire. It suggests to me the thought that the redeemed have gone through the fiery trials of this life, and now have been able to cross through the sea into the saving presence of God himself.

The sea reminds us of the occasion when God was leading Israel out from bondage in Egypt to the promised land. They came across the Red Sea on dry land, and when they reached the other side of the sea, they stood beside it. Moses joined with the multitudes of Israel singing the song of Moses, a song of victory, a song of triumph. It is recorded in Exodus 15:1-18. It begins with the words:

"I will sing to the Lord,

for he is highly exalted.

The horse and its rider

he has hurled into the sea."

We are a people who have been redeemed from bondage. As we see the scene in heaven, we see not only those who have been redeemed under the old covenant—those who were faithful to God, to the law of Moses—but also those who have been faithful to Jesus Christ, the Lamb of God, who takes away the sin of the world. Together, the redeemed of all the ages join in a mighty chorus praising God for his redemption. We see that they have come through the trials of life, across the sea, into the very presence of God himself.

Notice, in Revelation 15:3, what they sing as they stand victoriously in the presence of God:

"Great and marvelous are your deeds,

Lord God Almighty.

Just and true are your ways,

King of the ages."

I believe the King James says, "…thou King of saints," but I think the best reading is "King of the nations."

What are we seeing? Back in Revelation 13:3-4, the people of the world saw the beast that came up out of the sea which had one of its heads wounded so that it was about to die. But it revived and came to life, and it says of the people, "The whole world was astonished and followed the beast. Men worshiped the dragon because he had given authority to the beast, and they also worshiped the beast and asked, 'Who is like the beast? Who can make war against him?'" Here the people marveled at the beast, they marveled at those persecuting powers, governments that have oppressed the people of God. They were amazed because of the beast's seeming ability to resist all efforts to destroy him.

We have seen, finally, here in chapter 15, that the oppressive powers of government have been transcended by the people of God. They stand victorious in the presence of God, not marveling at the beast and his power, but saying, "Great and marvelous are your deeds,…King of the nations." Yes, God rules in the affairs of men. God is in control. The nations are nothing. The political powers of this age will come to their end, but God and his people will be victorious and triumph. The marvel is not in the nations of this world, the marvel is in the work of the Almighty God. In him can be seen power transcending all else.

Now, we come to Revelation 15:5-7:

> After this I looked and in heaven the temple, that is, the tabernacle of Testimony, was opened. Out of the temple came the seven angels with the seven plagues. They were dressed in clean, shining linen and wore golden sashes around their chests. Then one of the four living creatures gave to the seven angels seven golden bowls filled with the wrath of God, who lives for ever and ever.

The King James translation says, "vial," but "bowl" is a better term, because it refers to a rather deep, saucer-like vessel.

There were seven bowls filled with the wrath of God that were given to the seven angels. These angels came from the temple, the tabernacle of the

Testimony, in heaven. The word "temple" is a Greek word, "NAOS," which is actually a term referring to the innermost portion of the tabernacle, the sanctuary of God. It would be well translated as "the sanctuary of the tabernacle." The writer of Revelation is seeing a vision that takes us back, past the temple of Solomon, to the tabernacle in the wilderness. That was the very time period, when the people had escaped from slavery in Egypt and were being led to Sinai where God revealed his presence to them in a powerful way, when God said, "I am the Lord your God who has brought you out of slavery, and I can lead you now, if you're faithful to me, into the land I have promised you." In Revelation we see the angels coming from the sanctuary of the tabernacle of the Testimony in heaven, and they are given golden bowls.

Where did we last see the golden bowls, and what is their significance? Let's drop back to Revelation 5:8 for the first scene, where we are told: "And when he [the Lamb] had taken it [the scroll], the four living creatures and the twenty-four elders fell down before the Lamb. Each one had a harp and they were holding golden bowls full of incense, which are the prayers of the saints." Here are the golden bowls full of incense. What are they? They are the prayers of the saints.

Where next do we see the prayers of the saints connecting what takes place in heaven with what takes place on earth? It's in Revelation 8:3: "Another angel, who had a golden censer, came and stood at the altar. He was given much incense to offer, with the prayers of all the saints, on the golden altar before the throne." Then what happened? "The smoke of the incense, together with the prayers of the saints, went up before God from the angel's hand. Then the angel took the censer, filled it with fire from the altar, and hurled it on the earth; and there came peals of thunder, rumblings, flashes of lightning and an earthquake."

What do we see? We are seeing the prayers of the saints reach the throne of God, and they have effect on the earth. The little old lady sitting in her room may not have the strength and power to be able to go out into the world to make any great impression on it, but she can still lift her prayers to God and know that he hears her prayers and will respond. The prayers of God's people have power, far beyond that of any political potentate on earth, to affect the course of human history. The authorities that exist are simply established by God for man's well-being, but the prayers of the saints of God ascend to his throne and are heard. God does respond, and God does answer the prayers of his people. When we come to chapter 15 of Revelation, we see the angels with the bowls of incense, which are the prayers of God's people. But they are now bowls of God's wrath, for God is going to avenge his people. God is now going to pour out his wrath on impenitent humanity.

We come to verse 8: "And the temple was filled with smoke from the glory of God and from his power, and no one could enter the temple until the seven plagues of the seven angels were completed." What do we see here? We see the sanctuary of God now being filled with smoke so that no one could enter the sanctuary until the seven plagues of the seven angels were completed. And what does that say?

It is calling to mind again the occasion back in the wilderness of Sinai when the tabernacle was erected. The high priest was allowed, once a year, to go into the sanctuary, the innermost part of the tabernacle of God, to offer atonement for the sins of the people. But what happens here? In Revelation 15, the vision suggests that now the sanctuary is filled with smoke, so no one can enter the sanctuary to offer atonement for the sins of the people because these have been a rebellious people, an impenitent people, a people who have so continually hardened their hearts that God will not even permit atonement any longer for sin.

I believe the perfect comment on Revelation 15:8 is found in Hebrews 10:26-31 which says: "If we deliberately keep on sinning after we have received the knowledge of the truth, no sacrifice for sins is left…." In the imagery of Revelation 15:8, that's because the sanctuary is filled with smoke, so nobody can enter until the wrath of God is poured out. The writer of Hebrews 10 continues, in verse 27:

> …but only a fearful expectation of judgment and of raging fire that
> will consume the enemies of God. Anyone who rejected the law
> of Moses died without mercy on the testimony of two or three
> witnesses. How much more severely do you think a man deserves

to be punished who has trampled the Son of God under foot, who has treated as an unholy thing the blood of the covenant that sanctified him, and who has insulted the Spirit of grace? For we know him who said, "It is mine to avenge; I will repay," and again, "The Lord will judge his people." It is a dreadful thing to fall into the hands of the living God.

That is precisely what we have seen in Revelation 15:8. It is going to be revealed to us graphically, in detail, as we move next week into chapter 16. "It is mine to avenge; I will repay," says the Lord God. Why? Because a rebellious people have so hardened their impenitent hearts that it is, as the writer of the Hebrew letter elsewhere said, impossible to bring them back to repentance (Hebrews 6:6). The sanctuary of God, where he would come to forgive the sins of the people, is filled with smoke, preventing any from offering sacrifice for sins, because now the time of patience has ended. The time of judgment has come, the time for the justice of God to be vindicated for the benefit of the righteous people of all the ages.

God is almost ready to pour out the bowls of wrath on impenitent humanity. Will that be us? Will we have so hardened our hearts that God is unable to penetrate? Have we been sensitive to his love and his compassion and his tender mercy? What have we been doing with our lives? As we read through Revelation, it becomes quite clear that there are only those who have been sealed with the name of the Father written on their foreheads, who are servants of Almighty God, and there are those who have the mark of the beast, whose lives have become so characterized by Satan's ways that they are marked. They can be identified as his people because they have chosen to worship the image of the beast. They have chosen to give their allegiance to Satan.

Where do you stand? The choice is obvious and clear. You may choose to serve God and join the victorious multitudes who cross the fiery sea into the presence of God, or you will be numbered among those who are left for the outpouring of God's wrath. That is the message of Revelation. It's a message that comes to the heart of each of us.

If you are not a child of God, why not become one of his people, one of those who are victorious and triumphant, who are overcomers, who can rule their hearts because Christ is on the throne, who are reigning with Christ in this life, who have that power because Christ has given them the power to say "no" to Satan and to the allure and attraction of his ways and to follow the joy and the peace and the paths of God? If you believe in Jesus and will repent of your sins and confess your faith in him, we plead with you to be baptized into Christ immediately, so you will be prepared to meet God.

REVELATION 16:

The Seven Bowls of Wrath

W e are in the middle of studying through the book of Revelation chapter by chapter, and now we are studying from the 16th chapter of Revelation. This chapter deals with the pouring out of the seven bowls of God's wrath on the earth and mankind.

I believe if there is any one single verse in the entire Bible outside of Revelation that summarizes the message of Revelation 16, it is Romans 2:5 which says: "But because of your stubbornness and your unrepentant heart, you are storing up wrath against yourself for the day of God's wrath, when his righteous judgment will be revealed." I believe that to understand Revelation 16, you must read it in the context of the whole book. You can't just flip open your Bible to Revelation 16, leap in there, start interpreting, and understand the symbolism. You must see Revelation 16 in the context of the whole book of Revelation. Very briefly, by way of introduction, I want to review the first fifteen chapters of Revelation.

In chapters 1 through 3 of Revelation, we were shown—under the figure of the seven lampstands, or seven candlesticks—the surface issue, the fundamental problem of the book, which is the church struggling with sin and suffering persecution.

Chapters 4 through 7 showed us, under the figure of the seven seals, the church suffering trials, but under the overruling hand of God.

Chapters 8 through 11 showed us, under the figure of the seven trumpets, the warning judgments of God against those who persecute God's people. This is for the benefit of the persecutors, to cause them to repent.

Chapters 12 through 14 introduced us to the five enemies of God's people: the dragon, the beast of the sea, the beast of the earth, those who bear the mark of the beast, and Babylon.

In chapters 15 and 16, we see those who bear the mark of the beast and Babylon.

In chapters 14 and 16, we see those who bear the mark of the beast facing the wrath of God. In succeeding chapters, we see the destruction of the other four enemies of God and the ultimate victory of God's people.

In chapter 16, we see the seven bowls of wrath. They can only be understood against the background of the seven trumpets of warning seen in chapters 8 through 11. I believe it's the only way one can correctly understand Revelation 16, because, if you will compare the seven trumpets of warning found in chapters 8 through 11 with the seven bowls of wrath that are found in chapter 16, you will see that, in some sense, they are dealing point-by-point with exactly the same things.

Here's what I mean. The first trumpet sounded (in Revelation 8:7) affects the earth, and when the first bowl of wrath (in Revelation 16:2) is poured out, it also affects the land. Both the first trumpet and the first bowl affect the earth. The second trumpet (in Revelation 8:8) and the second bowl (in Revelation 16:3) both affect the sea. The third trumpet (in Revelation 8:10) and the third bowl (in Revelation 16:4) affect the rivers and springs of water. The fourth trumpet (in Revelation 8:12) and the fourth bowl (in Revelation 16:8) affect the sun. The fifth trumpet (in Revelation 9:1-11) and the fifth bowl (in Revelation 16:10-11) affect the pit of the abyss where the throne of the beast is, and they bring darkness and torment. The sixth trumpet (in Revelation 9:14) and the sixth bowl (in Revelation 16:17-21) involve the Euphrates River. I went through that meticulously to show that the trumpets and the bowls are dealing with identically the same things, and that's surely not just accidental. So, I believe we need to pay close attention to see the connection between the trumpets and the bowls. And when we see the connection, we will see what the whole message of Revelation 16 is. Well, what do we see?

In chapters 8 through 11, as we looked at the trumpets, we saw the judgments of warning from God against the wicked in response to the prayers and cries of the persecuted people of God. You recall, back in Revelation 8, when the prayers of the saints ascended to the altar and incense was added to the prayers that came before God, that fire was hurled on the earth. We saw the wicked begin to suffer all kinds of warning judgments of God designed for the very purpose of causing them to repent. In fact, if you look at Revelation 9:20-21, as we come down to the end of the passage on the sixth trumpet of warning, you see that that is precisely what this was all about, because the thought was repeated, they "...did not repent....Nor did they repent...."

The point is, God is bringing judgment against the wicked, against the oppressors of God's people, to cause them to turn back to God. Time and again the wicked are afflicted, and time and again they refuse to respond to the warnings of God. They continue in their evil ways and continually harden their hearts. Finally, at the very end, we are told they "did not repent....Nor did they repent...."

When we come to Revelation 16 and the bowls of wrath are poured out, we see that they are being poured out on people who did not repent. Here are people who continually have been warned by God, and continually have ignored the warnings of God, and continue to harden their hearts. Notice, in chapter 16, the description of the people on whom the bowls of wrath are poured. Verse 2 says that it was on the people who had the mark of the beast and worshiped his image. Verse 9 says they cursed the name of God, *but they refused to repent*! Verse 11 says they cursed the God of heaven, *but they refused to repent*! Verse 21 says they cursed God.

These are the people on whom the bowls of God's wrath are poured. They refused to repent; they refused to repent. They cursed the God of heaven; they cursed God. We see people who have heard the trumpets of warning, but they wouldn't turn to God. Finally, God's wrath is poured out on these people because they continually hardened their hearts. Revelation 16 is telling us that when men fail to repent and respond to the warning judgments of God, there will inevitably follow a final outpouring of God's wrath.

We are not dealing here only with things that happen at the end of time, but with that which is continually happening throughout the Christian age. The warnings of God come continually against the wicked. God is not reserving his warnings for people who just happen to be born at the end of the Christian age. God is always warning people through his messengers.

God's warnings continually come to us. Sometimes they come to us through natural calamities. There are people out in Washington who are, perhaps, seeing something of a warning judgment of God in the volcano that erupted today. Some were killed, and other people may begin to think more seriously about the brevity of life. Perhaps some will be caused to think more seriously about the fact that our life on earth will end someday. Maybe they will begin to think soberly about their relationship to God. Maybe they will decide they have not been thinking as seriously and soberly as they should have been about eternal realities, and they will turn to God.

This happens all the time. God is continually warning people and trying to turn them back to him. Warning judgments of God are brought against the wicked continually, and the terminal wrath of God is continually poured out, even in this lifetime, on those who remain impenitent and continue to harden their hearts. As we're told in Revelation 15:1, chapters 15 and 16 describe the last of the plagues. Here the final wrath of God is being poured out on man—something that can occur in one's earthly lifetime. It doesn't have to be something that happens at the end of time when the final judgment occurs after Jesus comes again. In this lifetime, you can so harden your heart that you become a terminal case. I believe the Bible reveals this to us continually.

The classic case in the Old Testament, which serves as almost a background against which all else can be considered, is the case of Pharaoh. Let's go back to Exodus 7 and notice a series of verses beginning with Exodus 7:13. It says, "Yet Pharaoh's heart became hard and he would not listen to them…." Chapter 8:15 says, "But when Pharaoh saw that there was relief, he hardened his heart…." Now look at verse 19: "But Pharaoh's heart was hard…." Verse 32 says: "But this time also Pharaoh hardened his heart…." You see what's happening?

Moses comes and says, "Look, you have seen the hand of God, Pharaoh. Repent, and let my people go." Pharaoh says, "No," and he hardens his heart. It isn't something that happened only one time when there was just one great hardening and then it was all over. We are told that he hardened his heart. Then, later, we are told he hardened his heart again. This means his heart was not completely hardened earlier, because you can't harden that which is already completely hardened. So there is a process involved here. He hardened his heart again. What is the final outcome of all this?

Let's go to Exodus 9:7, which says of Pharaoh: "Yet his heart was unyielding and he would not let the people go." Let's look at verse 12. Here's the clincher: "But the Lord hardened Pharaoh's heart…." Think about that a minute. Here was a man who had been in the process of hardening his heart. He had warning after warning, plague after plague after plague came on Egypt, and time after time after time Pharaoh ignored the warning judgments of God. Finally, in his own earthly lifetime, God stepped in and finished the process. God hardened Pharaoh's heart.

What are we seeing in Revelation 16? The same kind of thing. We're seeing one bowl of wrath poured out, another bowl of wrath poured out, another bowl of wrath poured out, another bowl of wrath poured out. These are judgments of God. Earlier, in Revelation 8 through 11, we saw warnings of God coming first. God sent his warnings to try to get people to repent, but they refused to repent, they refused to repent. Then we come to chapter 16, and still they refused to repent. In other words, they continually said "no" to God, and their hearts got harder and harder and harder. Finally, God stepped in and poured out the final judgment of wrath against them, and that can happen in this lifetime.

Let's move to other parts of the New Testament and look at a series of passages that suggest the same thing. In Romans 1, Paul speaks about the pre-Christian, Gentile world. The same process that had occurred in the life of that individual man, Pharaoh, was happening in the Gentile world. Notice how it is described for us in a series of verses in Romans 1, beginning with verse 21. It says, "For although they knew God, they neither glorified him as God nor gave thanks to him, but their thinking became futile and their foolish hearts were darkened." And now, verse 24: "Therefore God gave them over in the sinful desires of their hearts…." Now, verses 25-26: "They exchanged the truth of God for a lie, and worshiped and served created things rather than the Creator—who is forever praised. Amen. Because of this, God gave them over…." Let's go to verse 28: "Furthermore, since they did not think it worthwhile to retain the knowledge of God, he gave them over…."

What is happening here? These people had a knowledge of God, but they refused to seek after God, so God gave them up. They pursued the lusts of the flesh, and God gave them up. They refused to have God in their knowledge. God gave them up. That was the condition of the pre-Christian, Gentile world. God had given them up, because they had first given God up, and that can happen in this lifetime. In the course of our life here on earth, we may very well pass, or cross over, that line between God's patience and God's wrath—and woe to the man who has continued to so harden his heart that he passes that line in his lifetime.

Let's see other references to the same kind of thought. In Matthew 12:32, Jesus said: "…anyone who speaks against the Holy Spirit will not be forgiven, either in this age or in the age to come." In other words, in this world, before reaching the next, a person can reach a point where he can no longer be forgiven. He is dead even while he lives. He is hopeless even in this lifetime.

Let's look at 1 John 5:16, and we see the same thing: "If anyone sees his brother commit a sin that does not lead to death, he should pray and God will give him life. I refer to those whose sin does not lead to death. There is a sin that leads to death. I am not saying that he should pray about that." John is saying there are some men who have so persistently sinned in this life that even your prayers can no longer do them any good. They have crossed over the line. They have passed the patience of God.

Let's turn to Hebrews 6, which is the most convincing of all. Hebrews 6:4-6 says:

> It is impossible for those who have once been enlightened, who have tasted the heavenly gift, who have shared in the Holy Spirit, who have tasted the goodness of the word of God and the powers of the coming age, if they fall away, to be brought back to repentance, because to their loss they are crucifying the Son of God all over again and subjecting him to public disgrace.

The writer of the Hebrew letter says that there are people who, within their own lifetimes on earth, pass that point of no return. They cross the line from the patience of God into his wrath. They have tasted the good things of the world to come, and they have rejected them and fallen away. There comes a point where it is impossible to bring them back to repentance.

Turn to 1 Timothy 4:1-2. It says: "The Spirit clearly says that in later times some will abandon the faith and follow deceiving spirits and things taught by demons. Such teachings come through hypocritical liars, whose consciences have been seared as with a hot iron." Their consciences are seared. It's like taking a hot iron and putting it on your flesh and searing it so it is totally insensitive any longer to feeling. There are people who in their lifetimes have so continually rejected the warnings of God that their consciences are completely seared. They are totally insensitive to the appeals of the loving God, and it is impossible to bring them back to repentance.

There are those who are among the living dead. 2 Timothy 3:1-9 tells us the same thing. There are men who are never able to acknowledge the truth because they have become so evil. There is no point trying to teach them what's right. Timothy is told to just avoid them, keep away from them, have nothing to do with them. They have already gone beyond the point of repentance. It is impossible to bring them back to repentance. In Romans 1, we saw a hardened, pre-Christian world. I believe, as we move toward the end of time, that we will see a similar hardening, so that the impact of the Christian gospel in our world will be as insignificant as the impact of Judaism was in the pre-Christian world.

There is a paragraph in the commentary of Burton Coffman on Revelation which, I believe, suggests to us part of the message being seen in Revelation 16. He said,

> We have now seen all the bowls poured out. What do they mean? A very perceptive person suggested that they mean that a time will come when all the evil in the universe shall unite to oppose truth and righteousness, making it seem for a time that all is lost. This would certainly seem to be true; but evil shall not win; right shall prevail. God's answer to the first general hardening of mankind in Romans 1 was the First Advent of Christ; and his answer to the second and final general hardening of the human race will be the Second Advent of the Lord Jesus Christ, an event that follows very closely the pouring out of these seven bowls of wrath.

Revelation 11, 13, and 16 may hint at an idea, taught clearly in Revelation 20, about conditions prevailing on earth at the end of time. The gospel of Christ will be so hindered in its progress that it will almost seem as if Satan has totally overwhelmed and conquered. But, as those few remaining saints on earth are crying out to God, they will be delivered and be brought into the presence of God. Though that may be true, the more significant message of Revelation 16 is to men who continually refuse to repent at the warning judgments of God. They must understand that when a man is so hardened in sin, there is no hope for his salvation. Finally, God's patience can continue no longer. May it never happen to us!

We, unfortunately, haven't time to go into all the details of Revelation 16. That's the reason we have given you at least a background against which you can better understand the significance of Revelation 16 and a framework within which the details can be understood. Finally, let me call your attention to two small points in Revelation 16.

One is verse 15, which says: "Behold, I come like a thief! Blessed is he who stays awake and keeps his clothes with him, so that he may not go naked and be shamefully exposed." F. F. Bruce, in his commentary said: "According to the Mishnah, the captains of the temple in Jerusalem went their rounds of the precincts at night, and if a member of the temple police was caught asleep at his post, his clothes were taken off and burned, and he was sent away naked in disgrace." Why? Because he was not watching. It may very well be that John was drawing from that background when he wrote, "Blessed is he who stays awake and keeps his clothes with him, so that he may not go naked and be shamefully exposed."

Jesus, as he was speaking of his second coming, said you don't know when it will be, but watch because he's coming like a thief in the night. We need to be people who keep about us garments of righteousness, robes that have been washed in the blood of the Lamb and that are maintained pure and clean. Then, no matter when the Lord comes again, he will find us watching, will find us faithful, and will grant us the inheritance of the crown of life.

It is the very next verse after this that everybody wants to hear about, but about which I am going to say practically nothing. It is verse 16: "Then they gathered the kings together to the place that in Hebrew is called Armageddon." It seems there is an awesome fascination in our world concerning Armageddon. Mention Armageddon, and people will get their Bibles out and start trying to figure out where and when it is going to happen, this great battle that so many see as occurring at the end of time. Actually, I think it has nothing to do with any kind of battle that is going to take place over in the Middle East between the armies of China or Russia or any other country. Revelation is not concerned about that kind of warfare. It is concerned about spiritual warfare.

Where is Armageddon? Well, it seems to be the place of the final struggle between the powers of evil and the kingdom of God. But where does the final struggle between the powers of evil and the kingdom of God take place? Is it not in the hearts of men? Is that not where the real battle is? Throughout scripture, we are told that our struggle is not against flesh and blood. Our struggle is against authorities, against the powers of this dark world, and against the spiritual forces of evil in the heavenly realms. It's a struggle to overcome the temptations of Satan and to vigorously pursue the evangelistic work of God's kingdom, trying to lead men into the kingdom of God and to preserve their souls for Christ.

There's a battle that takes place daily in our hearts, and there's where the great battle is fought. We need always to be watching, ready, prepared, and active in the service of God so that, whenever he comes, we will be prepared for him. It doesn't matter whether there are masses of armies in the Middle East. That has nothing to do with the book of Revelation. The great issue of life is whether your allegiance is to Jesus, or your allegiance is to Satan.

That is the issue at this very moment. The cry of Jesus is, "Here I am! I stand at the door and knock. If anyone hears my voice and opens the door, I will go in and eat with him, and he with me." To you he leaves the answer as to whether you will open the door. Jesus says, "Come to me, all you who are weary and burdened, and I will give you rest." The issue is whether you'll come to Jesus for the rest that he offers you.

The issue of life is whether Jesus is Lord, or Caesar is Lord. The issue of life is what you will do with Jesus. What do you think about the Christ? Whose son is he? When these issues are properly decided in your life, then you are prepared for the coming of Jesus Christ, and you are prepared to hear those words, "Well done, good and faithful servant!" These are the great issues of Revelation.

If you hear his voice, don't harden your heart. Today is the day of salvation. Jesus is calling to your heart. Don't harden your heart, but give it to Jesus, so he can make your life something noble, something fit and prepared for entrance into the everlasting kingdom. If you believe in Jesus, and will repent of your sins and confess your faith in him, why not come and be baptized into him so you will be ready to walk in newness of life?

REVELATION 17:

Babylon, the Great Prostitute

W e have come to the 17th chapter of Revelation, the vision of the great prostitute. It was common among the leaders of the Protestant Reformation, including such men as Martin Luther, William Tyndale, John Wesley, and John Knox, to identify the great prostitute of the Revelation with the Roman Catholic Church. Alexander Campbell, in his debate in the 1800's with Bishop Purcell, defended the proposition that Babylon, the great prostitute, was the Roman Catholic Church.

Let me say, at the very beginning, that I do not believe that that is true. I am not saying that because I am trying to be nice to Roman Catholicism, but I do not believe that Babylon, the great prostitute, is a portrait of apostate Christianity. The picture given is not so much a picture of religious deception, as it is of worldly seduction. I believe the fact that Babylon is the symbol employed in Revelation is significant.

In the Old Testament, five cities are described as prostitutes: Nineveh, Tyre, Babylon, Jerusalem, and Samaria. Nineveh is so described in Nahum 3:1-4, Tyre in Isaiah 23:15-17, Babylon in Isaiah 47:1-7, and Jerusalem and Samaria in Ezekiel 23 and elsewhere. If God wanted to choose a city to represent apostasy from the true religion of God, which of these would he choose?

Only Jerusalem and Samaria were ever associated with faithful Judaism. Nineveh, Tyre, and Babylon were strictly pagan cities that were never identified with the chosen people of God. They could serve only as symbols of a world apart from God, offering only those pleasures the world can offer. And, of those, Babylon was the greatest city and the one that could most reasonably represent world-wide influence, a city of the world influencing the world with the attractions of the world.

That Babylon is the symbol of the power, influence, attraction, corruption, and seduction of the world, rather than the symbol of apostate Christianity, is further suggested by the fact that, as we move further into the chapter, Babylon begins to assume the form of another great city, Rome. At the time John wrote, Rome represented all those things that Babylon represented. Like Babylon, Rome was the capital city of a world empire, a totally pagan city, a perfect symbol of luxury, vice, and glamor seducing the world. At that time, Rome could not have been a symbol of apostasy from the true religion of God. But Rome, as the great prostitute, could be a symbol of the great seductive attractions of this world.

Even in that great prophecy in Hosea 2, the apostasy of Israel is attributed to the seductive attraction of this world, rather than to the deception of false religion. In Hosea 2:4-5, God said concerning Israel:

> I will not show my love to her children,
>
>> because they are the children of adultery.
>
> Their mother has been unfaithful
>
>> and has conceived them in disgrace.
>
> She said, "I will go after my lovers,
>
>> who give me my food and my water,
>
>> my wool and my linen, my oil and my drink."

Israel was not being seduced so much by other gods—although she involved herself in idolatry—as she was by the allure of the things of this world. So what we are seeing in Revelation 17, under the figure of Babylon, is not a representation of the apostate church. I believe that Babylon represents the seductive attractions of this world, the lusts of this world.

I believe that Satan employs three weapons to destroy the people of God. These three weapons are discussed in Revelation under the imagery of the beast that comes out of the sea, the beast that comes out of the earth, and the great prostitute, Babylon. Satan, the great dragon, is the one who is the force behind it all, but he uses these three instruments to cause people to bear the mark of the beast. The three instruments of destruction that Satan employs against the people of God are persecution, deception, and seduction.

In other words, Satan would like to destroy the people of God through persecution. If he can attack your body, if he can persecute you in a physical way, and cause you to deny your Lord, he will have won the battle.

But if that doesn't work, he has a second weapon. He can try to deceive you. He can use false religion to cause you to not seek true religion. He can produce a counterfeit so that, unless you are really seeking God with all your heart and soul and mind and strength, you can be deceived and be led away into a counterfeit religion. I do believe that Roman Catholicism and many other religions fit in that category.

There is a third instrument, seduction. Satan can attack your body with persecution, and attack your mind to deceive you, but he can also attack your emotions and your will. He can try to get you to anchor your life, tie your life, to this world and to center all your affairs in this life, without reference to a life that is to come.

In fact, I believe that in 1 John 2:15-17 you have an exact, clear, and direct statement of what Revelation 17 tells us. John said:

> Do not love the world or anything in the world. If anyone loves the world, the love of the Father is not in him. For everything in the world—the cravings of sinful man, the lust of his eyes and the boasting of what he has and does—comes not from the Father but from the world. The world and its desires pass away, but the man who does the will of God lives forever.

I believe that Babylon, under the figure of the great prostitute, is a symbol used to suggest this weapon of Satan to try to destroy you: the seductive allure of this world and what it has to offer, in opposition to that which God offers to his people.

Going to Revelation 17:1, I think it is significant that God did not choose the symbol of Jerusalem—which might have served as a good symbol of an apostate church—as the great prostitute, but he used Babylon as the symbol, because Babylon never was a part of God's people. Now Jerusalem once was, and Jerusalem, as a prostitute, would be a good symbol of an apostate church. But not Babylon; Babylon was always in opposition to the people of God. I believe, then, that what we are seeing is Satan's attempt to capture your heart and your affections by employing the enticements and lusts of this world. Revelation 17:1 says:

> One of the seven angels who had the seven bowls came and said to me, "Come, I will show you the punishment of the great prostitute, who sits on many waters. With her the kings of the earth committed adultery and the inhabitants of the earth were intoxicated with the wine of her adulteries."

I believe the symbolism comes out of a passage in Jeremiah 51. The same kind of imagery used there is employed in the Revelation. In Jeremiah 51:7, Jeremiah said,

> Babylon was a gold cup in the Lord's hand;
>
> she made the whole earth drunk.
>
> The nations drank her wine;
>
> therefore they have now gone mad.

Let's resume reading at Revelation 17:3:

> Then the angel carried me away in the Spirit into a desert. There I saw a woman sitting on a scarlet beast that was covered with blasphemous names and had seven heads and ten horns. The woman was dressed in purple and scarlet, and was glittering with

gold, precious stones and pearls. She held a golden cup in her hand, filled with abominable things and the filth of her adulteries.

Notice the similarity to Jeremiah 51:7. Babylon has been a golden cup in the Lord's hand that made all the earth drunk. The nations have drunk her wine; therefore the nations have gone mad.

Now, notice Jeremiah 51:12-13:

> Lift up a banner against the walls of Babylon!
>
> Reinforce the guard,
>
> station the watchmen,
>
> prepare an ambush!
>
> The Lord will carry out his purpose,
>
> his decree against the people of Babylon.
>
> You who live by many waters
>
> and are rich in treasures,
>
> your end has come,
>
> the time for you to be cut off.

Babylon is rich, and she seduces the people of God with her luxuries and treasures.

Note Revelation 17:3 again: "Then the angel carried me away in the Spirit into a desert. There I saw a woman sitting on a scarlet beast...." This beast is described as covered with blasphemous names and as having seven heads and ten horns. Back in Revelation 13, we were introduced to this beast, the beast that had the seven heads and ten horns. We identified it as representing all the persecuting governments of the world. What we are seeing here is Babylon, the great prostitute, sitting on the scarlet beast. In other words, she is in close association with the beast. The governments of this world so often gain the support of the people by promising economic prosperity and other earthly benefits.

Now John sees this woman in the desert. That's where the church was seen earlier, in Revelation 12. Satan goes where the church is. He is going to use the great prostitute to seduce the people of God. Babylon is described now in verse 5:

This title was written on her forehead:

MYSTERY

BABYLON THE GREAT

THE MOTHER OF PROSTITUTES

AND OF THE ABOMINATIONS OF THE EARTH.

We are seeing Babylon as representing seduction. That's the idea. The prostitute seduces. That's what she does. The prostitute does not persecute, the prostitute does not particularly deceive, the prostitute simply seduces.

We see, then, the seductive power Satan has to seduce God's people away from allegiance to God. These seductions include luxury, glamor, and all the vices—all these are suggested. Babylon is a good choice as a symbol of that kind of seductive power, because the great cities of our world are the places where these particular kinds of attractions are usually centered. Not only are they seemingly concentrated in the great cities of the world, but from those great cities the world is influenced by all these things.

In our own country, for example, where are Satan's greatest instruments for seducing people? You have Los Angeles and Hollywood constantly producing those things that are in opposition to what God wants for his people. The cities influence the world.

So God has chosen the greatest city he could choose in an ancient time, mighty Babylon. I don't think there was a greater city on the face of the earth in terms of its size and its influence. Babylon was chosen to suggest seductive power. Babylon later becomes a symbol for Rome. Interpreters agree the seven hills have reference to the seven hills of Rome. Rome is being suggested here, because Rome, in the time when John was living, was the perfect example of the great seductive city with all the luxury and vice and glamor that the world can offer.

Verse 6 says: "I saw that the woman was drunk with the blood of the saints, the blood of those who bore testimony to Jesus. When I saw her, I was greatly astonished." A good illustration of the kind of thing suggested here would be the coliseum in Rome where, for the amusement and entertainment of the people, the Christians were fed to the lions. There the blood of the martyrs flowed, all in the name of entertainment and great amusement.

Verse 7 says, "Then the angel said to me: 'Why are you astonished? I will explain to you the mystery of the woman and of the beast she rides, which has the seven heads and ten horns.'" All we have seen up to now may still seem rather mysterious, so the angel says, "I am going to explain all this to you now so you will understand better."

We go to verse 8: "The beast, which you saw, once was, now is not, and will come up out of the Abyss and go to his destruction." I believe that to understand Babylon, you must understand the beast. In our study of Revelation 13, we learned that the beast represents the persecuting political powers of all the ages. The emphasis I want to give here is *"of all the ages,"* because we learned that the beast was not just representing one particular government. It wasn't representing just the government of Rome. It was representing all the governments of the world that persecute God's people.

Now, as we see the woman riding the beast in chapter 17, we're seeing the same kind of association. The woman and beast are coextensive. The duration in which the beast is active is the duration in which the woman is active, which suggests that the woman is not a specific woman at some particular point in history, but that the symbol covers all of history. In other words, Satan has always been using governments to persecute God's people. Satan has always been trying to seduce God's people. So the symbols used here are ones that are comprehensive.

Notice again in verse 8, "The beast, which you saw, once was, now is not, and will come up out of the Abyss and go to his destruction." What does this mean? As we saw earlier, in chapter 13, the beast had seven heads, representing many governments. The beast received what seemed like a death stroke, and it looked like the beast would die because one of the heads was wounded. But it revived, and the world marveled. The point is that when one government seemingly is destroyed, the world gets excited, but then it always seems like a worse government comes along and takes its place. That has been the history of the world, one bad government after another bad government. When one falls, another comes up. So what we are seeing here is the beast that once was, and now is not.

But that's not the end of the story. It is about to come up out of the Abyss and then to go to its destruction. There are two pictures. One is of evil governments that continue to arise. One disappears, but then another comes up. The other picture is of evil governments that go to destruction. They all will finally fall. Notice the middle of verse 8: "The inhabitants of the earth whose names have not been written in the book of life from the creation of the world will be astonished when they see the beast, because he once was, now is not, and yet will come." This is the same thing we saw in chapter 13. Those who are not God's people, those who are not Christians, marvel at this, but the people of God don't marvel because they know. God revealed that this is the way things are. It's no marvel. But, Satan continues to bring about new governments and new persecuting powers, and he will continue to do so until the end of time.

Look at verse 9: "This calls for a mind with wisdom." In other words, the angel is saying, "Let me give you some wise insight into the whole situation to make clear what's going on." He says: "The seven heads are seven hills on which the woman sits. They are also seven kings. Five have fallen, one is, the other has not yet come; but when he does come, he must remain for a little while." Here the beast is portrayed in two ways. First, the seven heads are seven hills. That's one picture. But there is another picture he wants to develop, which is that the seven heads also represent seven kings.

There are two things suggested here. One is the seven heads, which are seven hills on which the woman sits, the seven hills of Rome. Rome was the present embodiment of a persecuting world government. That is one thing being suggested. But there is a second thing. There are seven kings; five have fallen, one is, the other has not yet come; but when he does come, he must remain for a little while.

He says there are five fallen kings. We must go back again to Daniel 2 and 7 in which the whole picture is rooted, because the beast of Revelation 17 (described more fully for us back in Revelation 13) was a composite of the four beasts in Daniel 7. The four beasts in Daniel 7 represented four successive world empires. That is made clearer as you compare it with Daniel 2. This suggests that the beast of Revelation 17 is the embodiment of all these governments which follow one right after the other.

You recall, also back in Daniel 2, when Daniel was interpreting the dream of King Nebuchadnezzar about the statue made of four different metals, that Daniel says these metals represent four kingdoms. In verse 39, Daniel said to King Nebuchadnezzar: "After *you, another kingdom* will rise…." In chapters 2 and 7, Daniel speaks of the kings as representing kingdoms. Since the symbolism of Revelation 17 emerges out of Daniel 7, let's let it set the context for interpreting Revelation 17. When it says in Revelation 17:9-10 that the heads are seven kings, I believe we must understand that as meaning the heads are seven kingdoms.

The heads represent seven kingdoms, and he says five have fallen, one is, and the other one has not yet come. What do we see as we look at the kingdoms of the world? There had been five kingdoms previously: The Egyptian, the Assyrian, the Babylonian, the Persian, and the Greek, and they had all fallen. Now, one kingdom is. The Roman Empire is the one that is. Then he says the other has not yet come; but when he does come, he must remain for a little while. Now, we'll learn in a moment what that is.

Let's move on to verse 11: "The beast who once was, and now is not, is an eighth king. He belongs to the seven and is going to his destruction." I believe the eighth king represents all the persecuting governments that are yet to come, because it says the beast that was, and is not, is himself also an eighth king. That beast represented all persecuting governments, so I believe the eighth is a composite of all persecuting governments yet to come. The fact that, since

Rome, no government has ruled the whole world may account for the eighth king representing a composite of governments.

Let's move to verse 12: "The ten horns you saw are ten kings who have not yet received a kingdom, but who for one hour will receive authority as kings along with the beast." Many interpreters have said these are actual kings that have ruled somewhere or will rule somewhere at some time. But notice it says that these who are called ten kings don't have any kingdom. So, in reality, they are not kings in the normal sense of the word.

What are "kings" anyway? They are men of power and influence in the world. But these are kings without a kingdom. It says they have not yet received a kingdom, and there is no necessary implication that they ever will. It says they received authority as kings. I think that's the whole point. It's speaking now of men who have authority as kings, that is, they are influential and powerful figures in the world.

Does this mean, literally, *ten* individual ones? In Revelation "ten" is a symbol of completeness. It has the significance of *all* the men in the future who are influential and powerful in our world who are not actually leaders of kingdoms, but who align themselves with the leaders of kingdoms. Men of great influence in the world will often align themselves with whomever is in power at the time for personal advantage and personal gain. We are seeing a picture of corrupt and persecuting governmental powers who have great and powerful men from all areas of life assisting them. For one hour they will receive authority as kings along with the beast. In other words, their influence is not going to be very permanent or very long. It is only for a brief time. Men who try to align themselves with the top dog, who try to get favors from the man on top, usually don't last very long in their ability to influence and affect things.

Now look at verse 13: "They have one purpose and will give their power and authority to the beast." In other words, they singlemindedly are giving their allegiance to the persecuting governmental powers of the world. They're not interested in following God or his Son, Jesus Christ.

Notice verse 14 which, I believe, is the theme and the key to the whole book of Revelation. Revelation 17:14 is the essential message of the book: "They will make war against the Lamb, but the Lamb will overcome them because he is Lord of lords and King of kings—and with him will be his called, chosen and faithful followers." So far, we have simply seen a rather discouraging and disgusting picture of oppressive governmental powers, of men aligned with them, and of those who are trying to seduce God's people.

But the message now is: "Cheer up, Christians!" These are all going to war against the Lamb of God, but the Lamb will overcome them. And the beautiful part for us is that we will overcome! That includes all who are called, chosen, and faithful. Didn't Jesus say already in Revelation 2:10: "Be faithful, even to the point of death, and I will give you the crown of life"? Yes, if you are faithful to Jesus. It doesn't matter what is happening out there in the world. It doesn't matter what's taking place there if you will keep your eye on the Lamb, on Jesus. Then you will be a conqueror. Then you will overcome the world.

Verse 15: "Then the angel said to me, 'The waters you saw, where the prostitute sits, are peoples, multitudes, nations and languages.'" In other words, the influence of that power is great and far-reaching.

Verse 16 says: "The beast and the ten horns you saw will hate the prostitute. They will bring her to ruin and leave her naked; they will eat her flesh and burn her with fire." Initially, you see the prostitute, the woman, riding on the beast, and they are working together. But a household cannot stand for long if it is divided against itself. Satan's hosts are divided against themselves. In the end, those who are among the associates of the beast will hate the prostitute.

They will begin to see that the world does not really have the answers, that the things of the world do not satisfy. Finally, they try to rebel against it all—but it's too late. They have been trapped. They can't throw it off. They have been caught in the snare of Satan, in the passions and the lusts of the world. They're slaves to their own passions and, even though they try to fight against them, it's too late. They have been caught. They hate the very thing they used to love.

Isn't that the way with sin? When we experience attractive things that God says are wrong, we find them bitter, we find they don't provide the satisfaction we expected. Yet if we continue in them, we reach a point where we just can't get out of the trap. We have developed habits that are wrong, and we can't break them.

Finally, notice verses 17-18: "For God has put it into their hearts to accomplish his purpose by agreeing to give the beast their power to rule, until God's words are fulfilled. The woman you saw is the great city that rules over the kings of the earth." The allure and the seduction of the world even control those who are the kings of the earth. Even the kings and rulers of governments are subject to the passions of the flesh. They are even slaves themselves to the allure of the world. They live restlessly, because they have not found the peace that lies and resides in a true relationship with God.

Revelation 17 is a very difficult chapter, admittedly, but we have tried to see what the message is. The message is, essentially, that the powers of Satan will fight against the Lamb, but the Lamb will overcome them because he is Lord of lords and King of kings—and with him will be his called, chosen and faithful followers. "…we are more than conquerors through him who loved us. For I am convinced that neither death nor life, neither angels nor demons, neither the present nor the future, nor any powers, neither height nor depth, nor anything else in all creation, will be able to separate us from the love of God that is in Christ Jesus our Lord." Be faithful to him and you need not worry about the rest, because God will be victorious and his people will be conquerors.

You can join that host of those who have given their allegiance to Jesus Christ. He's the way and the truth and the life. All else is a pathetic substitute that never satisfies, but Jesus gives life, and that life is eternal. If you believe in him and will repent of your sins and confess your faith in him, we urge you to come and be baptized into him to begin a new life.

Footnote: I originally preached these sermons using the text of the American Standard Version (ASV). Because of its archaic language, I have substituted the 1978 edition of the New International Version (NIV) for the transcription of these sermons. This has required some adjustments in the wording. The most important problem, not addressed in the written sermons, is the use of "adultery" in 17:2, 4; 18:3, 9; and 19:2. Babylon is a "prostitute," not an "adulteress." She is not described as a married woman, but as a "prostitute." The Greek word translated here is not the word for "adultery," but "fornication" or "sexual immorality." The point, in context, is not that she is unfaithful to a husband, falling from her loyalty to him. Rather, this is simply a promiscuous woman who seduces others.

REVELATION 18:

The Fall of Babylon

W e are taking our lesson from the 18th chapter of the book of Revelation. In Revelation 17, we were given a description of Babylon in terms of the great prostitute. Here, Babylon is described more in terms of the great city, although both ideas are found in both chapters. Previously, we introduced the idea of Babylon and its significance. As we begin our study of the 18th chapter, which describes the fall of Babylon, we want to add to what we had been studying regarding the meaning of Babylon.

What does Babylon represent in Revelation? I must say again, after more study, that I do not believe Babylon represents the Roman Catholic Church. I do not believe that it even represents false religion in the most general way. The reasons I believe that include the following: The idea of false religion has already been given a symbol and has been discussed previously in the book of Revelation. The beast seen coming up out of the earth in Revelation 13:11 is said to have done miraculous signs for the beast that came out of the sea, according to Revelation 13:14. And the earth beast which did that is identified in Revelation 19:20 as the false prophet. The same identification is seen in Revelation 16:13 and 20:10. Babylon is not discussed in association with the earth beast, which represents false religion, or with counterfeit Christianity in whatever form it might take.

Babylon is associated with the sea beast, which represents governments that persecute God's people. Babylon is spoken of as the great prostitute, which suggests seduction. The allure of this prostitute is the luxury, the vice, and the glamor of this world which will always be supported by governments opposing God's way of life and persecuting his people who live his way of life. Babylon could not be a symbol of apostate religion, because Babylon in the Old Testament, from which the imagery of Revelation is drawn, was never presented as apostate Judaism. Babylon was not a corruption of Judaism. Babylon represented a completely alien style of life caught up in the pleasures, the luxuries, the vices, and the glamor that the world can offer. Let's look at two examples of this.

In Isaiah 47:8, Isaiah describes Babylon and makes this statement:

> Now then, listen, you wanton creature,
>
> lounging in your security
>
> and saying to yourself,
>
> "I am, and there is none besides me.
>
> I will never be a widow
>
> or suffer the loss of children."

Babylon is portrayed as a place given to pleasures.

There is another description of Babylon found in the next prophecy of the Old Testament, in Jeremiah 51:13. Notice how Babylon is characterized:

> You who live by many waters
>
> and are rich in treasures,
>
> your end has come,
>
> the time for you to be cut off.

Here is a city that is identified as a wealthy city, one that can provide material things that people crave. Jeremiah speaks of the abundance of the treasures of Babylon, and Isaiah speaks of her pleasures. So, in the Old Testament, Babylon, rather than representing a corruption of God's religion, is portrayed as a place of treasures and pleasures. Babylon, then, represents a pleasure-oriented world.

That is the very aspect of Babylon that Revelation calls to our attention in this discussion in Revelation 17 and 18. For example, the first description of Babylon in Revelation 17:4 says, "The woman was dressed in purple and scarlet, and was glittering with gold, precious stones and pearls. She held a golden cup in her hand, filled with abominable things and the filth of her adulteries." The picture here is not of apostate religion. The picture is of luxury, of depravity, of a glamorous lifestyle. Here is a woman dressed in beautiful scarlet and purple, holding a golden cup of abominations, a woman who is engaged in filthy things, decked out with gold and precious stones. Here's a picture of a woman of luxury and ease and seduction, one who represents the enticements of the things of the world.

As we come to Revelation 18, the first description of Babylon in verse 4 says,

> Then I heard another voice from heaven say:
>
> "Come out of her, my people,
>
>> so that you will not share in her sins,
>>
>> so that you will not receive any of her plagues...."

Now, notice verses 11-13: "The merchants of the earth will weep and mourn over her because no one buys their cargoes any more—cargoes of gold, silver, precious stones and pearls; fine linen, purple...." And on and on it goes, naming luxurious things that appeal to those who have their hearts centered in this life.

Babylon, apparently, represents more than a single city of that name. Revelation 18:24 says,

> In her was found the blood of prophets and of the saints,
>
> and of all who have been killed on the earth.

Babylon is said to be the place where all who have been killed on the earth have lived. Babylon is, then, representing something more than one city in this world at one particular time in this world.

What was Babylon, anyway? Babylon was the great city that controlled the world. Babylon was the heart of the great empire whose influence spread to the ends of the earth. Babylon had worldwide influence. Babylon is, then, representative of the entire corrupting power of the world. Babylon had ruled the world, and its influence was worldwide.

When John wrote, Rome was the equivalent of Babylon, and John, in the Revelation, identified Rome with Babylon. Babylon sits on seven hills, according to Revelation 17:9. Revelation 17:18 says: "The woman you saw is the great city that rules over the kings of the earth." Well, the current manifestation of that was Rome. Rome was the city that ruled over the kings of the earth when John was writing.

Rome, at that time, was a perfect expression of the same thing Babylon was: a mighty city whose powerful, corruptive influence reached to the ends of the earth. Babylon, I believe, is not a single city and, certainly, not a religion. That doesn't seem to be the picture we are getting. We are getting a picture of the enticement of the world, simple worldliness, the corruptive influences of the world, the allure of luxury, the world's vices and its glamor. And that, it seems to me, is what we have seen in Revelation 17 and 18. Rome was, at that time, a perfect expression of the worldwide corrupting influence of luxury, glamor, and vice.

I believe that in Revelation we see the three great agents of Satan: the beast that comes out of the sea—representing governments that affect the people of God, the beast that comes up out of the earth (which is spoken of elsewhere as the false prophet)—deceiving the minds of men, and Babylon—which is seducing men. Satan uses persecution, deception, and seduction to destroy God's people. The fleeting satisfaction—but powerful attraction—of the things of this world are suggested in Revelation 18:2-3:

> With a mighty voice he shouted:
>
> "Fallen! Fallen is Babylon the Great!
>
> She has become a home for demons
>
> and a haunt for every evil spirit,

a haunt for every unclean and detestable bird.

For all the nations have drunk

the maddening wine of her adulteries.

The kings of the earth committed adultery with her,

and the merchants of the earth grew rich from her

excessive luxuries."

The angel spoke of her excessive luxuries.

Babylon represents luxury well. The things of this world hold such fascination and attraction. I doubt if there is any more powerful influence that Satan uses than the power and allure of the pleasures and treasures of this earth. This, I am confident, is a major consideration we are seeing here in Revelation. Those who are drunk on the wine of the world's immorality, as represented and presented in the figure of Babylon, will finally drink the wine of God's wrath.

Consequently, there is the appeal in verse 4:

Then I heard another voice from heaven say:

"Come out of her, my people…."

Then the voice explained why: "so that you will not share in her sins." This has been the appeal of God to his people throughout the ages, to come out from among the corrupting influences of the world and be a separate, holy, distinctive people who are committed to God and to his way.

In John 17:14-16 Jesus expresses the same idea: "I have given them your word and the world has hated them, for they are not of the world any more than I am of the world. My prayer is not that you take them out of the world but that you protect them from the evil one." That's the same thing Revelation 18:4-5 is saying. Come out from Babylon, come out from the world. How do you do this? Not by getting in a space ship and going to the moon. You come out by having no fellowship with the sins of the world. That's what Jesus is saying here. "My prayer is not," Jesus said, "that you take them out of the world but that you protect them from the evil one. They are not of the world, even as I am not of it."

I believe that 1 John gives the perfect elaboration on the point and makes it practical. It brings it down to earth. In 1 John 2:15-17, John said, "Do not love the world...." That's what Revelation 17 and 18 is saying to us. John said: "Do not love the world or anything in the world. If anyone loves the world, the love of the Father is not in him. For everything in the world—the cravings of sinful man...." Remember the great prostitute with whom the kings of the earth commit immorality? They mistakenly think that in this they will find the satisfaction of their yearnings and cravings. But John warned of the fleeting satisfaction of fleshly cravings of the world.

Then he warned about the lust of the eyes, and you can just see men looking at that golden cup filled with abominable things and thinking of that glamorous creature decked out in her scarlet and purple and holding the gleaming golden cup.

John warns of boasting of what one has and does. Babylon was saying, "I am, and I will always be, and I have everything to satisfy you." Here is the boasting, thinking that this world, this life, contains all that is necessary to provide us with all our needs, our happiness, and our joy. It doesn't. "...The cravings of sinful man, the lust of his eyes and the boasting of what he has and does—comes not from the Father but from the world." Next comes the verse that, I believe, best summarizes the entire 17th and 18th chapters of Revelation: "The world and its desires pass away, but the man who does the will of God lives forever."

It seems to me that Revelation 17 and 18 is simply a graphic, wildly symbolic picture of the very thing stated here. The world, the enticement, the allure of the things of this life that has ensnared hundreds of millions of people is going to pass away, but the only thing that really endures is the man who does the will of God.

In Psalm 17:14 the Psalmist speaks of "...men of this world whose reward is in this life." That describes, unfortunately, the great part of our world that has been captured by Satan. Remember, Jesus said we are not to be of the world. But there are men who are of the world, who have their reward in this life, and that's all they have. Some live a cradle-to-grave existence, trying to grab all the gusto they can right here, thinking this earthly life is everything.

Paul said, in 1 Corinthians 15:19, that if Christians have nothing to look for except the things of this life, then we are to be pitied more than all other men. Paul explained, in 2 Corinthians 5:2-4, that in this body of flesh "...we groan, longing to be clothed with our heavenly dwelling...so that what is mortal may be swallowed up by life." In every man there is a yearning for immortality. There is the intimation of immortality in life, and everyone knows it and feels it and senses it. There is the craving for what is yet to come. Eternity is, somehow, buried within the hearts of men (Ecclesiastes 3:11), and we can never rest until we have found the way to satisfy that yearning for it. The problem is that the world is filled with men who have extinguished, as best they can, that craving, who have sought to find fulfillment of that yearning in the things of this life, and who have been unable to find it.

In Revelation 18:6-8, judgment is pronounced on Babylon. And, again, I believe that Babylon simply represents all the seductions of the world, the things of the world, that attract us and turn our eyes away from God. They cause us to lose sight of eternity, of immortality, of the judgment to come, of the reality of heaven, of the reality of the coming again of Christ. They only distract our attention and cause us to occupy our lives in the things of this world. That's what Babylon represents. It's the allure, the seductions, of this life.

In verses 6 through 8, judgment is pronounced on Babylon. But those who are enamored with this world refuse to consider such a possibility. Look at Revelation 18:7:

> Give her as much torture and grief
>
> > as the glory and luxury she gave herself.
>
> In her heart she boasts,
>
> > "I sit as queen; I am not a widow,
>
> and I will never mourn."

"No, sir! I don't need to worry about the future. I'm not the one who is going to experience mourning. I'm going to live it up. I'm going to enjoy all the world can give me, and it's just going to go on and on." The materially prosperous in every age have lived under the illusion that their happy state will continue without interruption, but the deep realization that this really can't be is the source of relentless unrest.

I think we see a tremendous restlessness in our age. Many just can't seem to find peace. They can't seem to find real joy, and they're seeking it in a bottle, or they're seeking it in a succession of marriages or affairs. They're looking in every direction. The restlessness will finally cease when it is replaced by the genuine peace of a fulfilling relationship with the God who created us and with whom we will someday have fellowship, if we live faithfully to him. There is where peace is found. Yet those who have their whole lives centered in things of this world, and who do not look beyond, will surely be doomed to ceaseless restlessness.

In verses 9 through 19, we see the lamentation over the fall of Babylon, but I want you to notice the people who are sorry to see Babylon pass. They are sorry only because they can't get any more out of it. None is depicted as loving the city for herself, but only for what he could get out of her. She might seduce and enrich men, but there was nothing lovely in her. She had brought profit and pleasure to many, but affection to none. It distresses me to see so many in our time who are unable to establish really satisfying relationships with other people. They can't get along with their spouses, and they can't get along with the people at work. They can't get along because they are looking to other people to fulfill their cravings and their desires, and they are not able to look outward to be giving to others.

If you look at the people who are mourning over Babylon in verses 9 through 19, you find that these were people who had gotten all kinds of goodies, all kinds of pleasures and treasures, but now it was all cut off. They were sorry, but not because they had found that Babylon was really good. There's no goodness to be found, ultimately, in the thrills and the things of this life. The pleasures and the joys that are everlasting are those that are found in relationships with people and with God. In loving God and loving others as we love ourselves, there is peace. It is peace for which men are yearning and which God provides, if we will follow his procedures and his rules and not try to think that we can do it a better way. God does have the answer to our needs.

I think that most of us probably don't realize the degree of the luxury of the Roman world of that time. When you read in verses 11 through 13 of all the merchandise that was described by John, you are reading no exaggeration of the conditions that existed in the Roman world. We have confirmation of this from contemporary Roman historians. Let me just read you a description by Aristides, the Roman orator, on the way things flowed into the city of Rome back in that first century.

> Merchandise is brought from every land and sea, everything that every season begets, and every country produces, the products of rivers and lakes, the arts of the Greeks and the barbarians, so that, if anyone were to wish to see all these things, he would either have to visit the whole inhabited world to see them—or to visit Rome; so many great ships arrive from all over the world at every hour, at every season, that Rome is like some common factory in the world, for you may see such great cargoes from the Indies, or, if you wish, from the blessed Arabias that you might well conjecture that the trees there have been stripped naked; clothing from Babylon, ornaments from the barbarian lands, everything flows to Rome; merchandise, cargoes, the products of the land, the emptying of the mines, the product of every art that is and has been, everything that is begotten and everything that grows. If there is anything you cannot see at Rome, then it is a thing which does not exist and which never existed.

Rome was the center of commerce and luxury. The luxury of Rome is beyond description.

Let's look for a moment at the Roman emperors and some of the wealthier people of Rome. A man named Epicius squandered a fortune of about three million dollars in refined debauchery and committed suicide when he had only three hundred thousand dollars left, because he thought he couldn't live on such a pittance as that. Nero once gave a banquet at which the Egyptian roses alone had cost something like a hundred thousand dollars. Vitellius, who was emperor for less than a year, succeeded in that period of time in spending something like twenty million dollars, mainly on food. Suetonius tells of his favorite dish, and here's what that Roman writer in the first century said: "In this he mingled the livers of pike, the brains of pheasants and peacocks, the tongues of flamingoes, and the milk of lampreys, brought by his captains and triremes from the whole empire from Parthia to the Spanish strait." That was just his favorite dish.

The super-rich lived in almost unimaginable luxury in Rome, but even the common people were caught up in materialism. The historian Pliny tells us that women would only bathe in silver baths, that even soldiers had swords with silver hilts, and scabbards with silver chains, that even poor women had silver anklets, and the very slaves had silver mirrors. This was a materialistic age. You say we live in a materialistic age. We're just like Rome, as John described in Revelation. Here were people caught up in a luxurious manner of life, a life of ease, a life in which they were just looking for the trinkets and the amusements of this world. They were blinded to any realities beyond the immediate present and any immediate thing that would titillate their imaginations and cause them to have a few thrills along the way.

As we read again of the things being imported by Rome that are described in Revelation 18:11-13, you see things such as silk. Silk was so costly that it took one pound of gold to pay for one pound of silk. This passage describes a thing called citron wood. In another translation it is called "thyine wood." You won't even find that unless you look in an unabridged dictionary, because it was a very rare and aromatic sweet-smelling wood that came from North Africa. It was beautifully grained, and the best graining could be like a peacock's tail or like the skin of a tiger or a panther. It was used especially for table tops. Tables made of thyine wood could cost anything from about twelve thousand dollars to about forty-five thousand dollars. Seneca, who was Nero's prime minister, was said to have had three hundred such tables with marble legs. It was an age of luxury, a materialistic age, an age of trade and commerce, of money and finance, an age that was obsessed only with material things.

This was one of the great instruments and tools of Satan to turn people from God and from building character, and to turn their minds to just adorning their bodies with more trinkets. It was an age which turned the minds of people away from establishing helpful human relationships to merely acquiring more and more things. What God is revealing to us in Revelation 17 and 18 is simply this: "The world and its desires pass away."

The last five verses describe the destruction of Babylon, and the thought is expressed again and again: never found again, never heard again, never shine again. No more music to fill the spirit. No more craftsmen to make pretty things. No more lamps to give light. No longer the voice of the bridegroom. No love has been generated to last. There is no real compassion. There is no tenderness. There are only bodies and lust. Babylon has fallen. It provides nothing more at all for the satisfaction of the human spirit.

But notice verse 20:

"'Rejoice over her, O heaven!

Rejoice, saints and apostles and prophets!

God has judged her for the way she treated you.'"

Rejoice, saints, because you have seen reality. You have known that Babylon will fall. You have known that the allure of this world holds nothing of permanent value. You rightly sing, "Earth holds no treasures but perish with using. Heaven holds all to me." We look forward to a city with foundations, whose architect and builder is God. We walk through this life holding our heads up, looking to the future, and living triumphantly every day with the assurance that God is with us. And, as we live with him and enjoy the people about us, we are walking hand in hand with Jesus toward that eternal home with God.

Babylon is fallen. "Come out of her, my people," and give your allegiance to Jesus Christ. Won't you do that right now? Won't you let your joy and peace be found in him? Believe in Jesus and trust him. Repent of your sins, confess your faith in Jesus, and be baptized into him.

REVELATION 19:
The Banquet and the Battle

W e have come to Revelation 19. I would like to review, briefly, the last half of the book of Revelation, so we can look at chapter 19 in context.

In Revelation 12, 13, and 14, we were presented with the five great enemies of God's people. The first one introduced was Satan himself, and then, in succession, we saw four instruments of Satan presented. We saw the beast coming out of the sea, we saw the beast coming out of the earth, we saw those who wear the mark of the beast, and then we saw Babylon, later identified as the great prostitute.

Beginning with chapter 15, we saw the judgment of God on each of these. In chapters 15 and 16, we saw the final outpouring of God's wrath on those who wore the mark of the beast.

Then, in chapters 17 and 18, we saw the doom of Babylon, the great prostitute.

Now, as we come to chapter 19, we see the doom of the beast that came out of the sea and the beast that came out of the earth. That beast is identified here, as it is elsewhere, as the false prophet.

Finally, in chapter 20, we will see the doom of Satan himself.

This leaves the last two chapters of Revelation for us to see that glorious vision of the triumph of the redeemed and their eternal enjoyment of the presence of God.

Now, we come to chapter 19. These various agents of Satan have been identified—reasonably, we hope—through their scriptural contexts. The dragon is identified for us as Satan. The beast that comes out of the sea, we identified as being persecuting governmental powers throughout the Christian age. We saw the beast that comes out of the earth as representing false religion, counterfeit Christianity. We saw those who have the mark of the beast as simply meaning all those whose allegiance is to Satan, rather than to Christ, and we saw Babylon as representing the seductive allure of the world, the lusts of the world.

I sometimes think it is difficult for us to get hold of these very bizarre and unusual symbols so that we can handle them. But what God is doing in the book of Revelation is something like what the political cartoonist attempts to do in his work. I believe there is an analogy here that could help us appreciate what we are dealing with.

From time to time, you see political cartoons on the editorial pages of the newspaper with various things represented. For example, you might see a partial view of the globe and a great big bear looming up over the edge of the earth with one great paw placed on Afghanistan. Another paw may be reaching over into Iran, and out of a blackish-looking pool his paw is scooping up liquid and he is drinking it. On the bear there is a symbol of a hammer and sickle. As you look at that, you get the picture. This is all done in very rich symbolism. The bear represents Russia coming down from the north. Russia is trampling Afghanistan underneath its foot and is reaching over into Iran to get some of that precious oil. The hammer and sickle represent Communism.

In another political cartoon, you may see a donkey and an elephant tugging on a rope. The donkey is a symbol of the Democratic party, the elephant represents the Republican party, and the tugging on the rope symbolizes the struggle for dominance by the two parties. We see these kinds of things, and we very quickly get the point of these political cartoons. They are not necessarily intended to be funny, either. They usually have a very serious message.

I believe that what we have in the book of Revelation is something like this. But instead of being done visually, it is done verbally. Pictures are painted with words, and the pictures are representations of things. For example, we have identified the strange looking beast that comes out of the sea as representing governments that persecute God's people. The beast is simply a representation of that, just as the elephant in a political cartoon may be a representation of a political institution. If you see the animal being destroyed, you're to understand that portrays the destruction of the political power it represents.

At the end of Revelation 19, we are going see the destruction of the beast that came out of the sea and the false prophet, the beast that came out of the earth. As we look at these, we must understand that when we see warfare taking place, we should not necessarily be thinking in terms of an actual military battle taking place here on earth with guns and military hardware. What we are seeing is the struggle that those symbols represent, the struggle between God and Satan, between God's people and those people who are antagonistic to him. When we see the beast of the sea destroyed, we learn that oppressive political and governmental powers are going to come to an end. God's people will be relieved, finally, of that kind of oppression.

When we see the false prophet being destroyed, being thrown alive into the fiery lake of burning sulfur, we are seeing that what the false prophet represents, false religion, finally meets its doom.

Let's look at Revelation 19, beginning with verse 1:

After this I heard what sounded like the roar of a great multitude in heaven shouting:

"Hallelujah!

Salvation and glory and power belong to our God,

for true and just are his judgments.

He has condemned the great prostitute

who corrupted the earth by her adulteries.

He has avenged on her the blood of his servants."

I believe this reflects the statement found in Revelation 18:20 which says,

Rejoice over her, O heaven!

Rejoice, saints and apostles and prophets!

God has judged her for the way she treated you.

Here, in Revelation 19:1-2, we see precisely that occurring. Heaven is rejoicing over the fall of Babylon. Those seductive influences in the world—drawing people's minds away from allegiance to God and enticing them with the lust of the flesh—have finally come to an end. There will come a time when we will be freed from the temptations that trouble us in this lifetime.

Verse 3 says:

And again they shouted:

"Hallelujah!

The smoke from her goes up for ever and ever."

Incidentally, the word "Hallelujah" occurs four times in Revelation 19, and it is the only place in the New Testament where it occurs. The word "Hallelujah" means "praise God," or "praise the Lord." It strikes me as strange that that expression is used so frequently among many people while it is used in the New Testament only at the throne of God in heaven. But there, in the final moment of judgment, when God's righteousness is vindicated, we hear the heavenly hosts singing, "Hallelujah, praise the Lord."

Now, let us look at verses 5-9:

Then a voice came from the throne, saying:

"Praise our God,

all you his servants,

you who fear him,

both small and great!"

Then I heard what sounded like a great multitude, like the roar of rushing waters and like loud peals of thunder, shouting:

"Hallelujah!

For our Lord God Almighty reigns.

Let us rejoice and be glad

and give him glory!

For the wedding of the Lamb has come,

and his bride has made herself ready.

Fine linen, bright and clean,

was given her to wear."

(Fine linen stands for the righteous acts of the saints.)

Then the angel said to me, "Write: 'Blessed are those who are invited to the wedding supper of the Lamb!'" And he added, "These are the true words of God."

We have come now to that exciting day when the people of God will gather together, rejoicing at the wedding of the Lamb.

Verse 7 begins with the statement: "Let us rejoice and be glad." There is only one other place in the New Testament where that expression is found, and I think it is significant. It is in Matthew 5:12 where Jesus said, as he concluded the beatitudes: "Rejoice and be glad, because great is your reward in heaven...." That is the ultimate reason for the rejoicing of God's people—there is a reward in heaven. But that's not all. The reason that is the cause of such rejoicing is found in the next statement of Jesus: "...for in the same way they persecuted the prophets who were before you."

God's people will always be persecuted in one way or another. Everyone who wants to live a godly life in Christ Jesus will be persecuted. So, it is the source of great joy to know that when we enter heaven, we have the reward, among other things, of no longer having to experience persecution. We should rejoice and be glad, because great is our reward in heaven where we will sit down at the wedding banquet of the Lamb.

I believe there is tremendous symbolism here in this passage where the wedding of the Lamb has come and his wife has made herself ready. The Jewish marriage custom was different from ours today. There was, first, the betrothal, which was a more decisive pact than our engagement, which we might break off. The betrothal was the legal ceremony of marriage. The betrothed were considered legally husband and wife, yet they were not allowed, at that point, to live together as husband and wife. That was the circumstance that Joseph and Mary were in when Jesus was conceived by the Holy Spirit. Mary was betrothed to Joseph, but they were not living together as husband and wife, although, legally and technically, she could be referred to as his wife.

This is the relationship between Christ and the church. In 2 Corinthians 11:2, Paul said to the church, to Christians, "I am jealous for you with a godly jealousy. I promised you to one husband, to Christ, so that I might present you as a pure virgin to him." Here is the picture of the betrothal. The church is espoused to Christ, but the church is to remain as a virgin until that time when, finally, the church is presented to Christ. The point is that now, in this lifetime, we, as we enter Christ, are betrothed to him. So, in some sense, it can be said that we are the bride of Christ.

A similar thought is suggested in Ephesians 5 where there is that beautiful picture of the husband-wife relationship and where, finally, in verse 32, Paul says: "This is a profound mystery—but I am talking about Christ and the church." This is the husband-wife relationship. It is as though the church is the wife of Christ.

But, in view of Revelation 19, we are only in a technical and legal sense the wife of Christ. By Jewish custom, the consummation, the actual time when they lived together as husband and wife, began at the wedding. During the period between the betrothal and the wedding, there was a period of preparation. We are not yet fully joined to Christ. Yes, we are his. We are united with Christ in baptism, but we are not joined to him in the same sense that one day we will be when we stand in his presence in the life that is to come. There will be a great reunion there with him, suggested in this picture in Revelation 19. But now is the time for us to prepare for the great wedding, when we will begin our life in eternity with our husband, with Jesus Christ.

Verse 8 says:

> Fine linen, bright and clean,
>
> was given her to wear.
>
> (Fine linen stands for the righteous acts of the saints.)

Remember Ephesians 5:25-27: "Husbands, love your wives, just as Christ loved the church and gave himself up for her to make her holy, cleansing her by the washing with water through the word, and to present her to himself as a radiant church, without stain or wrinkle or any other blemish, but holy and blameless." That's what God wants of his people. He wants a holy people, a people without stain or blemish, a people who have been preparing themselves, dressing themselves in fine linen that is bright and clean, because the fine linen is the righteous acts of the saints.

We are to adorn our lives with good deeds. We are to put on the wedding clothes, the clothing of a pure life. Failure to do that is pictured in the wedding banquet, described in Matthew 22:11-13, where Jesus said:

> But when the king came in to see the guests, he noticed a man there who was not wearing wedding clothes. "Friend," he asked, "how did you get in here without wedding clothes?" The man was speechless.
>
> Then the king told the attendants, "Tie him hand and foot, and throw him outside, into the darkness, where there will be weeping and gnashing of teeth."

It is obvious that Jesus uses this as a picture of the final judgment when men come unprepared. They come without having been adorned with the clean clothes that are appropriate for the wedding banquet. Consequently, because they have not been preparing in this life, they will be thrown outside, into the darkness, where there will be weeping and gnashing of teeth. But God's people who come to him prepared, clean and ready, will enjoy that marvelous occasion, the wedding of the Lamb.

Notice Revelation 19:10: "At this I fell at his feet to worship him. But he said to me, 'Do not do it! I am a fellow servant with you and with your brothers who hold to the testimony of Jesus. Worship God! For the testimony of Jesus is the spirit of prophecy.'" Here John falls down to worship before an angel. Certainly, it was not God, and the angel said to John, "Don't fall down before me." He said, "Worship God! I am just a fellow servant like you." God is the only one who is to be worshiped. That is expressed throughout the scriptures. Jesus said to Satan, "Worship the Lord your God, and serve him only." God is the one to be worshiped.

That suggests to us, indirectly, something about Jesus, because Jesus, throughout his earthly ministry, continually accepted the worship of many people. When we come to Hebrews 1:6, we have the Father saying of Jesus: "Let all God's angels worship him." Jesus is worthy of worship. This means, since the only one who is to be worshiped is God, that Jesus is God. The rich young ruler saw Jesus as only a good teacher. But Jesus was not merely good. Jesus was God. Jesus was God in the flesh, as John 1 tells us more vividly.

There is the strange expression at the close of verse 10, "For the testimony of Jesus is the spirit of prophecy." What does that mean? I think it means one of two things, which may be the same thing. The message concerning Jesus is what prophecy is all about. Or another way to put it is that the true spirit of prophecy is always concerned about Jesus.

I think there are two verses of scripture that say essentially what is meant by that phrase. One of these is in Luke 24:44, where Jesus is recorded by Luke as having said: "This is what I told you while I was still with you: Everything must be fulfilled that is written about me in the Law of Moses, the Prophets and the Psalms." Jesus said the entire Old Testament is a message concerning him. The testimony of Jesus is the spirit of prophecy. In John 5:46, Jesus said, "If you believed Moses, you would believe me, for he wrote about me." Jesus is the essential content of prophecy. That's what prophecy, which has been given by God and which has been delivered in the form of scripture, is all about. The theme of the Bible is Jesus. He is the heart of the whole matter.

We have been presented with the picture of the wedding, and we have seen the wife, or the bride. Now we are prepared to see the groom, or the husband, come in, but, instead, we see a warrior. Verses 11-16 present a new scene:

> I saw heaven standing open and there before me was a white horse, whose rider is called Faithful and True. With justice he judges and makes war. His eyes are like blazing fire, and on his head are many crowns. He has a name written on him that no one but he himself knows. He is dressed in a robe dipped in blood, and his name is the Word of God. The armies of heaven were following him, riding on white horses and dressed in fine linen, white and clean. Out of his mouth comes a sharp sword with which to strike down the nations. "He will rule them with an iron scepter." He treads the winepress of the fury of the wrath of God Almighty. On his robe and on his thigh he has this name written:
>
> KING OF KINGS, AND LORD OF LORDS.

2 Thessalonians 1:7-9 speaks of the same thing when it says:

> ...and give relief to you who are troubled, and to us as well. This will happen when the Lord Jesus is revealed from heaven in blazing fire with his powerful angels. He will punish those who do not know God and do not obey the gospel of our Lord Jesus. They will be punished with everlasting destruction and shut out from the presence of the Lord and from the majesty of his power....

We see Jesus leading from heaven armies which, apparently, are the angels. But notice that he doesn't really need the angels in this warfare. In the Greek text of verse 15, the pronoun "he" is emphasized. I want to read it with that emphasis. Notice what happens after the armies are mentioned. It says: "Out of his mouth comes a sharp sword with which to strike down the nations. '*He* will rule them with an iron scepter.' *He* treads the winepress of the fury of the wrath of God Almighty." Jesus is the one who does this. The armies are the retinue that follows him, but he alone is sufficient and adequate for this task.

We are told that he is dressed in a robe dipped in blood. That's before the battle. I take it, then, that that blood represents the blood of Jesus shed on the cross for the forgiveness of our sins. In that act, in that great sacrificial act in which the blood flowed on Calvary, the victory was won. There Satan was defeated. There is where the battle was actually won. So now he comes dressed in a robe that is dipped in blood, and his weapon is a sharp sword which comes out of his mouth. This reminds us of the sword of the Spirit which is the word of God, because it is the word of God that is both the power to save and the power to destroy.

Jesus is King of kings and Lord of lords. Notice he is both of those things before he ever goes to battle against Satan's forces. Jesus, right now, is King of kings and Lord of lords. Jesus reigns now. It is up to us to submit to his reign so we may enter his kingdom now and be prepared for entrance into the everlasting kingdom.

Let's notice verses 17-18:

> And I saw an angel standing in the sun, who cried in a loud voice to all the birds flying in midair, "Come, gather together for the great supper of God, so that you may eat the flesh of kings, generals, and mighty men, of horses and their riders, and the flesh of all people, free and slave, small and great."

Here the angel cries out to the birds of the heavens to gather and to consume the enemy. It reminds us of a passage back in Ezekiel 39:4 where God says: "On the mountains of Israel you will fall, you and all your troops and the nations with you. I will give you as food to all kinds of carrion birds and to the wild animals."

I think that is significant, because in the very next chapter of Revelation, in Revelation 20:8, we have the battle described again, the climactic battle in which the forces of evil are finally and ultimately destroyed, the battle that was described earlier as Armageddon. The battle is described several times as we go through Revelation because, as we move through Revelation, we see again and again the scene of judgment.

We simply see the application of judgment to different groups as we go through. We see the judgment of those who wear the mark of the beast. Later, we see the judgment of Babylon. Still later, we see the effect of God's judgment in other applications. We're seeing the same period of time and the same struggle between God and Satan and between God's people and those who are followers of Satan. We see judgment depicted in Ezekiel in terms of the birds of the heavens coming. We see in Revelation 19 the same kind of terminology.

Now, we see the climax of Revelation 19:

> Then I saw the beast and the kings of the earth and their armies gathered together to make war against the rider on the horse and his army. But the beast was captured, and with him the false prophet who had performed the miraculous signs on his behalf. With these signs he had deluded those who had received the mark of the beast and worshiped his image. The two of them were thrown alive into the fiery lake of burning sulfur. The rest of them were killed with the sword that came out of the mouth of the rider on the horse, and all the birds gorged themselves on their flesh.

The devastation and the destruction are total. The enemies of God's people are destroyed. There is only one of these enemies yet to be described for us as having been conquered, and that is Satan himself. But that victory has already been assured. Jesus already has died on the cross, has been raised from the dead, and has broken the power of Satan. He has ascended to the throne of God, to reign with God until he has put all his enemies under his feet—and the last of those enemies is death. Then, according to 1 Corinthians 15, Jesus will hand the kingdom over to God the Father.

We hope you are in that kingdom that Jesus will hand over to the Father. In the end, you will be able to sit down with all the saints at the wedding of the Lamb, enjoying the fellowship of God. You'll be free from temptations and struggles, from persecution, and from the deceptions and seductions of this life, and you'll fully and freely enjoy God's presence and his blessings forever and ever. That's the essential message of Revelation.

If you are not a Christian, why not be born again into the kingdom of God, born of water and the Spirit, believing in Jesus, repenting of your sins, confessing your faith in him, and being baptized into him?

REVELATION 20:

The Meaning of the Thousand Years

C hapter 20 of Revelation is the only place in the Bible where a thousand-year reign is mentioned, but there it is mentioned six times in seven verses. This has served as the basis for all kinds of speculation through the years. Many have made Revelation 20 the central feature of a scheme for trying to interpret future events. And, I suppose, it is understandable that people might presume that when we come toward the end of the book of Revelation, a reference to a thousand-year period would refer to something yet to come.

But as we have been studying Revelation I believe we have begun to see that Revelation is not put together to give us a consecutive, chronological picture of events from the time that Christ came the first time until he comes again. Rather, we are seeing a series of visions that give us a view of the Christian age from various perspectives, calling attention to various aspects of our relationship to God and God's dealing with our world.

For example, we have already seen in our journey through the book of Revelation the scene at the end of the world, the judgment of God, six times in the first nineteen chapters. We saw it back in chapter 6 toward the end of that chapter, we saw it again in chapter 11, we saw another view of the judgment of God in chapter 14, we saw it again in chapter 16, chapter 18, and another view in chapter 19.

After each of these descriptions of the final judgment of God on mankind, we are taken back for another look at God dealing with mankind while we are living here on this earth. So, it should be no surprise when we suggest that, as we come to chapter 20 of Revelation, we are being shown another view of the Christian age from the first coming of Jesus until the time when he comes again.

There is no more dramatic example of this kind of transition in Revelation than is found at the end of the 11th chapter where we clearly see the judgment of God and the people of God victoriously living in his presence. Then, when we come to chapter 12, we're taken back to the birth of Jesus Christ again, then taken forward to the events that followed: the death of Jesus, the resurrection, then the church coming into existence, and the persecution of the church.

We see the same kind of transition from chapter 19 to 20. In chapter 19, we see the final judgment of God again. We see Jesus going to war against the enemies of God and being victorious. Revelation 19:17-18 says:

> And I saw an angel standing in the sun, who cried in a loud voice to all the birds flying in midair, "Come, gather together for the great supper of God, so that you may eat the flesh of kings, generals, and mighty men, of horses and their riders, and the flesh of all people, free and slave, small and great."

At the end of chapter 19, all mankind is destroyed. If we were to look at this chronologically, then in chapter 20 there wouldn't be anybody around to be enjoying any reign for a thousand years. All mankind was destroyed at the end of chapter 19.

You recall that we saw the three major enemies of God, Christ, and his people presented in chapters 12 through 14 in sequence. First, we saw Satan himself, the dragon, presented in chapter 12. Then, in chapter 13, we saw the beast coming out of the sea, and then we saw the beast coming out of the earth.

As we move on toward the end of Revelation, we see one by one, in reverse order, the final judgment of God poured out on each of these. We see the judgment of the beast that came out of the earth, later referred to as the false prophet. Then we see the beast that came out of the sea and the judgment of God on it. Now, in chapter 20, we will see a description of the judgment of God on Satan himself.

So, although we have seen a series of views of the final judgment of God, we are seeing the same time of judgment as it applies to different groups and from different perspectives. Now, we are going back and looking at Satan's activity in our world and how his final judgment comes about.

Revelation 20 begins by saying:

> And I saw an angel coming down out of heaven, having the key to the Abyss and holding in his hand a great chain. He seized the dragon, that ancient serpent, who is the devil, or Satan, and bound him for a thousand years. He threw him into the Abyss, and locked and sealed it over him, to keep him from deceiving the nations any more until the thousand years were ended. After that, he must be set free for a short time.

In these first three verses of Revelation 20, we see the binding of Satan. It is understandable that people might assume that this must be something that is going to take place in the future, because, in view of all the evil in our world, it doesn't look as though Satan has already been bound. Yet that is precisely what I would argue, that Satan has already been bound.

He was bound almost two thousand years ago. He was bound when Jesus died on the cross, rose from the dead, and ascended into heaven. The binding of Satan happened way back then. It is not something we look forward to in the future. You might be inclined to say, "He's got to be crazy, because surely, in view of all the misery in our world, Satan is not bound." Let's allow the Bible to interpret itself and tell us what "binding" means. Then we'll be able to understand the rest of the 20th chapter of Revelation. We'll see that the popular theories—suggesting that Jesus someday is going to come back to the earth, set up his kingdom here, and reign for a thousand years—are not true.

Revelation 20 speaks of the binding of Satan in the very introductory portion of the chapter. Revelation, as we have seen, is a set of visions of the Christian age, each looking at it from a different perspective. Revelation is not written as one series of events described in chronological order. That means, then, that what is described at the end of the book is not necessarily discussing those things that happen at the end of the world.

The fact is, the binding of Satan in Revelation 20:2 refers to the very thing that Jesus was speaking of in Mark. The binding of Satan was associated with the first coming of Christ, not with the second coming.

In Mark 3:27, Jesus said: "In fact, no one can enter a strong man's house and carry off his possessions unless he first ties up the strong man. Then he can rob his house." The context is one in which Jesus had been driving out demons, and he was being accused of driving out demons by the power of Beelzebub. Jesus replied that that could not be true because, "If a kingdom is divided against itself, that kingdom cannot stand. If a house is divided against itself, that house cannot stand. And if Satan opposes himself and is divided, he cannot stand; his end has come." Then Jesus makes that statement, "In fact, no one can enter a strong man's house…."

Now, who's the strong man? The strong man is Satan. No one can enter his house and carry off his possessions unless he first ties up the strong man. The meaning of Mark 3:27 is well expressed by J. W. McGarvey in his commentary when he said: "Satan is the strong man, his house the body of the demoniac, and his goods the evil spirit within the man. Jesus had entered his house and robbed him of his goods…to demonstrate the fact that he was making successful warfare against the dominion of Satan."

In Luke 10:17-19, we find another suggestion of Jesus winning the war against Satan. Jesus sent seventy-two out on an evangelistic mission, preaching that the kingdom of heaven was at hand. Luke says:

> The seventy-two returned with joy and said, "Lord, even the demons submit to us in your name."

He replied, "I saw Satan fall like lightning from heaven. I have given you authority to trample on snakes and scorpions, and to overcome all the power of the enemy; nothing will harm you."

Jesus was entering the strong man's house and tying him up. Satan's power now was limited so that Jesus' messengers could carry out their evangelistic activity. The victory over Satan was being achieved as the message of the gospel of the kingdom advanced.

But the consummation of the victory is pinpointed by John as occurring at the cross. We have looked at Mark, we have looked at Luke, and now let's turn to John 12:31-33. Jesus said: "'Now is the time for judgment on this world; now the prince of this world will be driven out. But I, when I am lifted up from the earth, will draw all men to myself.' He said this to show the kind of death he was going to die." You see, when Jesus died on the cross, the prince of this world was driven out. According to Revelation 12, Satan—in connection with the events of the death, burial, resurrection and ascension of Jesus into heaven—was hurled out of heaven. Then and there the power of Satan was broken at last.

The binding of Satan at the cross as an accomplished fact is suggested in other passages of scripture. In Hebrews 2:14-15, the writer said: "Since the children have flesh and blood, he too shared in their humanity so that by his death he might destroy him who holds the power of death—that is, the devil— and free those who all their lives were held in slavery by their fear of death." It was through death that Jesus destroyed the power of the devil. That's when it was accomplished.

Look at Colossians 2:15. Paul said of Jesus, "And having disarmed the powers and authorities, he made a public spectacle of them, triumphing over them by the cross." If we read the previous verse, we see he is speaking about the death of Jesus Christ on the cross. It was when Jesus died on the cross that he disarmed the powers and authorities and made a public spectacle of them.

Let's look at 1 John 4:4, where John said: "You, dear children, are from God and have overcome them, because the one who is in you is greater than the one who is in the world." We are overcomers, because there is one who is greater than the one who has been giving us so much trouble. Jesus Christ has made it possible for us to overcome Satan. Satan is bound. He is tied up. He is limited. There is only so much that Satan can do. Mark 3:27 implies that, in some very real sense, Satan was being tied up, bound, or else the Lord could not have driven out the demons.

It must be understood that the binding of Satan does not mean his destruction. That's where so many people fail to understand Revelation 20. Binding Satan does not mean destroying him. In fact, when you read Revelation 20, you see that the purpose of binding Satan was not to punish Satan. The purpose of binding Satan was to limit Satan. It means a limitation of his power, rather than a total curtailment of his power. Some assume that, although the world is in bad shape today, it could be in infinitely worse shape if Satan were only turned loose on the world. That, in itself, indicates a recognition that Satan must be limited and restrained by some divinely imposed boundaries.

We know, from a number of references found in the New Testament, that Satan can only go so far in his attacks on Christians. 1 Corinthians 10:13 says no temptation can overtake you that you cannot bear, because God provides a way of escape with every temptation. That means that Satan cannot overpower you as long as you are willing to stand for God.

We know that he can only act as God will permit. In Luke 22, Jesus told Peter that Satan had to ask permission to sift the apostles like wheat. Satan is on a leash. He can only go so far. He's limited. He's bound in that sense. He's bound like a dog on a chain. It's true that Peter describes Satan as one who prowls around like a roaring lion looking for someone to devour. But I am sure you have seen dogs on leashes that looked like roaring lions about to devour you. You were grateful for the fact that they were on a leash, because they would snap their teeth and snarl at you, but they couldn't get to you. That's the way Satan is. He can only go so far. Now, if you want to walk over there within the boundaries of the chain, Satan can tear you to pieces, but God is not going to permit him to get to where you are, if you don't want him to. Satan is bound in our world now, and his binding began when Jesus died, rose from the dead, and ascended to heaven.

We know that Satan and his angels are presently in chains of darkness to be "held for judgment" (2 Peter 2:4). They are bound. Jude 6 presents the same thought: "And the angels who did not keep their positions of authority but abandoned their own home—these he has kept in darkness, bound with everlasting chains for judgment on the great Day."

The fact that demon possession does not exist today—contrary to what many claim, but which none can prove—ought to be evidence that the binding of Satan is an accomplished fact. Demon possession was peculiar to the age in which Jesus lived. It seems that God permitted Satan, at that time, to give some unusual proofs of his existence, his power, and his malice by frequently attacking men's bodies. This proves what a dangerous enemy he is and how great a need there was for the aid of one who had power over Satan. The driving out of demons, then, was a proof to the senses and evidence of the victory of Christ over Satan. No kind of wonder could be more suited for demonstrating the nature of Christ's mission, or for drawing men to him. Certainly, it was evidence of the binding of Satan.

If you need any further evidence that "binding" does not mean the total elimination of the power and ability of Satan to do anything, I simply invite your attention to Romans 7:2 where exactly the same word, "bound," is used that is used in Revelation 20:1-3. There Paul said, "For example, by law a married woman is bound to her husband as long as he is alive, but if her husband dies, she is released from the law of marriage." Paul said a woman is "bound" to her husband. Does that mean she is totally incapacitated and can never do anything from then on? Of course not. Well, what does it mean? It means that there are some boundaries, there are some limitations now, on what the woman can do with respect to her husband. She is bound to him. She is not free to go and run around with every other man that comes along. It is the same with Satan. Satan is limited. He can only do so much; he can only go so far.

Satan was to be bound for a thousand years. If Satan was bound when Jesus came the first time, hasn't that time long since expired? Not if we understand that thousand-year period in the same way we have already understood other numbers used in Revelation, as numbers that are symbols. The number seven is the symbol of completeness, and even ten is sometimes the number of completeness. The number 1,260 days, the number forty-two months, the time, times and half a time of Revelation, and the 144,000 we have already seen previously are not literally those numbers of days or months or years or people. Rather, they are numbers suggestive of something else; they are symbols.

So it is with a thousand, a perfect symbol of completeness or fullness. Ten cubed, ten times ten times ten, is a thousand, a symbol of fullness or completeness. In other words, throughout the entire period from the first coming of Christ to nearly the second coming of Christ, Satan is bound, limited, and Christians are able to reign. I'm suggesting that the thousand-year period is the period from the first coming of Jesus Christ until just about the time when Jesus comes again.

That is a symbolic figure. The Bible uses the expression "a thousand" in other contexts in the same way, not meaning literally nine hundred ninety-nine plus one, but a figure of largeness or completeness. For example, in 2 Peter 3:8, Peter said, "With the Lord a day is like a thousand years, and a thousand years are like a day." He simply is using a thousand years as a symbol for a gigantic period of time, an enormous period of time, in contrast to a single day.

In the Old Testament, the number is used in the same way. For example, Psalm 90:4 says:

> For a thousand years in your sight
>
> are like a day that has just gone by,
>
> or like a watch in the night.

In Psalm 50:10 God says:

> ...for every animal of the forest is mine,
>
> and the cattle on a thousand hills.

God didn't mean that if there are 1,263 hills that 1,000 of the hills that have cattle on them are his, and the other 263 are not. It is simply a figure of speech meaning they are all his. It's a symbol of fullness, of completeness. We use the expression in our own language when we say, "I wouldn't believe that in a thousand years." We don't treat other things in chapter 20 in such a literal way. Nobody really believes that a literal chain was taken by an angel to bind Satan in a literal pit somewhere. That approach is contrary to the whole spirit of the book of Revelation.

We have seen the binding of Satan taking place. Let's read on in verses 4-6:

> I saw thrones on which were seated those who had been given authority to judge. And I saw the souls of those who had been beheaded because of their testimony for Jesus and because of the word of God. They had not worshiped the beast or his image and had not received his mark on their foreheads or their hands. They came to life and reigned with Christ a thousand years. (The rest of the dead did not come to life until the thousand years were ended.) This is the first resurrection. Blessed and holy are those who have part in the first resurrection. The second death has no power over them, but they will be priests of God and of Christ and will reign with him for a thousand years.

Where does this reign take place? There is not a word in Revelation 20 about this reign taking place on the earth, which is what so many today believe. The thousand-year reign occurs in heaven, where the throne is. Forty-eight times in Revelation the throne is mentioned, and, with the exceptions of the throne of Satan and the throne of the beast, which is his servant, the thrones are always in heaven. So that is where the disembodied souls of the martyrs are.

It is important to notice that the writer says, "…I saw the souls of those…." John didn't see *them*. He saw the *souls* of those who were at the throne of God. Back in Revelation 6, we saw a scene of those people who had been put to death because their allegiance was to the Lord. The seal of the book was opened, and we saw the souls of those who had been put to death because of their loyalty to the Lord at the altar in heaven. There's where the souls are. Their bodies were not there yet, but their souls had gone to be in the very presence of God.

The souls reign until the second coming. Who are these? They are martyrs and those who have washed their robes and made them white in the blood of the Lamb. We have learned that when Revelation speaks of those who have the mark of the beast, it simply means all those who give their allegiance to Satan, as opposed to those who have been sealed on their forehead with the name of God. That simply means all of God's people, all who are faithful to God.

This passage means that when you die, you're not just going to be lying there in the grave and sleeping until Jesus comes again, but your soul is going to be in the presence of God. That's what we are seeing in Revelation 20. The souls of those who did not have the mark of the beast, which means all of God's faithful people, are going to enter his presence.

That's why Paul said he had the "desire to depart and be with Christ…." (Philippians 1:23). That's what happens when a faithful person in the service of God dies. He goes to be with the Lord. He doesn't go and stay in the cemetery. His body does, until Jesus comes again, and then his body will be transformed, and he will receive a new body. In the meantime, the souls of the righteous reign now with Jesus Christ throughout this entire period of human history until Jesus comes again. Then the saints reign, not for a thousand years, but, according to Revelation 22:5, for ever and ever. According to 1 Corinthians 15, they will have received transformed bodies. Then the final judgment will have been pronounced, and heaven will be their eternal home.

What's the first resurrection? It is when you die and your soul goes to be with God to reign with him. What's the second resurrection? It is when Jesus comes again. Then all who are in their graves will hear his voice and come out, and all who are still alive will be caught up to meet the Lord in the air. We will be with the Lord forever. The second resurrection occurs at the second coming when the body, too, is glorified. Who participates in this reign? Those who do not worship the beast. The rest of the dead—that is, the unbelievers—don't live until the thousand years are finished. Then they will experience the second death, which is the lake of burning sulfur.

What happens after the thousand years? Revelation 20:7-10 says,

> When the thousand years are over, Satan will be released from his prison and will go out to deceive the nations in the four corners of the earth—Gog and Magog—to gather them for battle. In number they are like the sand on the seashore. They marched across the breadth of the earth and surrounded the camp of God's people, the city he loves. But fire came down from heaven and devoured them. And the devil, who deceived them, was thrown into the lake of burning sulfur, where the beast and the false prophet had been thrown. They will be tormented day and night for ever and ever.

This particular scene corresponds to scenes that we have already seen in Revelation 11 and 13.

Apparently, right at the end of time there is going to be a brief period, a short time, when Satan is going to be able to dominate the minds of men in greater measure. He will have made such inroads among humanity that it will seem as though the church has been wiped off the face of the earth. There will be a few righteous souls left, and they will be spared at the end. But, apparently, there is going to be a very terrible period right at the end of time when Satan will be released.

Up to this time, the point of his being bound is that he can't deceive the nations. That is to say, the gospel can be carried throughout the world, and men throughout the world are capable and willing to receive the message of Jesus Christ. But at the very end, Satan will again be able to deceive the nations. Men will have become so corrupted and so debased that the power of the gospel of Christ will not even be able to penetrate their hearts. So the question can properly be asked, "...when the Son of man comes, will he find faith on the earth?" The answer is: The faithful may be hard to find, but there will be a few when Jesus comes again.

We have a reference here to Satan gathering his forces together, just as we saw in chapter 19. We saw Satan gathering his armies together. The beast, the kings of the earth, and their armies gathered together to make war against the rider on the white horse and against his army. But do you know what happens? We're ready for a great battle scene, and all of a sudden the beast is captured and thrown alive into the fiery lake of burning sulfur. There isn't any battle. In other words, Satan is totally impotent in his battle against Jesus Christ and against God. He can muster all his forces, but he cannot even begin to create a battle, because God is the victor before the battle ever begins.

Here again, in Revelation 20, we see Satan gathering nations in the four corners of the earth—Gog and Magog. In Jewish literature at that time, Gog and Magog were terms that referred to all the forces of evil combined. The point is that Satan brings all his powers to bear to destroy the efforts of Jesus Christ, and it looks like a great war is going to take place. We're not talking about literal warfare with bullets, machine guns, tanks, and atomic bombs. We're talking about the kind of warfare the Bible speaks about from beginning to end, the battle for the minds of men. It's a spiritual battle, and Satan, at the end, is going to seem to be winning. Then the end comes, and Satan is thrown into the fiery lake of burning sulfur. God's people are victorious and reign with him for ever and ever.

Finally, we have the great judgment scene, beginning with verse 11:

> Then I saw a great white throne and him who was seated on it. Earth and sky fled from his presence, and there was no place for them. And I saw the dead, great and small, standing before the throne, and books were opened. Another book was opened, which is the book of life. The dead were judged according to what they had done as recorded in the books. The sea gave up the dead that were in it, and death and Hades gave up the dead that were in them, and each person was judged according to what he had done. Then death and Hades were thrown into the lake of fire. The lake

of fire is the second death. If anyone's name was not found written in the book of life, he was thrown into the lake of fire.

There's the final judgment, the scene of the judgment of God when all the nations of the earth will be gathered together before the throne of God. They will be judged, and they will be judged comparing their deeds to the things written in the books, which must refer to the books of the Bible. What's going to happen is that your life, what you have done in your life, is going to be put up beside the standard of God's truth as revealed in scripture. The books of the Bible comprise the final examination book for your life.

Where do you stand with reference to it? Are you prepared for the final judgment when all will stand before the throne of God and you will be judged out of the books that God has given us in scripture? If not, you need to prepare so you may have your name written in the Lamb's book of life and be able to enjoy the presence of God forever. If you are not a Christian, we urge you to surrender your life to Jesus now, so you may enjoy victory over Satan and may enjoy the triumph of the people of God, and so that you may avoid being among that number who will be thrown into the fiery lake of burning sulfur. If you believe in Jesus, and will repent of your sins and confess your faith in him, we plead with you to be baptized into Christ, so you can begin to walk in a new and victorious life.

REVELATION 21:

The New Jerusalem

Our lesson is from the 21st chapter of Revelation. Here we have that marvelous description of the new Jerusalem. Back in Revelation 20:11, John said, "Then I saw a great white throne and him who was seated on it. Earth and sky fled from his presence, and there was no place for them." We reach the point now where there are no longer the earth and the sky as we know them. This fits in perfectly with what Peter said in 2 Peter 3:10-13:

> But the day of the Lord will come like a thief. The heavens will disappear with a roar; the elements will be destroyed by fire, and the earth and everything in it will be laid bare.
>
> Since everything will be destroyed in this way, what kind of people ought you to be? You ought to live holy and godly lives as you look forward to the day of God and speed its coming. That day will bring about the destruction of the heavens by fire, and the elements will melt in the heat. But in keeping with his promise we are looking forward to a new heaven and a new earth, the home of righteousness.

You recall that Jesus had previously said in Mark 13:31 that heaven and earth will pass away. There will come a time when Jesus comes again, and the heavens and the earth will be destroyed. So we have the scene in Revelation

21:1: "Then I saw a new heaven and a new earth, for the first heaven and the first earth had passed away, and there was no longer any sea." What is meant by "there was no longer any sea"? Perhaps it merely means that the sea, as being part of the earth, also had passed away. But, as we see the use of the word "sea" in prophetic literature, and in Revelation particularly, it seems as though the sea is symbolic of the masses of humanity who are under the power of Satan.

Even in the Old Testament, that thought seems to be expressed in one of the prophecies of Isaiah. In Isaiah 57:20-21, Isaiah said:

> But the wicked are like the tossing sea,
>
> which cannot rest,
>
> whose waves cast up mire and mud.
>
> "There is no peace," says my God, "for the wicked."

There is no peace for the wicked. They are restless as the waves of the sea.

The sea forms a fine symbol for the restless masses of humanity who have never found their peace in God. You will recall in Revelation 13:1 that the beast that represented the oppressive governments of the earth came up out of the sea. This suggests the thought that it is that portion of humanity that is alienated from God and has not found rest in him from which emerge those great oppressive powers. Notice, also, Revelation 17:15: "Then the angel said to me, 'The waters you saw, where the prostitute sits [and she was sitting on the beast that came out of the sea], are peoples, multitudes, nations and languages.'"

Perhaps what we are seeing in Revelation 21 is not merely the suggestion that now the heavens and the earth as we know them have passed away, have burned up, have been destroyed, and are no more, but also that the wicked—the masses of humanity who have turned their backs on God and allowed themselves to be subject to the power of Satan—are no more. So, all who remain to enter the presence of Almighty God are those who have been faithful and loyal to God and to the Lamb.

Verse 2 says: "I saw the Holy City, the new Jerusalem, coming down out of heaven from God, prepared as a bride beautifully dressed for her husband,"—

the new Jerusalem, the city of God. You recall that even back in Old Testament times, according to Hebrews 11:10, Abraham was looking forward to the city with foundations, whose architect and builder is God.

As we come to Hebrews 12:22, the writer says, "But you have come to Mount Zion, to the heavenly Jerusalem, the city of the living God. You have come to thousands upon thousands of angels in joyful assembly, to the church of the firstborn, whose names are written in heaven." Paul said in Philippians 3:20: "But our citizenship is in heaven." Our names are written in the Lamb's book of life. In Hebrews 13:14, the writer said: "For here we do not have an enduring city, but we are looking for the city that is to come."

Our goal and our destination in life is the new Jerusalem that has its origin in God. It comes down out of heaven as a bride beautifully dressed for her husband. We saw that figure back in the 19th chapter of Revelation as a symbol of the church. The church, as the bride of Christ, was dressed in clean clothing and prepared for the wedding of the Lamb. Now we see the bride again in Revelation 21:3. "And I heard a loud voice from the throne saying, 'Now the dwelling of God is with men, and he will live with them. They will be his people, and God himself will be with them and be their God.'" The dwelling of God is now with men.

Again, going back to Hebrews 8:1-2, the writer said: "The point of what we are saying is this: We do have such a high priest, who sat down at the right hand of the throne of the Majesty in heaven, and who serves in the sanctuary, the true tabernacle set up by the Lord, not by man." That tabernacle that was erected in the wilderness of Sinai—under the leadership of Moses and under the direction of God—was only a temporary tabernacle to be replaced by the temple. It was simply a foreshadowing of that great tabernacle which finally God makes his dwelling with his people for eternity.

In the very next chapter, Hebrews 9:11-12 says:

> When Christ came as high priest of the good things that are already here, he went through the greater and more perfect tabernacle that is not man-made, that is to say, not a part of this creation.

He did not enter by means of the blood of goats and calves; but he entered the Most Holy Place once for all by his own blood, having obtained eternal redemption.

Jesus Christ entered the true tabernacle. The earthly tabernacle was merely a type and a foreshadowing of that eternal one yet to come in which God's people will be able to dwell eternally in the presence of God.

Returning to our text, Revelation 21:4 says: "He will wipe every tear from their eyes. There will be no more death or mourning or crying or pain, for the old order of things has passed away." The picture we get of the final home of God's people is a place where there are no tears, no death, no mourning, no crying, no pain and, according to verse 6, no more thirst. It is a place where the needs and the desires and the yearnings and longings of men are finally fully satisfied. They find fulfillment in God's presence where he supplies all our needs and relieves us of the difficulties and pressures of this life.

Verse 5 says: "He who was seated on the throne said, 'I am making everything new!' Then he said, 'Write this down, for these words are trustworthy and true.'" "I am making everything new!" God has made a new home for a new people. In 2 Corinthians 5:17, Paul said: "Therefore, if anyone is in Christ, he is a new creation…." God is trying to create in this world new people, people prepared for the new home that God has prepared where everything finally has become new.

Verse 6 of our text in Revelation 21 says: "He said to me: 'It is done. I am the Alpha and the Omega, the Beginning and the End.'" He is saying, "I am the originator, and I am the one who brings the consummation of all things." The fulfillment of human purpose, human destiny, is to be found in the one who originated us, who created us, and who now is calling us into his eternal presence. Verse 6 continues: "To him who is thirsty I will give drink without cost from the spring of the water of life." God will provide for our every need.

Verse 7 says: "He who overcomes will inherit all this, and I will be his God and he will be my son." Notice, God said he will inherit all this. That expression, "inherit," is used throughout the New Testament of various things, but all suggest the same kind of thing. We are told in Matthew 19:29 that we will inherit eternal life, everlasting life; in Hebrews 1:14, we will inherit salvation; in 1 Peter 3:9, we will inherit a blessing. In Matthew 25:34, those who are judged to be righteous in the great judgment day of God were told they would inherit the kingdom prepared since the creation of the world. Who will inherit? Who, in this life, are those who inherit? It is the children who inherit. So God tells us in Revelation 21 that the person who overcomes will inherit these things, and "I will be his God and he will be my son." What a beautiful thought!

It is expressed more clearly for us in Galatians 3 and 4 where we learn how we can become children who have the right to inherit all these great blessings that God has prepared for his people. In Galatians 3:26-27, Paul said: "You are all sons of God through faith in Christ Jesus, for all of you who were baptized into Christ have been clothed with Christ." Now, verse 29: "If you belong to Christ, then you are Abraham's seed, and heirs according to the promise." The promise that God made to Abraham so many centuries before, the promise that through him all peoples on earth would be blessed, is for our benefit. We are made sons of God through faith in Christ Jesus, because we have been clothed with Christ in baptism.

As we read on into chapter 4, in verses 6 through 7, Paul said: "Because you are sons, God sent the Spirit of his Son into our hearts, the Spirit who calls out, '*Abba*, Father.' So you are no longer a slave, but a son; and since you are a son, God has made you also an heir." We have the right of inheritance because of sonship, sonship in relationship to Almighty God. No wonder the apostle John could say in 1 John 3:1: "How great is the love the Father has lavished on us, that we should be called children of God! And that is what we are!" What great plans God has for us that we can become sons of God, able to inherit eternal life, and able to inherit the blessings of the new Jerusalem!

We return to our text in Revelation 21 and read on in verse 8: "But the cowardly, the unbelieving, the vile, the murderers, the sexually immoral, those who practice magic arts, the idolaters and all liars—their place will be in the fiery lake of burning sulfur. This is the second death." There is no annihilation of the wicked. The wicked do not simply cease to exist. The Revelation given to John was that they will be thrown into the fiery lake of burning sulfur. That is punishment.

Who will be punished? The cowardly. Remember, Jesus frequently said, and God has often expressed to his people throughout the Bible, "Do not be afraid, for I am with you." If we really trust God and believe that he is with us, then we need never be afraid.

There is another sense of fear, however. Remember the man who was given one talent in Matthew 25:25? He said, "…I was afraid and went out and hid your talent in the ground. See, here is what belongs to you." Notice what the judge said of him in verse 30: "And throw that worthless servant outside, into the darkness, where there will be weeping and gnashing of teeth."

God does not want worthless servants, those who are cowardly, who are ashamed or afraid to say, "I believe that Jesus Christ is the Son of God, the savior of the world, and the one who can save my soul." Are we ashamed? Are we afraid? Heaven is not for the cowardly. It is for the courageous, those who trust in God, who understand his promise: "I will be with you always, to the very end of the age."

Hell is the place prepared for the cowardly and for the unbelieving. You recall that Jesus said, "…if you do not believe that I am the one I claim to be, you will indeed die in your sins." James said in James 2:18, "Show me your faith without deeds, and I will show you my faith by what I do." My obedience is the expression of the fact that I believe and trust my God, but hell is the place for the unbelieving. It is the place where the vile will be.

Remember the picture shown in Revelation 17:4-5:

> The woman was dressed in purple and scarlet, and was glittering with gold, precious stones and pearls. She held a golden cup in her hand, filled with abominable things and the filth of her adulteries. This title was written on her forehead:

MYSTERY

BABYLON THE GREAT

THE MOTHER OF PROSTITUTES

AND OF THE ABOMINATIONS OF THE EARTH.

God simply will not tolerate men who give themselves over to the abominations, to the enticements, to the allure and the attractions of the world and the things that it offers, because the things of the world will pass away.

Hell is the place for the cowardly, the unbelieving, the vile, the murderers, the sexually immoral, those who practice magic arts—the modern equivalent of which are those who use drugs and potions and enchantments to bring others under their power. Astrologers, drug pushers, psychics, faith healers are all modern versions of the ancient sorcerers who tried to lead men under their power by their enchantments, by their fakeries, by their sorceries, and by deception. Hell is the place for idolaters, including the greedy, for whom money has become God, according to Ephesians 5:5. It is a place for liars. What a terrifying list of things that will send people to hell! None of these will be found in heaven.

Back to our text in Revelation 21:9-10:

> One of the seven angels who had the seven bowls full of the seven last plagues came and said to me, "Come, I will show you the bride, the wife of the Lamb." And he carried me away in the Spirit to a mountain great and high, and showed me the Holy City, Jerusalem, coming down out of heaven from God.

An interesting thing happens here, as it has happened before in Revelation. Recall on one occasion that John was told about the Lion of the tribe of Judah, and when he turned to see it, he saw a Lamb. Now he is being told about the bride, the wife of the Lamb, and when he is taken to see her, he does not see the bride, he sees a city.

He sees, according to verses 11-12, the holy city, Jerusalem: "It shone with the glory of God, and its brilliance was like that of a very precious jewel, like a jasper, clear as crystal. It had a great, high wall with twelve gates, and with twelve angels at the gates. On the gates were written the names of the twelve tribes of Israel." Here is a city that has a great, high wall, suggesting protection. God's people need have no fears, for they are protected. Yet, in a moment, we will see that that wall is really not necessary anyway. In fact, we have already seen it, for the sea is no more. Heaven and earth have passed away, and now all the redeemed are in the presence of God—and in his presence alone. Nevertheless, we see a great, high wall.

Then, in verses 13-14, "There were three gates on the east, three on the north, three on the south and three on the west. The wall of the city had twelve foundations, and on them were the names of the twelve apostles of the Lamb." Here on the gates we have the names of the twelve tribes of Israel, and on the foundations the names of the apostles, suggesting God's people under the old covenant and God's people under the new covenant. In other words, as we have seen previously, the holy city, the new Jerusalem, represents the redeemed of all the ages. It's God's people, and under the new covenant, those who are his people—his church—are finally found in the presence of God.

Revelation 21:15-16 continues: "The angel who talked with me had a measuring rod of gold to measure the city, its gates and its wall. The city was laid out like a square, as long as it was wide. He measured the city with the rod and found it to be 12,000 stadia in length, and as wide and high as it is long." What we see here is a figure that staggers the imagination. In fact, it is totally incomprehensible. A stadium is an eighth of a mile. Twelve thousand stadia would be something like 1,400 or 1,500 miles long.

This city is a city that would stretch all the way from New York City to Houston, Texas. It's a city that would in length and width cover more than half of the United States. This is a city of immense proportions, but it is not a city that simply extends geographically in such directions. It extends the same length into the heavens, into the sky, because the length and width and height of that city are all the same. A massive city is described—something we can't even visualize and conceive in our minds.

Here is the place where God resides, in the holy city that defies description. John has to produce the most exaggerated figure to convey to us the immensity, the grandeur, the scope of this glorious city, a city that has walls of jasper which, apparently, is something more like our diamond. Imagine a city with walls composed of diamonds. John, obviously, is not trying to give us a literal description of the city, but is using figures and symbols to suggest something that is beyond physical description, because he's describing spiritual realities. If a physical description of this is so great and marvelous and immense, think of what the spiritual reality behind it must be, of the reality of God's presence, and of the preparations that God has made for his people.

Verse 17 says: "He measured its wall and it was 144 cubits thick, by man's measurement, which the angel was using." We are told that the wall is great and high and, in fact, 144 cubits is about 218 feet in height. That's something like a 20-story building. That's a big, tall wall. That is a great, high wall by any human standard, so, after the wall is presented to us, we think security is suggested. But, on the other hand, what is a 218-foot wall going to do for a city that is 1,500 miles tall? We have here a description of something that is, in essence, indescribable.

Notice verse 18: "The wall was made of jasper, and the city of pure gold, as pure as glass." Again, we have something here that staggers the imagination. There's nothing like this on the earth. Here you have gold that is translucent. It's gold that you can see through. Gold like crystal—what a phenomenal picture that is! What would somebody pay if they could get hold of such a thing as that, something that is far beyond the most precious jewel that could be conceived? The city was pure gold like clear glass.

Continuing in verses 19 and 20:

> The foundations of the city walls were decorated with every kind of precious stone. The first foundation was jasper, the second sapphire, the third chalcedony, the fourth emerald, the fifth sardonyx, the sixth carnelian, the seventh chrysolite, the eighth beryl, the ninth topaz, the tenth chrysoprase, the eleventh jacinth, and the twelfth amethyst.

There is no point going into detail trying to examine each of these precious jewels. Obviously, these were the most precious jewels available to the ancient world, and John is describing a city composed of the most precious things men knew.

This suggests that God has prepared something for us far beyond our wildest dreams and imaginations. 1 Corinthians 2:9 summarizes the whole thing, where Paul said:

> However, as it is written:
>
> "No eye has seen,
>
> no ear has heard,
>
> no mind has conceived
>
> what God has prepared for those who love him."

It is something you have never seen. It is something you have never heard. It is something that is beyond your capacity to see or hear or imagine. God has prepared something great and glorious for those who love him.

Now we come to verse 21: "The twelve gates were twelve pearls, each gate made of a single pearl. The street of the city was of pure gold, like transparent glass." Speaking of pearls, somebody suggested that the pearl is the only precious jewel in existence that is created through suffering. Perhaps the gates each being of a single pearl is suggestive that it is the suffering, persecuted people of God who pass through those gates into the presence of God and the Lamb.

Notice verse 22: "I did not see a temple in the city, because the Lord God Almighty and the Lamb are its temple." Here we see the fulfillment of what was said back in Revelation 3:12: "Him who overcomes I will make a pillar in the temple of my God. Never again will he leave it. I will write on him the name of my God and the name of the city of my God, the new Jerusalem, which is coming down out of heaven from my God; and I will also write on him my new name." Those who overcome will be the ones who participate in the new Jerusalem which comes down from God.

Let's look at verse 23: "The city does not need the sun or the moon to shine on it, for the glory of God gives it light, and the Lamb is its lamp." Here we see that the glory of God fills the new Jerusalem. It's interesting to trace the glory of God through the Bible. Back in Exodus 40:34, the glory of God filled the tabernacle. In 1 Kings 8:11, the glory of God filled the temple built by Solomon. John 1:14 says of Jesus that, "We have seen his glory, the glory of the one and only Son, who came from the Father…." And now, at the culmination of the ages, the glory of God fills the new city, the holy city, Jerusalem, which is prepared for the people of God.

We come to verses 24-25: "The nations will walk by its light, and the kings of the earth will bring their splendor into it. On no day will its gates ever be shut, for there will be no night there." The nations will walk in the light, and the kings of the earth will bring their splendor into it because those who are God's people, as we have seen elsewhere in Revelation, come from every tribe and people and language and nation, and their citizenship is in heaven. So, finally, those from all the nations populate heaven itself.

Verse 26 continues: "The glory and honor of the nations will be brought into it. Nothing impure will ever enter it, nor will anyone who does what is shameful or deceitful, but only those whose names are written in the Lamb's book of life." Dishonor and shame will only be outside the city. Only those people who have brought glory and honor to God will enter that eternal city.

The Bible presents a marvelous symmetry. The first three chapters of Genesis and the last three chapters of Revelation serve as a glorious beginning and an exciting climax to the revelation of God's will for mankind. Genesis tells us God created the heavens and the earth, and Revelation tells us he will create a new heaven and a new earth. Genesis tells us that God created the sun and the moon and the stars, and Revelation 21:23 says: "The city does not need the sun or the moon to shine on it, for the glory of God gives it light, and the Lamb is its lamp." Genesis tells us of the cunning and the power of Satan, and Revelation tells us that Satan was thrown into the fiery lake of burning sulfur. Genesis tells us of man fleeing from the presence of God, but God searched us out, and Revelation 21:3-4 tells us: "And I heard a loud voice from the throne saying, 'Now the dwelling of God is with men, and he will live with them. They will be his people, and God himself will be with them and be their God. He will wipe every tear from their eyes.'"

A great preacher in the church some years ago was on his deathbed in great agony, and someone who stood at the bedside gently asked him, "How are you doing?" The preacher replied, "I am almost well." And for God's people, that's the way it is. Even when we walk through the valley of the shadow of death, we will fear no evil because we know,

> ...you are with me;
>
> your rod and your staff,
>
> they comfort me.

We're almost well when we reach the point of death, because there remains for us the entrance into the new Jerusalem, into the new heaven and the new earth. But those joys are only for those whose names are written in the Lamb's book of life. It is for those who are sons of God.

If you have faith in Jesus Christ, you can become a child of God with a right to inherit all the blessings of God, for all of you who were baptized into Christ have been clothed with Christ. Don't you want him in your life? And don't you want to be able to eagerly anticipate that great day when Jesus comes again to receive his own? Will you be in that number? It's your choice right now. You can make things right with God, restore a lost relationship with him, and find paradise regained.

REVELATION 22:

The Climax of the Bible

W hen God created man, he placed him in the most beautiful part of his creation. He put him in a beautiful garden called Eden, and there he provided for all his needs. But Satan entered that garden, and Satan was able to convince man to disobey God. The consequence was that God had to drive man out of that garden. This is explained in Genesis 3:22-24:

> And the Lord God said, "The man has now become like one of us, knowing good and evil. He must not be allowed to reach out his hand and take also from the tree of life and eat, and live forever." So the Lord God banished him from the Garden of Eden to work the ground from which he had been taken. After he drove the man out, he placed on the east side of the Garden of Eden cherubim and a flaming sword flashing back and forth to guard the way to the tree of life.

God banished man from the Garden of Eden because the tree of life was there, and it would have been the greatest tragedy for man to live forever in that cursed state in which he found himself.

God was merciful, however, because it was not his intention that man should suffer and die, but that man should live, and that man should live with him forever. So, in the process of time, God provided a way to bring man back.

Ultimately, that way was provided through his own son, Jesus Christ. Man's hard heart made it difficult for him to realize the awfulness of his condition. Only in such an ultimate sacrifice as the giving of God's precious son to die was there the hope that that heart, that hardened heart, might be so softened that it would be drawn to God and to Jesus. God made provision so that one day man could be restored to the kind of paradise that he had once enjoyed. So, in Revelation 2:7, Jesus said, "He who has an ear, let him hear what the Spirit says to the churches. To him who overcomes, I will give the right to eat from the tree of life, which is in the paradise of God."

Now we have come to the climax of the Bible. We have come to eternity. We have come to man's home with God forever. We have come to Revelation 22. Listen to the reading of verses 1-5:

> Then the angel showed me the river of the water of life, as clear as crystal, flowing from the throne of God and of the Lamb down the middle of the great street of the city. On each side of the river stood the tree of life, bearing twelve crops of fruit, yielding its fruit every month. And the leaves of the tree are for the healing of the nations. No longer will there be any curse. The throne of God and of the Lamb will be in the city, and his servants will serve him. They will see his face, and his name will be on their foreheads. There will be no more night. They will not need the light of a lamp or the light of the sun, for the Lord God will give them light. And they will reign for ever and ever.

As we come now to the climax and conclusion of the book of Revelation, I think it would be appropriate for us, very briefly, to drop back to the beginning of this great book and see in one broad, sweeping scope what God has revealed.

In chapters 1 through 3 of Revelation, we see the church as the light of the world, a light shining brightly in some places at some times and sometimes barely flickering—but, nevertheless, a light. But light and darkness cannot coexist, so the church will inevitably face persecution. "In fact, everyone who wants to live a godly life in Christ Jesus will be persecuted," Paul told Timothy, in 2 Timothy 3:12. But let us see things in their proper perspective.

First, then, we must see God, and in Revelation 4 we do see God seated on the throne. We realize that the world is not operated by blind chance and by blind forces, but that our benevolent God is still in charge of our universe, and he still controls the destiny of man.

We also need to see Jesus—and see him we do in chapter 5 of Revelation. The head of the church is the king on the throne who controls the future. Knowing who is ultimately controlling our world, the Lamb who was slain to show his love and to draw us to him, we are ready to face the persecution which comes with chapter 6.

Here we find that those who die in the Lord go to be in his presence. This reassurance provides us with courage to view the awesome judgment finally to be inflicted on the world. Even then, the church triumphant is seen rejoicing before the throne of God. But, will the persecuted be avenged? Yes! The seals of persecution give rise to the trumpets of judgment.

In Revelation 8 God is seen constantly sending his judgments in response to the prayers of his people. Here we are introduced to the warning trumpets, judgments of God designed to cause men to repent and persecutors to relent. But, for the most part, it doesn't work, according to Revelation 9:21.

Consequently, we see in chapters 10 and 11 the gospel-proclaiming, cross-bearing church being afflicted, but emerging victorious. But the book does not end here. Two questions cry out for an answer: Why is the church being so vigorously persecuted? And what will be the ultimate fate of the impenitent? So far, we have seen the surface and the conflict on the earth. Now we see what is behind it all.

Behind the struggle on earth between the church and the world is the cosmic struggle between Christ and Satan. In chapter 12, we see the dragon, Satan, trying to destroy the Christ. Failing in this, he directs his persecution against Christ's people, the church.

Then, in chapters 13 through 14, we see Satan employing the beast out of the sea (representing anti-Christian government), the beast out of the earth (representing anti-Christian religion), and the great prostitute, Babylon (representing anti-Christian seduction of the world), to destroy the church. But Satan fails, and in chapter 14, we see the Lamb standing victoriously on Mount Zion initiating the harvest of God's final judgment.

What is the fate of those who, being warned by the trumpets of judgment, remain impenitent? In chapters 15 and 16, we see the bowls of God's wrath being given to the angels and poured out on the wicked.

But what of the great prostitute, Babylon, and the two beasts? In chapters 17 and 18, we see Babylon described and destroyed. In chapter 19, we see the beasts thrown alive into the fiery lake of burning sulfur.

In chapter 20, the devil, death, and Hades are all thrown into the fiery lake of burning sulfur.

Finally, in chapters 21 and 22, the great Revelation closes with a vision of the new heaven and new earth where the saints are seen reigning with God and the Lamb forever and ever.

Things are not as they seem. God and his people are ultimately victorious and triumphant, Jesus reigns, and God is on his throne. Therefore, we need to heed the advice and warning, the caution and exhortation of Jesus in Revelation 2:10: "Be faithful, even to the point of death, and I will give you the crown of life." That is an absolute promise of God. His promises do not fail. Our task is to be faithful to him.

As encouragement to us to be faithful, we have this magnificent book of Revelation to challenge us and to make us see that victory is indeed at the end of the road for the people of God, that they cannot be defeated, that Satan cannot snatch God's people out of his hand, that we are those who are able to continue and hold out to the end, if we will. It is true, unfortunately, that we can leave God, that we can choose to turn our backs on him, but God is faithful, and he will continue to aid us and give us strength.

Before us, finally, is that beautiful picture of the paradise of God: "Then the angel showed me the river of the water of life, as clear as crystal, flowing from the throne of God and of the Lamb…." Psalm 46:4 says: "There is a river whose streams make glad the city of God…." We have seen that river described for us before in Revelation 7:17 where it says:

For the Lamb at the center of the throne will be

their shepherd;

he will lead them to springs of living water.

And God will wipe away every tear from their eyes.

Then again, in chapter 21:6: "He said to me: 'It is done. I am the Alpha and the Omega, the Beginning and the End. To him who is thirsty I will give to drink without cost from the spring of the water of life.'" God provides it for us. He does not force us to drink of it in this life nor in the life to come, but it is provided by a gracious and loving God.

The picture of the river is one of a river that flows from the throne of God. We have a song that we sometimes sing, "Shall We Gather at the River?" and there is a phrase in it that speaks of the river flowing by the throne of God, but this river does not flow by the throne. The river in the paradise of God flows from the throne, because he is the source of the life-giving water. It will quench the thirst of those people who are seeking for the fullness and joy that God provides.

We see here the throne of God and of the Lamb. It is not the thrones of God and the Lamb, because they share the throne together. That is because, as Ephesians 5:5 tells us, it is the kingdom of Christ and of God. Therefore, they sit together on the throne and reign.

In Revelation 22:2, we are told that "On each side of the river stood the tree of life, bearing twelve crops of fruit, yielding its fruit every month. And the leaves of the tree are for the healing of the nations."

Man, who was cursed in Eden, is now restored to the very presence of God on his throne. It's a beautiful description. There will be no curse anymore. In Eden, God cursed the ground, and he cursed the serpent. But now,

> No longer will there be any curse. The throne of God and of the Lamb will be in the city, and his servants will serve him. They will see his face, and his name will be on their foreheads. There will be no more night. They will not need the light of a lamp or the light of the sun, for the Lord God will give them light. And they will reign for ever and ever.

I am convinced, in view of what we have seen here in Revelation, that these faithful servants will reign forever and ever, and that they share in the glory and majesty of those who sit on the throne. They reign, perhaps, over themselves, able to achieve finally that perfect balance of life and spiritual equilibrium that we seek so much to find in this sin-cursed world. We are able to reign effectively now over our passions in this world through the help of the Spirit of Christ; but in the next, we will be able to do so not merely effectively, but perfectly.

In verse 6 through the end of this chapter, we have the final summation of the book of Revelation and of the Bible. We have seen the redeemed sharing the joy of eternity with God in the paradise prepared for them. Now, in the remaining verses, we find warnings, we find confirmations, we find exhortations to each of us to live now the life that God is expecting of us.

Verses 6 and 7:

> The angel said to me, "These words are trustworthy and true. The Lord, the God of the spirits of the prophets, sent his angel to show his servants the things that must soon take place."

> "Behold, I am coming soon! Blessed is he who keeps the words of the prophecy in this book."

Three times in these final verses Jesus says, "I am coming soon." (The Greek word translated "soon" is an adverb telling the manner of his coming. It is better translated "quickly.") When Jesus comes, it will be in a flash, in the twinkling of an eye, at the last trumpet. Then there will not be time for us to suddenly make new resolutions and determine that we will change the course of our lives, because then it will be too late. He comes quickly. There is the warning to us. There is the encouragement provided for us that, right now, we should be living and acting according to the words of the prophecy in the book so that we will be found watching, waiting, and ready when finally Jesus comes quickly.

Verses 8-9: "I, John, am the one who heard and saw these things. And when I had heard and seen them, I fell down to worship at the feet of the angel who had been showing them to me. But he said to me, 'Do not do it! I am a fellow servant with you and with your brothers the prophets and of all who keep the words of this book. Worship God!'"

This is the second time we have seen something of this nature where John falls down before an angel. However, back in Revelation 19:10 John said, "At this I fell at his feet to worship him." In Revelation 22, it does not say John fell down before the angel to worship the angel. It simply says he "…fell down to worship at the feet of the angel" who had been showing him these things. It may very well be that what we are seeing here is John falling down at the feet of the angel, but for the purpose of worshiping God.

The significance is not merely that God does not want us to worship angels. The angel here said he was a fellow servant of the prophets. In other words, the angel is saying that angels, prophets, and apostles are all servants of God, and worship that is accommodated by kneeling before the servants of God—or even the creation of God or man—cannot be acceptable and genuine worship of God.

Even in our world today, people fall down and kneel before religious leaders, not with the idea that they are worshiping them, but as a way of expressing their worship to God. But here the angel will not allow John to fall down before him in his presence, even though the worship may well be directed toward God. Perhaps John thought he was worshiping God acceptably. In reality, he was not, because no one is to bow down in worship to any angel or any man, but to God alone.

Notice verses 10-11: "Then he told me, 'Do not seal up the words of the prophecy of this book, because the time is near. Let him who does wrong continue to do wrong; let him who is vile continue to be vile; let him who does right continue to do right; and let him who is holy continue to be holy.'" I believe that in this passage we are seeing three things: number one, that character is progressively set; number two, that character can be permanently set; and number three, that character must be determined now.

Remember, "I come quickly, I come quickly, I come quickly." We cannot wait until the end of our lives to begin making these adjustments. Let him who does right continue to do right. Let him who is holy continue to be holy. Let him who is vile continue to be vile. The idea is that as we live our lives, we are progressively setting what, finally, will become an irreversible course of life. We are constantly engaged in gathering the materials which go into the foundation and fixing of character, no matter whether it be good or bad. All our pursuits, our pleasures, our companionships, all our thoughts, works, words, and deeds tend, ultimately, to result in character which remains steadfastly the same. This would not be as important if at any time we could turn over a new leaf, or if it were never too late to mend, but there comes a time when that new leaf will not be turned over, and it is too late to mend.

You know, when the great suspension bridge was built over Niagara Falls, first a slender wire was carried over by a kite to the other side, and that one drew over a stronger wire, and that one a chain, and that one a heavier chain. As by degrees the bridge was put together and completed, the bridge became firm and fixed. And so it is with our character. Some slight, insignificant action, as we might consider it, draws after it some others which are not so insignificant, and these draw others that are more important, and even more important still. At length the whole structure of our completed character, whatever it be, is brought together and remains permanently fixed.

There are whole harbors that have drawn large trading ships and that have produced important towns which have been destroyed by the slow deposit of silt—producing sand bars—until eventually the port has been closed and prosperity has ended.

Right now, we are building temples or tombs. We are building a life, we are building character, and those who are building righteously will, more than likely, continue in that direction.

There is reason to believe that moral character can become unalterable even in this life. We find in the Bible, for example, such expressions as: "My Spirit will not contend with man forever,"

Ephraim is joined to idols;

let him alone!

"If you, even you, had only known on this day what would bring you peace—but now it is hidden from your eyes." "…whose consciences have been seared as with a hot iron," and "…without fruit and uprooted—twice dead." If these passages mean anything, they mean that in this life corrupt character may become unalterable. The alteration of character requires deep thought and earnest resolve. It requires effort of the most strenuous and determined kind. If it is not altered before death, it will not likely be altered at death, and it cannot be altered after death. We need to take seriously the day by day living that builds or destroys character.

Verse 12, "Behold, I am coming soon! My reward is with me, and I will give to everyone according to what he has done." Constantly through Revelation we have been cautioned that we are going to be judged according to our work. It is true that we are saved by faith, but it is not dead faith, it is a faith that is active and living. It is a faith that works, and we are going to be judged according to what we have done.

"I am the Alpha and the Omega, the First and the Last, the Beginning and the End," is what Jesus said in verse 13. He is the author and perfecter of our faith, as the writer of the Hebrew letter said in chapter 12:2. His name, Jesus, is in the very first verse of the New Testament. His titles introduce the New Testament, and his blessing concludes it. He is the beginning and the end.

Verse 14, "Blessed are those who wash their robes, that they may have the right to the tree of life and may go through the gates into the city." The King James says, "Blessed are they that do his commandments." In essence, it's the same, because in either case it is doing the will of God. It is something that is continually done. Ananias, you recall, told Saul of Tarsus in Acts 22:16, "Get up, be baptized and wash your sins away, calling on his name." The washing of the robes does not end with baptism, because, as we see elsewhere in Revelation 19:8,

"Fine linen, bright and clean,

was given her to wear."

(Fine linen stands for the righteous acts of the saints.)

John continues in verse 15: "Outside are the dogs, those who practice magic arts, the sexually immoral, the murderers, the idolaters and everyone who loves and practices falsehood." Heaven will be a place where the fellowship of the wicked will be excluded, where they will never enter, so those who have served God faithfully are freed from the temptations that have so beset them in this life.

In Revelation 22:16, Jesus says: "I, Jesus, have sent my angel to give you this testimony for the churches. I am the Root and the Offspring of David, and the bright Morning Star." He is the one who opens and lights the way to the eternal day: Jesus Christ, the Root and the Offspring of David. He has written these things for the churches. It is not merely for the church of the first century, it is not merely for the churches of Asia Minor, but for the churches then, and for the churches now, and until Jesus comes again.

Verse 17 says, "The Spirit and the bride say, 'Come!' And let him who hears say, 'Come!' Whoever is thirsty, let him come; and whoever wishes, let him take the free gift of the water of life." The invitation is for whoever will come. Salvation is a free gift from God, but it is something that we still must accept to be able to enjoy.

Finally, there is a warning: "I warn everyone who hears the words of the prophecy of this book: If anyone adds anything to them, God will add to him the plagues described in this book. And if anyone takes words away from this book of prophecy, God will take away from him his share in the tree of life and in the holy city, which are described in this book." Man must not tamper with

God's message and with God's words. When God has spoken, we must simply obey. It is not for us to try to improve on the Revelation God has given. In fact, God says if you tamper with it, if you change it, he will take away your share in the tree of life.

The Revelation ends with these words: "He who testifies to these things says, 'Yes, I am coming soon.' Amen. Come, Lord Jesus. The grace of the Lord Jesus be with God's people. Amen." I think it is appropriate that as we come to the very last verse of the Bible, we are told it is not for the curiosity seeker or for the religious fanatic, but it is for the faithful people of God who have found and continue to find in him grace for every trial. This is the message of Revelation. Though we find troubles and tribulations and suffering and anguish in this life, God provides grace sufficient for our needs so that, finally, we may be the victors, having overcome the world because Jesus overcame the world.

In a previous generation, the skeptic Robert Ingersol made a speech over the grave of a little child, and here is what he said:

> We do not know which is the greatest blessing, life or death. We cannot say that death is not good. We do not know whether the grave is the end of life or the door of another, or whether the night here is not somewhere else a dawn. Every cradle asks us, "Whence?" and every coffin, "Whither?" The poor barbarian weeping over his dead can answer the question as intelligently and satisfactorily as a robed priest of the most authentic creed. The tearful ignorance of the one is just as consoling as the learned and unmeaning words of the other.

But the answer to such skepticism rings from the empty tomb through two millenniums of human history: "He is not here; he has risen." No tombstone bears the name of Christ, for it is a fact of history that on a hill called Olivet outside the city of Jerusalem, eleven men watched and heard the words, "This same Jesus, who has been taken from you into heaven, will come back in the same way you have seen him go into heaven."

God's people can confidently say that the throne of God is there in heaven, the Lamb of God is there, our hope is there, our treasure is there, our citizenship is there, and our names are written there. And there is much more.

The story is told of an old man who said, "When I was young I thought of heaven as a faraway place of golden domes and spires with mansions and a world of light and angels tripping about, none of whom I knew. And then my little brother died, and I thought of heaven as a place of golden domes and spires, streets of gold, and gate of pearl and one tiny little precious face that I knew."

> "No eye has seen,
>
> no ear has heard,
>
> no mind has conceived
>
> what God has prepared for those who love him."
>
> (1 Corinthians 2:9)

The questions now are simply, "Do you love him? Is Jesus Christ the center and soul of your life? Are you prepared for him? Do you realize that God loves you so much that Jesus died for you and has prepared for you an eternal paradise where you can drink freely of the water of life?"

The Spirit and the bride say, "Come!" Jesus invites you. Are your robes washed in the blood of the Lamb? Have you been baptized into Christ? If you believe in Jesus and will repent of your sins, do that now. You will be prepared for that time when Jesus comes quickly.

Graduate Paper

The following is a portion of a term paper written as a prelude to my doctoral thesis. It is included here because the professor for whom it was written said, "This ought to be published." After reading the paper, he also wrote, "I hereby resolve to do a sermon series from Revelation."

Connecting Revelation with the Contemporary Audience

The book of Revelation is the climax of the Bible, and it should be the source of some of the most exciting preaching imaginable. Yet it has suffered a history of neglect. The leaders of the Protestant Reformation responded to it in ways that have been typical. Donald Guthrie summarized it by saying, "Luther regarded the book as a dumb prophecy, while Calvin never commented on it, and Zwingli could make no sense of it."[1]

Neglect of Revelation has continued to the present. A survey of 538 sermons published in religious periodicals in the first four years of the 1990's reveals only eleven based on texts in the book of Revelation.[2] Seven of these are from chapters 21-22. In fact, another survey suggests that the great majority of sermons from Revelation are drawn from only five chapters (1-3 and 21-22). Clymer and Lowery indexed the sermons on Revelation found in 113 English language journals from the first date of publication through 1973 or the last date of publication.[3] Of the 199 sermons, 121 were from these five chapters.

In fact, neither survey found any sermons from chapter 10 nor from chapters 15-18. Only nine sermons could be found from the middle half of the book, chapters 8-18. Even in 1935 Daniel Russell expressed what these surveys have suggested: "with the exception of certain monumental texts, and of passages used at funerals, few preachers turn for their material to the Apocalypse."[4]

Why has preaching from Revelation been so neglected? Fred B. Craddock mentioned both the obvious difficulty of the book and a reaction against abusers of the book.[5] Regarding the latter, Thomas G. Long noted that "hawkers of last day superstition keep in perpetual motion a cottage industry of fear, ignorance, and Armageddon anxiety."[6] But as Eugene H. Peterson said, the book "is the revelation of Jesus Christ, not the end of the world, not the identity of antichrist, not the timetable of history."[7] It is the presumption that the book of Revelation is the latter that has driven much of the popular preaching frequently heard on radio that capitalizes on fear, a fascination with the bizarre, and a craving to know the future.

But how does one responsibly connect Revelation with the contemporary audience? Craddock suggested, "First of all, immerse yourself in the text of Revelation as a whole."[8] Robert H. Mounce once wrote, "It is difficult to say what anything means until one has decided in a sense what everything means."[9] Before connecting his audience to Revelation, the preacher must connect himself to the book. He should develop a coherent conception of the book so he can see the relationship of the parts to the whole.[10]

Many preachers have undoubtedly been discouraged from developing a sense of competence in handling Revelation due to the massive and often conflicting scholarly material dealing with the relationship of the book to intertestamental apocalyptic material and the contemporary historical setting. But without denying the value of such studies, Michael Wilcock has sensibly stated that "the real, central, message of Revelation can be understood without the help of any 'background knowledge' drawn from beyond the limits of the Bible itself."[11] However, a knowledge of the Old Testament is extremely important. Westcott and Hort found nearly 500 allusions to the Old Testament in Revelation.[12]

After studying and analyzing Revelation itself in its Biblical setting, the preacher will undoubtedly study secondary literature on Revelation to get help in understanding the book. He will then be confronted with various approaches to interpreting the book, such as the preterist, futurist, historical, and idealist. Wilcock has said, "It is impossible for a commentator to avoid plumping for one of these views, unless he waters his comments down to the point where they cease to be nourishing."[13] The preacher must also make a decision concerning the proper approach to the book and how it is structured. Space here does not permit a defense of the choice, but one must be made. Something akin to the "progressive parallelism" developed in William Hendriksen's *More Than Conquerors* is the choice viewed in this paper as reasonable.[14]

More important for this paper in attempting to determine how to connect Revelation to the contemporary audience is the issue of relevance. Many have assumed that the central purpose of Revelation "is to strengthen and to encourage persecuted communities."[15] If this were the case, the book would seem to have little relevance to people more apt to face apathy than persecution. However, the messages to the seven churches of Asia Minor suggest at least three major threats facing the church: deception by false religion (2:2, 6, 14-15, 20-24; 3:9), seduction by the world's attractions (2:9, 14, 20-22; 3:17-18), and persecution by authorities (2:9-10, 13). The threat behind all threats is Satan (2:9-10, 13, 24; 3:9). These threats seem to be portrayed by the Dragon, the beasts of the earth and sea, and Babylon, the great prostitute, in chapters 12-19. In fact, David L. Barr has gone so far as to say:

> John's task was not so much to give comfort to those afflicted as it was to help them remember who their enemy was and to know which side they were on. Revelation is a clarion call to faithfulness to a people whose general hostilities to Rome are in danger of being overwhelmed by the attractiveness of Greco-Roman culture.[16]

Eugene H. Peterson expressed a similar thought:

Emperor worship, a feast to the senses that also guaranteed a certain worldly security, was far more impressive than the Christian belief in an invisible God and crucified Savior that put its followers in danger of their lives.[17]

Paul S. Minear has provided a good summary:

When one isolates the hortatory sections of the book, and analyzes the thrust of these sections, he is impressed with the diversity of external conditions, the variety of Christian responses, and the manifold shape of the author's purpose.[18]

All of this is to say that the circumstances of the Christians to whom Revelation was initially addressed may have been far more similar to ours than many have previously supposed. And the purpose of the book was not necessarily even primarily to comfort persecuted Christians. David A. deSilva has said,

By understanding how Revelation sought to transform the way in which these churches in Asia viewed and responded to their situation in the world, Christians today are given a means of examining their attitude toward their own societies.[19]

Although persecution was a threat, at a more fundamental level the Christian lived in the midst of an ideological struggle in society. It could be expressed in terms of whether Caesar or Christ would be Lord. Each could be seen as a threat or an attraction. The same is essentially true today. Revelation serves a purpose at this point. DeSilva has noted:

Apocalyptic literature may function not as solace for the oppressed—as it certainly has at times in history—but as ideological warfare, calling for a strengthening of boundaries and response to a larger society which reflects those ideological commitments and boundaries—as has also been the case in history.[20]

Although the possibility of physical persecution has always been a prospect for the church, the attraction of conflicting ideologies has always been a greater threat to the Christian faith. The emperor cult presented such an ideology to John's initial readers.

His use of the symbols of the "image" and the "beast" and all that surrounds them can be fruitfully understood as an attempt to decentralize the ideology which he understands to be communicated through the cult and to raise up a counter-ideology on which the churches may take their stand.[21]

How does all of this relate to preaching? Craig A. Loscalzo has said, "In biblical preaching, we hope that the sermon will do in the lives of our hearers what the biblical text did and does in the lives of its readers."[22] This echoes what Craddock has said, that the preacher of Revelation should "attempt to do what the text does."[23] But what does the text of Revelation do? Peterson said,

> I have taken the position that the book does not primarily call for decipherment, as if it were written in code, but that it evokes wonder, releasing metaphors that resonate meanings and refract insights in the praying imagination.[24]

Therefore, "I read the Revelation not to get more information, but to revive my imagination."[25] William H. Willimon has said, "Only when our imaginations are transformed are we transformed by the 'renewing of our mind' as Paul might put it; only when there is a shift in the paradigmatic images by which we construe the world."[26] This is precisely what Revelation does. Accordingly, Long has said that the message of Revelation is not "pay day, someday....It claims, 'Things may be hopeless in this world, but there is another, parallel world where things have already been set aright, and you belong to that world and to this one.'"[27] He presents an analogy of an inmate in a prisoner of war camp being tortured, but who sees on a TV set in the room a picture of liberation forces moving victoriously into the capital city. This is illustrated in Stephen's experience in Acts 7:54-60.[28]

Revelation reinterprets human experience. When one has been to the mountaintop and has seen the promised land, his definition of his experience changes. For example, Revelation reinterprets death in a perpetually relevant way. Adela Yarbro Collins said,

The conviction that death is not the end can empower a person to die for a principle dearly held….Alternatively, the narrative, in another situation, can empower a person to "practice dying," to let go of whatever needs to be relinquished: a destructive relationship, an inadequate understanding of a complex matter, or a less-than-helpful behavior pattern.[29]

Revelation is so constructed and developed that it has relevance for vast areas of concern to the contemporary audience. Collins noted:

The symbols and plot fit other situations, other times and places, as well as their original situation. One way of expressing the significance of these visions for our own time is to say that the vision of the beast from the sea is a narrative about counterfeit power and the vision of the beast from the earth about counterfeit cult.[30]

There are related ways in which Revelation is relevant to our circumstances. It reminds us that things are not always as they seem. Counterfeit religions and counterfeit power can appear benevolent. The Roman government "built the roads, kept the peace, and ran the post office."[31] But even grotesque evil can appear benevolent. Worldly religion and governments vie for the allegiance of God's people. Revelation can help the church to see itself as a gathering of worshiping exiles joining the fantastic, celebrative, unending party of praise and thanksgiving in heaven. As it disperses from the real world of the worshiping people of God, it enters a world of illusions by which it must never be deceived.

Revelation provides hope for people in crisis. Long pointed out that cancer, divorce, and serious accident provide crises for individuals more real and gargantuan than political and military crises between nations.[32]

In discussing the relevance of Revelation, Craddock has suggested that the book offers a response to faith's struggle, conviction that Jesus is Lord, a picture of the enthronement of the crucified one, a vision of the throne of God and the vulnerability of the Lamb, the importance of the church, the reality and power of evil, and an invitation to worship.[33]

In reading through the book of Revelation, it becomes apparent that it does many things. The following 40 items are some of the things it does. These are offered as indications of the relevance of Revelation. They are designed to stimulate the mind of the preacher and to suggest ideas that might help the preacher in connecting Revelation to the contemporary audience. The book of Revelation:

1. provides an unspecified but genuine blessing (1:3).

2. tells about Jesus Christ (1:5-18). He:

    is a faithful witness – Dependable (1:5).

    is the firstborn from the dead – Our hope (1:5).

    is ruler of the kings of the earth – Sovereign (1:5).

    loves his people – Lover (1:5).

    freed his people – Savior (1:5).

    made his people a kingdom and priests – Empowerer (1:6).

    is coming – Deliverer (1:7).

    is with his people – A present help (1:13).

3. encourages the testing of religious claims (2:2).

4. challenges to never give up (2:3).

5. provides instruction for rekindling lost love (2:4-5).

6. reminds of the importance of hating evil (2:6).

7. emphasizes the relationship of the Spirit to the churches (2:7).

8. provides incentive to overcome (2:7).

9. emphasizes that Somebody does know the troubles I've seen (2:9).

10. encourages faithfulness even in the face of persecution (2:10).

11. provides warnings against false teachings and teachers (2:14-16).

12. tells of the need to give people time to repent (of patience, not expecting too much too soon) (2:20-21).

13. teaches the necessity of repentance (2:22).

14. reminds of God's (Christ's) omniscience (3:1).

15. says to be prepared always for Christ's return (3:3).

16. says that God's people are worthy—not worms (3:4).

17. encourages to patient endurance (3:8-12).

18. challenges lukewarmness (3:15-20).

19. thrills with a vision of God that leads to worship (4:1-11).

20. reminds that God is still in charge of his universe (4:1-11).

21. fills the listener with a sense of awe, wonder, and joy in being in God's presence (4:1-11).

22. provides a poignant and powerful picture of the crucified and ascended Christ (5:1-14).

23. reveals the true status of God's people on earth (5:9-10).

24. shows the victory of the militant church over its obstacles (6:1-17).

25. encourages the Christian with the assurance of God's protection and a scene of his ultimate residence with God (7:1-17).

26. offers dramatic evidence of God's response to the prayers of his people (8:1-5).

27. helps in understanding that the wicked do not escape God's warning judgments (8:6-9:21).

28. confirms the fact that the Christian experience includes the bitter and the sweet (10:1-11).

29. assures that even when it appears that the church has been destroyed God's people will be victorious (11:1-19).

30. takes the listener behind the scenes to help in understanding that the sufferings of the church are due to Satan who, having failed in destroying the Christ, seeks to destroy God's people (12:1-17).

31. introduces two of the enemies Satan uses to try to destroy God's people: the persecution of governments and the deception of false religion (13:1-18).

32. assures of the redemption of God's people and the certainty of a final harvest (14:1-20).

33. assures the listener that the redeemed of both covenants will have emerged victorious through life's fiery trials (15:1-8).

34. guarantees that the final wrath of God will be poured out on an impenitent humanity (16:1-21).

35. directs attention to a third weapon Satan uses in his effort to destroy God's people—the seduction of the attractions this world offers (17:1-18).

36. reminds the listener that the world and its desires pass away; that "earth holds no treasures but perish with using" (18:1-24).

37. assures that God will put an end to all persecution and deception and God's people will be united with him at the wedding supper of the Lamb (19:1-21).

38. guarantees the doom of Satan and his followers and the certainty of final judgment (20:1-15).

39. provides a thrilling picture of the ultimate dwelling place of the redeemed in the city of God where there will be no more death or mourning or crying or pain (21:1-27).

40. offers an invitation to eternal life from Jesus, who is coming again (22:1-21).

These are 40 things Revelation does. There still remains the question of how one may translate these into sermons that will connect with the listener. Collins has cautioned, "If the symbols and plot of Revelation are translated into logical propositions or timeless principles, they lose much of their power to evoke emotion and to persuade."[34] This calls attention to the fact that God is doing something in Revelation that is different from what he has done in most of the rest of Scripture. Wilcock put it this way, "What he has in store for his last unveiling is a word of a different sort: an acted word, a word dramatized, painted, set to music—a word you can see and feel and taste."[35] The preacher must approach this book in a different way. Peterson said, "If the Revelation is not read as a poem, it is simply incomprehensible....We do not have more information after we read a poem, we have more experience."[36]

While the preacher must allow his mind to be transformed by the images of Revelation, it is encouraging to know that the contemporary audience has been well prepared to receive a message conveyed through such wild and fantastic imagery. Cornish P. Rogers has said,

> The contemporary mind, addicted to visual imagery through daily doses of television, cinematic portrayals of interplanetary travel, and far-out science fiction, seizes on the lurid images, grotesque figures, violent conflict, and interstellar action described in Revelation. It is, in a word, great theater.[37]

He added:

> Like Picasso, Revelation paints in lurid cartoon images in order to evoke the true likeness of created reality. It is more than cartoon, more than poetic imagery; it is the stuff of which dreams are made....Those realities, or images, are the subliminal force of the book. Moved by this current, readers take away more than the text actually says.[38]

How can the preacher create in the minds of the listeners the effect Revelation was intended to produce? Craddock argued,

> It is through the process of hand-to-hand engagement with a text that listeners become participants in the search for meaning....They are better joined to the Scripture if they experience their pastor doing workmanlike exegesis with them.[39]

All that has been said to this point is theory. But what does it all look like when developed into a sermon? To illustrate with a sermon is risky because no given sermon can perfectly achieve what even good theory suggests. Nonetheless, an effort must be made to demonstrate an attempt to connect the book of Revelation with the contemporary audience. The sermons in this book are an attempt to achieve what the theory requires.

SUPPLEMENTARY
NOTES

I n the year 2000 I was awarded the Doctor of Ministry degree from the Harding University Graduate School of Religion after gaining approval of my thesis, *Preaching the Messages of Revelation: From Hermeneutics to Homiletics*. The thesis can be borrowed from the Harding School of Theology through interlibrary loan.

However, for the purposes of this book I have adapted portions of that thesis as a supplement to the 22 sermons. This is to provide additional insights into the book of Revelation. It is also to provide help and to encourage preachers and teachers to inspire their congregations with messages from Revelation.

A portion of the Abstract to the thesis explains the material that follows. In part, the Abstract says:

> In response to the frequent neglect and abuse of the book of Revelation, this thesis attempts to demonstrate a process for preaching the messages of the book from seeking the interpretation of the text (hermeneutics) to the application in preaching the text (homiletics). It develops from texts in Revelation sermons designed to convey the messages of those portions of the book. A blending of preterist and idealist approaches as adopted

by William Hendriksen serves as the hermeneutical basis for the development of texts for preaching.

After discussing hermeneutical and homiletical principles and insights bearing on selected texts in Revelation, three annotated sermons are included. The conclusion contains an additional sermon developed from the same text as the first sermon to demonstrate another approach in preaching the text.

CHAPTER 1:

Introduction

The body of material explicitly designed to help the preacher preach Revelation is rather small and with limited purposes.[1] However, there are three areas that point the way to a fresh approach for preaching Revelation. One is general works in homiletics. It seems to be commonly assumed and occasionally expressed that the task of preaching is to communicate the message intended by the passage being preached. For example, John MacArthur, Jr. advocates "preaching in such a way that the meaning of the Bible passage is presented *entirely and exactly* as it was intended by God."[2]

Statements such as this from the field of homiletics converge with a common view in hermeneutics, a second related area. As expressed by John Bright, the task of exegesis is "reading from the biblical text the meaning its author intended to convey."[3] This corresponds to the statement made by E. D. Hirsch, Jr. in the opening sentence of his important work on hermeneutics, *Validity in Interpretation*,[4] published the same year (1967) Bright expressed his view. Hirsch spoke of "the sensible belief that a text means what its author meant."[5] In explaining and building on Hirsch's views, Vern Sheridan Poythress said, "Interpretation of a biblical passage, narrowly speaking, determines the meaning of the human author. Application involves the exploration of the significance *for us* of the one meaning, and actions in accordance with it."[6] Millard J. Erickson has suggested the need to expand the search for meaning:

It has often been thought that the meaning of language was to be found in the meaning of the individual units or words. Logical positivism modified this by contending that the proposition, rather than the word, was the basic unit of meaning. Now, however, it is apparent, based on some of the insights of narrative literary interpretation, that the unit must be made even broader, extended to the whole story.[7]

If this be true, applying the concept to Revelation, exegesis should begin by seeking to determine the purpose of the whole book. Then one might attempt to determine the purpose of smaller units as they relate to the whole.

All of this suggests that preaching from Revelation demands an investigation of the intention or purpose of the writer of the work. This leads to a third area for help in preaching Revelation. Recent studies in Revelation have challenged previous views concerning the purpose of the book. Typically, in the past, writers have agreed with Elisabeth Fiorenza's assessment that the central purpose of the book "is to strengthen and to encourage the persecuted Christian communities."[8] David L. Barr said, "That such encouragement was John's purpose is the nearly uniform conclusion of the commentators."[9] Elsewhere he expressed *his* view:

> John's task was not so much to give comfort to those afflicted as it was to help them remember who the enemy was and to know which side they were on. Revelation is a clarion call to faithfulness to a people whose general hostilities to Rome are in danger of being overwhelmed by the attractiveness of Greco-Roman culture.[10]

Richard Bauckham has said of John,

> By no means all of his readers were poor and persecuted by an oppressive system: many were affluent and compromising with the oppressive system. The latter are offered not consolation and encouragement, but severe warnings and calls to repent.[11]

Bauckham added, "The call to 'conquer'…transcends both consolation and warning."[12] So Paul S. Minear wrote:

When one isolates the hortatory sections of the book, and analyses the thrust of those sections, he is impressed with the diversity of external conditions, the variety of Christian responses, and the manifold shape of the author's purpose.[13]

Adela Yarbro Collins has observed that "on the deepest level, the Apocalypse expresses an interpretation of reality and exhorts its audience to live in a way that is an appropriate response to that interpretation."[14] Wilfrid J. Harrington said John chose to "depict history as a stark struggle between the forces of evil and the worshipers of God and of the Lamb."[15] Barr concluded that Revelation gave its readers "a new understanding of their world....They live in a new reality in which lambs conquer and suffering rules. The victims become the victors."[16] In fact, the concluding words of Arthur W. Wainwright in his book on Revelation are that "it gives assurance of the victory of God and the triumph of the Lamb."[17]

Michael Wilcock has seen the purpose of Revelation fulfilled in another dimension. Of Revelation he said, "Jesus has given it to us as a sacrament of the imagination, to quicken the pulse and set the soul aflame over the gospel which all too often we take for granted."[18]

Out of all of this emerged a conception that the circumstances of the Christians to whom Revelation was initially addressed may have been far more similar to ours than many have previously supposed. David A. deSilva has said,

By understanding how Revelation sought to transform the way in which these churches in Asia viewed and responded to their situation in the world, Christians today are given a means of examining their attitude toward their own societies.[19]

This review of related literature has surfaced two considerations relevant to the abuse and neglect of preaching Revelation. One is the importance of connecting hermeneutics and homiletics. The other is the relevance of the message of Revelation to the contemporary audience.

Regarding connecting hermeneutics and homiletics, much of the abuse in preaching Revelation has arisen when the preaching has been a reflection of bizarre or indefensible interpretations of the book. Biblical preaching should communicate the message and meaning of the text. It should not present speculation as truth.

Regarding relevance, it may be that some of the neglect in preaching Revelation has been due not only to the difficulty in interpreting it, but to a failure to see its relevance in the present time in the United States and other countries where the church is more ignored than persecuted. If it is seen only as a book to encourage persecuted Christians, the book may seem to have little relevance in a time when the church is more ignored than persecuted. Recent Revelation studies have indicated the book's purpose is much broader. William Hendriksen agreed with this. He said the "main purpose" of Revelation was "to comfort the militant church in its struggle against the forces of evil."[20] But the forces of evil are diverse:

> The beast that comes up out of the sea is satan's antichristian persecution, embodied in world governments, directed against the *bodies* of believers. In John's day, the *Roman government*.

> The beast that arises out of the earth is *satan's* antichristian religion, aimed to deceive the *minds* and enslave the *wills* of believers. At the time when these visions appeared to John that beast out of the earth was incorporated in the *pagan religion and emperor-worship of Rome*.

> The great harlot, Babylon, is *satan's* antichristian seduction, striving to steal the *hearts* and pervert the *morals* of believers. In the *city of Rome* the harlot at that time manifested herself.[21]

Hendriksen recognized that persecution, deception, and seduction each posed major threats to Christians. The potential threat, if not the presence, of persecution and the reality of deception and seduction continue to confront Christians, and make preaching from the book of Revelation important for this present time.

CHAPTER 2:

Hermeneutical Principles and Insights Used in Preaching Selected Texts in Revelation

T his chapter is designed to lead the preacher through major hermeneutical issues involved in Revelation, and to provide suggestions on how to preach from the book in view of those concerns. Opposing points of view will be presented, but a judgment will be made concerning the approach that is most faithful to the text and appropriate for preaching. It is beyond the scope of this thesis to provide an exhaustive defense of the choices made, but as Wilcock has said, "It is impossible for a commentator to avoid plumping for one of these views, unless he waters his comments down to the point where they cease to be nourishing."[1]

Books which survey the ways in which Revelation has been interpreted will usually mention the preterist, historicist, futurist, and idealist views.[2] The theory that drives the preterist view says the book had to be understood by and have a message for its original recipients. This is reasonable, and surely this much of preterist theory must be accepted. However, the book does claim to be a prophecy (Rev. 1:3; 22:19). Isaiah was a prophecy with a message for its original recipients which they could understand. But the fulfillment of its prophecies concerning the Christ could not be *fully* understood by them (Acts 8:30-35). Yet it still was valuable for them as it gave them a message of hope.

The preterist view also says that all or nearly all of the book had its fulfillment in the first century or, at most, the first 300 years or so of the history of the church. Leon Morris has noted that "some variant of this view is adopted by most modern scholars."[3] This view rests heavily on Rev. 1:1, 3 and 22:6, 10 which indicate the book was written "to show his servants what must soon take place."[4] But this may put too much weight on one meaning of a time referent, the duration of which must be determined by context. For example, Rev. 12:12 says the devil's time is "short" (comp. Rom. 16:20) in spite of the fact that he is still very active over 1,900 years later. Nevertheless, Revelation certainly did show even God's first century servants what, from their perspective, would soon take place. But in the process the book accomplishes much more. It continues to provide a blessing even for God's servants who now read, hear, and keep it. And even by verse 7 John spoke concerning an event that did not "soon" take place and that has still not occurred more than 1,900 years later.

The historicist (or continuous historical) view has seen Revelation as a consecutive, prophetic history of the church through the ages. It has attempted to match up specific historical events, people and movements with the symbols of the book. The history of this approach presents a classic study of eisegesis with each interpreter in each century making his time "the last days." It has assumed, contrary to the structure of the book, that Revelation was intended to present a consecutive history of future events. Commentators from Victorinus of Pettau in the third century to Elizabeth Schüssler Fiorenza in the present day have noted recapitulation as a feature of the book's structure.[5] For example, Hendriksen's first proposition is that Revelation consists of seven parallel sections, each spanning the period from the first to the second coming of Christ.[6] If this is correct, then the historicist position is wrong.

A view more often seen today is the futurist approach. A typical futurist view takes off from Rev. 1:19, "Now write what you have seen, what is, and what is to take place after this." It treats the verse as a table of contents for the book. According to this interpretation chapter 1 is what John had seen, chapters 2 and 3 represent what is, and everything after chapter 3 is what is to take place in the future beyond even our own time. If chapters 2 and 3 describe literal churches in the first century, the futurist view forces the "after this" of Rev. 4:1 to leap at least 1,900 years into the future. There is no linguistic basis justifying such a leap from the words themselves. But the futurist assumes the symbols are to be taken literally and, since a literal fulfillment cannot be found in human history since the book was written, the fulfillment is said to be in the future. But it is difficult to accept a position that demands a literal interpretation of what appears to be symbolic and pictorial language.

Furthermore, to regard practically the entire book as referring exclusively to events many centuries in the future strains the meaning of the word "soon." Although the meaning of the word "soon" involves no absolute time frame and must be understood in context, it is difficult to believe it had no application to the time of the recipients of the book.

The idealist view has been identified with such terms as "spiritual," "symbolic," and "philosophy of history." It says that Revelation is not attempting to trace the history of the church by identifying specific events, but through symbolic language it shows the principles and ways God deals with the church in history. It shows the conflict between Christ and Satan, and the church and the world, and the ultimate victory of God and his people.

In extreme form the idealist view could separate Revelation from its first century historical setting. This need not be the case. Idealists can see the symbols of Revelation arising from both their Biblical and contemporary settings and having immediate application to the first century reader's situation. However, the symbols are seen as encompassing forces at work in heaven and on earth that are larger and descriptive of more than what was occurring in the time of the Roman empire. Perhaps this may more aptly describe a blending of some preterist and idealist views. This approach sees a perpetual relevance in Revelation. It showed what shortly came to pass for Christians in the Roman empire, but it shows what Christians will continue to experience. The same forces that created their specific problems will always create similar problems in different forms at every point in history as long as Satan has power. God still provides the same encouragement, help, and hope for his people today as he did for his people in the past. This is the view adopted in this thesis, and a view that can make preaching from Revelation a relevant and exciting event.

Robert W. Wall presumes to present a fifth approach to interpreting Revelation, a "canonical critical approach." It involves "a concern to recover allusions to or echoes of the OT as the primary context within which John first understood his visions as the word of God."[7] However, it is less than clear that this presents a view mutually exclusive of the others. Those who hold to the other views would not necessarily disagree with that concern.

What Wall said does raise another hermeneutical consideration—the relationship of Revelation to other writings. George Eldon Ladd said, "Revelation belongs to the genre of apocalyptic."[8] Collins explained: "The idea that there is a body of ancient literature which may be called 'apocalyptic' has been prevalent since the first attempt was made in 1832 to interpret Revelation in light of similar texts."[9] What is apocalyptic literature? Collins noted that even by 1970 "there was still great confusion about just what it was that these books had in common and precisely which should be included."[10] Collins became a member of a Forms and Genres Project of the Society of Biblical Literature. Out of that came this definition of "apocalypse":

> A genre of revelatory literature with a narrative framework, in which a revelation is mediated by an otherworldly being to a human recipient, disclosing a transcendent reality which is both temporal, insofar as it envisages eschatological salvation, and spatial, insofar as it involves another, supernatural world.[11]

Since then, as might be expected, even that definition has been challenged as being inadequate.[12]

In spite of all of this, it has become almost a given in scholarly circles that "the Apocalypse must be studied in a manner congruent with the forms of apocalyptic literature rather than discursive or narrative works of history."[13] In fact,

Collins assumed that Revelation should be interpreted in the context of those texts which are "*most similar* to biblical apocalypses."[14] This implies that Revelation was influenced by and therefore must be interpreted against non-biblical apocalypses. This would make a knowledge and grasp of non-canonical Jewish apocalypses essential to understanding Revelation. This must be challenged.

While there are similarities between Revelation and non-canonical apocalypses, Morris describes eight significant "marked differences from typical apocalyptic."[15] It is clear that imagery of Revelation is rooted in the rest of the Bible. It is not surprising that even though, as M. Eugene Boring pointed out, John "never once formally cites an Old Testament passage,"[16] Westcott and Hort found nearly five hundred allusions to the Old Testament in Revelation.[17] Revelation fairly breathes the atmosphere of the Hebrew scriptures from Genesis to Malachi. Henry Barclay Swete noted that the writer of Revelation "belongs to the order which in older days produced the books of Isaiah, Ezekiel, and Zechariah."[18] There and in Daniel, and even Genesis, one will find clues to understanding some of the more complex imagery found in Revelation.

Those who assume, because of some similarities, that Revelation must be understood in the context of non-canonical apocalypses, would be well advised to read the writings of James L. Blevins. Blevins looks at Revelation from a totally different perspective. He has adopted a "dramatic-literary approach" which "views Revelation as a literary whole with plot, characters, and themes. Greek tragic drama is viewed as the literary medium of the author."[19] In fact, Blevins goes so far as to say that "the writer of Revelation...used the dramatic medium of Greek drama and the stage of Ephesus to ensure the book would be heard and seen."[20] The latter comment derives from his observation that the stage of the giant amphitheater in Ephesus was unique in that it "contained seven windows (*thuromata*) for scenery consisting of painted panels."[21] From there he moves on to note that "Revelation can easily be divided into seven acts with seven scenes."[22] His outline of Revelation so divided is worth studying.[23]

The point is that similarities between Revelation and non-Jewish apocalyptic literature no more prove dependence of the former on the latter than similarities between Revelation and Greek drama prove dependence of the former on the latter. Neither case is strong enough to demand acceptance.

Blevins finds many striking points of similarity between Revelation and the Greek dramatic form. Nevertheless, it is difficult to see that he has *proven* his case. Craddock has observed that some traits of apocalyptic literature in general have been improperly imported into Revelation.[24] It is hard to believe that this is not what Blevins has done with the Greek dramatic form. The natural home of Revelation is in the field of Old Testament and New Testament literature.

In giving attention to major issues and approaches involved in the interpretation of Revelation, mention must be made of a minor matter. Blevins explains: "Although there are only three verses concerning the millennium in Revelation, many Bible students place exaggerated importance on the subject. The millennium becomes 'the tail that wags the dog.'"[25] The reason for this is the sensationalized futurist interpretation of the millennium that has captured the popular imagination through means such as Hal Lindsay's multi-million bestseller, *The Late Great Planet Earth*.[26] Blevins gives a fair summary of the three basic views of the millennium:

> The premillennial school teaches that Christ will come to earth before the thousand years and reign on earth. The postmillennial school asserts that Christ will reign in heaven during the thousand years and return to earth at the end of that period. The amillennial school views the millennium symbolically: Christ began his reign at his victory over Satan at the cross; he will reign for a complete time.[27]

The appropriate conclusion concerning the millennium will be reached within the framework of one's approach to the book as a whole. Boring has correctly said,

> the Apocalypse must be grasped as a whole, for it simply cannot be understood verse by verse. It is a narrative, a drama with action and movement that conveys the message of each part within the context of the story in its totality.[28]

He elaborated by saying: "Sermons and lessons may certainly deal with smaller units, but preaching and teaching from any text in these larger units must be aware of how the unit as a whole is composed and functions theologically."[29]

It is from this perspective that Craddock makes three suggestions, among others, concerning procedure in preaching from Revelation.[30] First, immerse yourself in the text of Revelation. Read and reread it before planning a single sermon from it. Second, make an original rough outline of the book. Third, ask how the message to be preached from this part of the book fits the whole book.

Behind all of this lies the fundamental assumption that the best interpreter of the Bible is the Bible itself, and the part must always be interpreted by and be in harmony with the whole. How is the book of Revelation to be seen as a whole, and how are its parts related?

This leads to the interpretive issue of parallelism. This has typically been associated with the idealist approach. However, the term "parallelist" focuses attention on the structure of the book of Revelation. Perhaps the most dominant structural aspect of the book one would notice is four groups of "sevens" which cover more than half the book. This immediately suggests a tentative, incomplete outline from which to work:

Chapters	1-3	Seven Lampstands
	4-7	Seven Seals
	8-11	Seven Trumpets
	12-14	?
	15-16	Seven Bowls
	17-22	?

A striking feature noticed regarding the seven trumpets and seven bowls is that they affect or pertain to the same things. A kind of repetition and intensification seems to occur. There is a kind of parallelism here.

As one reads Revelation one is also struck by what appear to be scenes, scattered through the book, of Christ coming in final judgment, e.g., 7:9-17;

11:15-18; 14:14-20; 16:13-21; 19:11-21. These also suggest that the events of Revelation are not strictly sequential from beginning to end. Rather there seems to be recapitulation and a paralleling of events. This enables one to complete a basic outline of Revelation by seeing 12-14 as "Christ Opposed by the Dragon and the Beasts," and dividing the end of the book into 17-19 "The Fall of Babylon and the Beasts," and 20-22 "The Dragon's Doom and Christ's Victory." Within this structure one begins to see in each section the way God is dealing with the church and the world during this age that lies between the time Christ was here the first time and the time when he comes again. This view of Revelation has been most carefully and eloquently detailed by Hendriksen.[31] It seems basically to be the view suggested by the book itself. It provides a framework that seems to make sense of the book and will be applied in the sermons.

Sermons from texts of the Bible should be developed with an awareness of the flow of the book from which they come. What follows is a brief narrative description of the movement of the book of Revelation in view of the structural suggestions given above, according to an idealist approach, and along the general lines of Hendriksen's treatment of the book.[32]

Chapter 1 of Revelation presents Jesus Christ as "the firstborn of the dead, and the ruler of the kings of the earth," as one who is coming again. John sees a vision of Jesus among seven churches. John is told to write to the churches. Here and in chapters 2-3 the church is seen as the light of the world, a light shining brightly in some places at some times, and sometimes barely flickering. Light and darkness cannot coexist. So the church will inevitably face opposition and persecution. Encouragement and perspective are needed for a struggling church. So in chapter 4 John is shown a scene of God sitting on the throne in heaven. As bad as things may seem, there is a reminder that God is still in control of his creation. In chapter 5 the crucified Lamb of God is seen, having ascended to the throne of God from where he controls the destiny of history. With such reassurance it is easier to face the opposition and persecution portrayed in chapter 6. Chapter 7 provides encouragement in the knowledge that God's people will be victorious.

What about those who have opposed God and his people? Chapters 8-9 reveal God's continual warning (trumpet) judgments against the wicked to cause them to repent. Once again in chapters 10-11 there is encouragement that even when the impenitent wicked seem to be winning, God's people emerge victorious.

What has been seen so far is the struggle between the church and the world. Chapter 12 goes behind the scenes to reveal the reason for the conflict. There was a conflict between Christ and Satan. Satan was cast to the earth. Unable to destroy Christ, Satan set out to destroy God's people. Chapter 13 introduces the first of three weapons Satan uses to destroy God's people. One is described under the image of a beast from the sea which appears to represent persecution embodied in government opposing God's people. The other is described under the image of a beast from the earth that appears to represent deception embodied in false religion. But Satan's efforts will not be completely successful. Chapter 14 reveals the Lamb standing victoriously on Mount Zion initiating the harvest of God's judgment.

What will happen to those who had experienced the warning judgments of God? Chapters 15-16 reveal the outpouring of the bowls of God's wrath on those who did not repent. Chapters 17-18 develop the third weapon Satan uses to destroy the people of God. It is described under the image of the great whore/Babylon that seems to represent seduction as expressed in the pleasures and treasures of this world. Chapter 19 describes the rejoicing of heaven over the destruction of Babylon, and reveals the destruction of the beasts. Chapter 20 reveals the doom of Satan. The great Revelation concludes in chapters 21-22 with the vision of the new heaven and earth where the saints are seen reigning with God and the Lamb forever and ever.

A final hermeneutical issue that needs to be addressed is the matter of symbolism. How are the symbols to be understood? C. S. Lewis made some worthwhile observations:

> All the scriptural imagery (harps, crowns, gold, etc.) is, of course, a merely symbolical attempt to express the inexpressible….

Crowns are mentioned to suggest the fact that those who are united with God in eternity share His splendor and power and joy. Gold is mentioned to suggest the timelessness of Heaven (gold does not rust) and the preciousness of it. People who take these symbols literally might as well think that when Christ told us to be like doves, he meant that we were to lay eggs.[33]

The symbols of Revelation should be noticed against their biblical background. Two examples will serve to illustrate. First, in Rev. 7:1-3 the servants of God are marked with a seal on their foreheads. Placing a mark on the foreheads of the godly for the sake of protection has a precedent in Ezek. 9:1-6. Further biblical background for appreciating the significance of a seal on the forehead may come from Ex. 28:36-38. There the high priest wore a signet on the forehead inscribed with the words, "Holy to the Lord."

Second, one may wonder as to the identity of the bizarre creatures portrayed in Rev. 4:7-8. One need not speculate, but turn to Ezekiel 1 where such creatures are seen. Although not identified there, they are revealed later in Ezek. 10:20 as cherubim of God.

Finally, a survey of hermeneutical issues related to Revelation leads to some implications and suggestions for preaching from Revelation. It is appropriate that Revelation is placed at the end of the Bible because it is based on what has come before. Accordingly, the preacher will be wise to save his preaching on Revelation until he has a good knowledge of the *whole* Bible and the *whole* of Revelation. It might also be wise to wait until the congregation has a reasonable overall grasp of the Bible.

The first suggestion must be tempered by the observation of Boring, "John expected the ordinary men and women of the churches of Asia to understand the book, though they were not Bible scholars, historians, or theological experts."[34] Some balance is required here. For example, Wilbur Smith said,

Because of its symbolism, its saturation with Old Testament passages and themes, the various schemes of interpretation that have developed concerning this book through the ages, and the profundity and vastness of the subjects that are here unveiled, I believe that the Apocalypse, above every book of the Bible, will yield its meaning only to those who give it prolonged and careful study.[35]

Yet the book itself promises a blessing on those who read, hear, and take to heart what is written in it (Rev. 1:3). The Christian is to grow in knowledge (2 Pet. 3:18). Even though one may not understand much on the first hearing of Revelation, one will be blessed and prepared to understand more on the next hearing. If the impression received on first hearing Revelation is nothing more than, "We're going to win!" the person has been blessed and probably has understood the main point of the book. Job did not understand suffering after God spoke to him, but he was strengthened. So may it be with the hearer of Revelation.

After having read and analyzed Revelation for himself, the preacher will do well to read several good commentaries to test his conclusions.

As Craddock says, the preacher of Revelation should "attempt to do what the text does."[36] John was surely not just teaching a lesson or passing on some information in Revelation. The rich imagery of Revelation stirs the heart and elevates the spirit. If something like that happens to the preacher as he allows himself to be caught up in the visions of the book, he needs to seek to communicate not merely the information but those feelings to his audience. He needs to help them experience what he experiences and feel what he feels. This is another reason to read good commentaries. Good commentators, who are not mere exegetes, may capture the spirit of the text and express themselves with such eloquence that the preacher may be ignited to articulate his feelings in a way that will motivate his audience. Herein lies an additional value of commentaries.

J. Ramsey Michaels expresses well the role of the preacher as he meditates on the text in preparation to preach, "All the author asks is that we, his readers, stand beside him in his visions, see what he saw, hear what he heard, and share his wonder at things even he did not fully understand."[37]

Michaels also expresses well the role of the preacher as he stands in the pulpit,

> The purpose of preaching from the Revelation is to evoke first wonder and then faithfulness to the slain Lamb, not to explain the book away or reduce it to a blueprint of the future. The preacher's task is to stand out of the way and let the book's images do their work.[38]

The preacher of Revelation must never lose sight of the central message of the book as he preaches. Michaels has also said, "At the heart of the Book of Revelation *is* a story, the same gospel story that echoes through-out the entire New Testament, about a slain Lamb victorious over death and evil and a God who makes everything new."[39]

Westcott and Hort found allusions in Revelation to 28 of the books of the Old Testament.[40] The preacher who is alert to such associations can make the whole Bible come to life and develop the great themes that run through the Scriptures. The entire purpose of God for humanity is revealed in Revelation. It provides the preacher the opportunity to lift the hearer out of the limited perspective of his day-to-day existence, and enable him to see his place in God's eternal purpose.

When the preacher feels he has a good grasp of the whole of Revelation, and if he has become excited by its message, he would do well to present the sweep of its message in a series of sermons. Most people are fascinated by Revelation and wish to hear the book explained. What they may not realize is the extent to which they may receive not only information but inspiration. The potential of preaching from Revelation is great for edification and evangelism. The book, for example, can be preached effectively chapter by chapter or, possibly, as a series of seven sermons.

Finally, David L. Larsen once wrote, "It was only a matter of time before the new hermeneutic should be followed by the new homiletic."[41] New or old, a good hermeneutic should be followed by a good homiletic. And the preacher who has captured the heart of the message of Revelation is prepared to capture the heart of the hearer, to bring it into captivity to the Christ who wishes to claim it as his own.

CHAPTER 3:

Homiletical Principles and Insights Used in Preaching Selected Texts in Revelation

P reaching from the book of Revelation presents unusual challenges. God is doing something in Revelation that is different from what he has done in most of the rest of Scripture. Various scholars have described it in different but similar ways. Wilcock has described it in terms of dramatization.[1] Cornish R. Rogers has called it "great theater,"[2] and compared it to "cartoon images."[3] Hendriksen has compared it to watching a movie.[4] Peterson says it should be read as a poem.

The effect of Revelation is not just to provide information, but to evoke wonder.[5] It reaches beyond the intellect to the emotions and the will. For example, Revelation does not attempt to attack the problem of temptation by listing five easy steps to combat it. Instead, it seeks a transformation of affections and allegiance by a total reorientation of the understanding of reality. Revelation seeks to accomplish this by exposing us to dimensions of reality that extend beyond our normal vision. As Hendriksen expresses it, "The Apocalypse intends to show...that things are not what they *seem!*"[6]

So what does this mean for preaching from Revelation? Craddock has said the preacher of Revelation should "attempt to do what the text does."[7] Craig A. Loscalzo expands: "In biblical preaching, we hope that the sermon will do in the lives of our hearers what the biblical text did and does in the lives of its readers."[8] What Revelation does is present visions of reality enabling the reader or listener to see things as he or she has never seen them before, to see things as God sees them. Rules and instructions are important for knowing what to do. But where does one find the motivation and courage to obey? Walter Brueggemann has said:

> Our obedience will not venture far beyond or run risks beyond our imagined world. If we wish to have transformed obedience… then we must be summoned to an alternative imagination, in order that we may imagine the world and ourselves differently.[9]

Revelation does this. William H. Willimon has expressed it this way:

> Only when our imaginations are transformed are we transformed by the "renewing of our mind" as Paul might put it; only when there is a shift in the paradigmatic images by which we construe the world.[10]

Long has stated that the claim of Revelation is, "Things may be hopeless in this world, but there is another, parallel world where things have already been set aright, and you belong to that world and to this one."[11] He presents an analogy of an inmate in a prisoner of war camp being tortured, but who sees on a TV set in the room a picture of liberation forces moving victoriously into the capital city.[12] This is illustrated in the experience of Stephen who, while facing the antagonism of a murderous crowd, was permitted to see "the heavens opened and the Son of Man standing at the right hand of God!"[13]

Revelation opens the heavens and permits the Christian to see his circumstances from the perspective of the throne of God. It reinterprets human experience. When one has been to the mountaintop and has seen the promised land, his definition of his experience changes. For example, Revelation reinterprets death in a perpetually relevant way. Collins said,

> The conviction that death is not the end can empower a person to die for a principle dearly held....Alternatively, the narrative, in another situation, can empower a person to "practice dying," to let go of whatever needs to be relinquished: a destructive relationship, an inadequate understanding of a complex matter, or a less-than-helpful behavior pattern.[14]

The key word here is "empower." It might be said that the purpose of Revelation is to empower the Christian to live the life described elsewhere in scripture.

So how can the preacher translate the texts of Revelation into sermons? Commonly in the past the exegetical and homiletical task has been seen as extracting from the text the main thought which became the thesis which would then be subdivided into "points." But, as Lowry has observed, "Powerful stories *do* something, *effect* something, in ways not captured by the response, 'Oh, yes, I now understand the point.'"[15]

The significant word here is "stories." In recent years narrative theologians and homileticians have responded to the fact that the literature of the Bible consists of a variety of genres. A major portion of scripture consists of narrative or stories. A major portion of recent homiletical *literature* has focused on how to preach from such material. One positive contribution from this source has been attention to the importance of the emotional as well as the intellectual content of some texts. As Long put it, "Biblical texts *say* things that *do* things, and the sermon is to say and do those things too."[16]

But is this relevant to the book of Revelation? Is Revelation narrative? The recent focus on narrative preaching has been on the stories of the Old Testament and the gospels, particularly the parables, in the New Testament. Long in his book on *Preaching and the Literary Forms of the Bible* includes chapters on several literary forms including one on preaching on narratives. No mention of Revelation was made there. Later he dealt with Revelation in a journal article, "Preaching Apocalyptic Literature."[17]

Part of the difficulty of discussing Revelation in the context of narrative homiletics lies in the problem of defining "narrative." Charles L. Campbell said,

"There is no simple way to define 'narrative preaching.'"[18] In a similar way Long noted: "The understandings of 'story preaching' are, it seems, almost as numerous as the homileticians who use the phrase."[19] Some homileticians emphasize story telling, while others emphasize the sermon's narrative shape. "Narrative" has been defined as "a story or account of events, experiences, or the like, whether true or fictitious."[20] Surely by that definition John's record of his visions would qualify. The visual content of Revelation suggests that John wanted us to see something we would not see otherwise, or to see things in a new way.

But the goal of narrative preaching is not just to help the listener see something, but to experience something. Campbell said, "Narrative is valued for its distinctive ability to produce or evoke experience....The sermon becomes an 'experiential event' in which transformation is supposed to happen experientially in individuals."[21] As Peterson has said, "We do not have more information after we read a poem, we have more experience."[22]

It is this "experience" that narrative preaching intends to provide. But how is that to be achieved? Collins has cautioned, "If the symbols and plot of Revelation are translated into logical propositions or timeless principles, they lose much of their power to evoke emotion and to persuade."[23] Campbell expressed this characterization of Lowry's position regarding narrative preaching: "the hearer should experience the gospel existentially, rather than know it propositionally."[24] Campbell also characterized preaching as taught by Craddock by saying, "The preacher seeks not primarily to convey propositional information or develop a logical argument, but rather to effect an experience of the gospel in the hearers."[25] The preacher, however, should not necessarily have to choose between providing understanding and providing an emotional experience. Neil Postman said of Jonathan Edwards, "audiences may have been moved emotionally by Edwards' language, but they were, first and foremost, required to understand it."[26]

A reaction against cognitive-propositional preaching has resulted in a move toward "indirect" conveyance of meaning.[27] Narrative homileticians have seen this approach as less manipulative, violent, and coercive. To this Campbell dared to say:

> A straightforward, direct argument can be less violent or manip-
> ulative than stories that yank people all over the place emotion-
> ally. In addition, much of the emphasis on noncoercive preaching
> among contemporary homileticians draws not on the non-violent
> gospel, which dares to speak truth and challenge the powers, but
> rather on a kind of pallid liberalism, which is intent on making
> no daring claims in order to respect each person's right to think
> what he or she wants.[28]

Narrative preaching could enable the avoidance of propositional truth, but that is not necessary. Stories and narratives can have a variety of purposes. Some may be designated to inspire or encourage, but others might intend to make a "point." So how is the preacher to handle a particular text? And how can the preacher create in the minds of the listeners the effect Revelation was intended to produce? Craddock argued,

> It is through the process of hand-to-hand engagement with a text
> that listeners become participants in the search for meaning....
> They are better joined to the Scripture if they experience their
> pastor doing workmanlike exegesis with them.[29]

Exegetical study may be seen as merely a tedious academic exercise. But the end result of exegesis may be the insight of discovery resulting in seeing something so radically different as to create a profound emotional experience and a transformation of both understanding and behavior. Frequently texts in Revelation are filled with symbols and imagery that can only be understood or fully appreciated by seeing them against the background of other portions of scripture. And when that understanding and insight is achieved, an emotional experience consistent with that insight can occur.

Revelation presents an alternative world to the one experienced by the five senses. How can the preacher present this to his listeners? Jensen asks, "What stories can we tell to picture an alternative world?"[30] Actually we do not have to make up stories on our own. Revelation has already provided a fresh perspective on our world, a new way to see it and our place in it. It remains for the preacher to impress it on the minds of the listeners to enable transformation to occur.

So how is it to be done? Campbell has insisted there is "no paint-by-numbers formula."[31] However, Long has suggested an approach. He argued that the preacher is to bring to the listeners both what the text says and does. The final step in the exegetical process should be to complete this sentence: "In relation to those who will hear this sermon, what this text wants to say and do is…."[32] What the sermon aims to say (focus) and do (function) should reflect the purpose of the text. A focus and function statement should guide the development of the sermon. Long defines them as follows:

> A *focus statement* is a concise description of the central, controlling, and unifying theme of the sermon….A *function statement* is a description of what the preacher hopes the sermon will create or cause to happen for the hearers.[33]

These should grow directly out of the exegesis of the biblical text, be related to each other, be clear, unified, and relatively simple.[34]

What form should the sermon take? Lowry suggests some options. The one that seems most usable for the more complex visions in Revelation: "Highlight, elaborate, amplify, and creatively enflesh certain portions while moving through the text."[35] This sounds similar to Campbell's description of a sermon of Brueggemann's which "represents a kind of dramatic, expository preaching, in which text, exposition, and application are inseparably and dramatically woven together in the sermon."[36] Long said some texts are "too complicated to be utilized without giving textual or contextual comment."[37]

Texts from Revelation generally are complicated. The first task of the preacher (after praying for God's help) is to do the appropriate exegetical work to achieve understanding for himself. As he moves through the text he is apt to gain insights that will enrich his understanding and enable him to see applications. He can then lead his listeners through the text enabling them to share his experience as he weaves in the insights and applications he has discovered.

The goal is to allow the text as illumined by the preacher's discoveries to do its own work in the experience of the listener. To the extent the preacher has been faithful to the text, the message God intends can be communicated with fidelity and the concomitant emotional impact. The degree to which it will be communicated may still depend in part on such factors as the preacher's communicative skills and the receptivity of the hearers.

God did not write a manual on homiletics. There may be minimal rights and wrongs in preaching. The conscientious preacher strives for the better and best. It would surely be presumptuous to suggest there is only one way a text from Revelation, or any other portion of scripture, can be preached. Nonetheless, the effort to preach faithfully and effectively must be made, and the rewards can be all out of proportion to the effort expended.

What has been said to this point is theory. But what does it all look like when developed into a sermon? To illustrate with a sermon is risky because no given sermon can perfectly achieve what even good theory suggests. Nonetheless, an effort must be made to demonstrate an attempt to communicate a portion of the book of Revelation with the contemporary audience. Chapter 4 presents three annotated sermons. These sermons were preached before chapter 3 was written. In chapter 5 I will reflect and evaluate the sermons in light of current homiletical theory. In addition, these manuscript sermons differ from the ones I actually preached at the Newberg church, though they are based on the same texts.

CHAPTER 4:

Annotated Sermons

<u>The Beast of the Sea</u> (Rev. 13:1-10)[1]

The apostle Peter said, "Like a roaring lion your adversary the devil prowls around, looking for someone to devour" (1 Pet. 5:8). The apostle John said, "we have an advocate with the Father, Jesus Christ the righteous, and he is the atoning sacrifice for our sins, and not for our sins only but also for the sins of the whole world" (Jn. 2:1-2).

God wants you to know that your life is being played out in a world in which you face a powerful adversary, but in which you have an even more powerful advocate. This colossal struggle was even dramatized in the vigorous, vivid imagery of the book of Revelation.[2]

In chapter 12 the devil is portrayed not as a roaring lion, but as "a great red dragon, with seven heads and ten horns, and seven diadems on his heads." He tries to destroy the Christ, but having failed at that he begins to make war on his people, "those who keep the commandments of God and hold the testimony of Jesus." We are told, "Then the dragon took his stand on the sand of the seashore."

God does not want us to be "outwitted by Satan," nor "ignorant of his designs" (2 Cor. 2:11). So in Revelation 13 we are introduced to one of the weapons the devil uses in his effort to destroy God's people. John said,

> And I saw a beast rising out of the sea, having ten horns and seven heads, and on its horns were ten diadems, and on its heads were blasphemous names. And the beast that I saw was like a leopard, its feet were like a bear's, and its mouth was like a lion's mouth. And the dragon gave it his power and his throne and great authority (Rev. 13:1-2).

What is this ghastly creature? It is a composite of the dragon and the four beasts described in Daniel 7. Daniel, in a vision, saw "four great beasts come up out of the sea." "The first was like a lion" followed by "a second one, that looked like a bear." Then "another appeared, like a leopard" and had four heads. The fourth beast "had ten horns." The beast of the sea in Revelation 13 combines aspects of the dragon and each of the four beasts of Daniel 7.

But what were these four beasts? Dan. 7:17 says, "As for these four great beasts, four kings shall arise out of the earth." Daniel uses the term "kings" to represent "kingdoms" as indicated in verse 23, "As for the fourth beast, there shall be a fourth kingdom on earth that shall be different from all the other kingdoms." This is indicated also in Daniel 2 where Daniel said of Nebuchadnezzar,

> You are the head of gold. After you shall arise another kingdom inferior to yours, and yet a third kingdom of bronze, which shall rule over the whole earth. And there shall be a fourth kingdom" (Dan. 2:38-40).

The beasts of Daniel 7 parallel the materials that comprised the statue of Daniel 2, and they represent successive world empires beginning with the Babylonian empire and extending through the Medo-Persian and Greek to the Roman empire. Each of these were worldly governments that stood in opposition to the empire of God and represented a threat to their well-being that sometimes expressed itself in persecution.[3] In these the persecuting power of Satan found expression.

In John's time that persecuting power found embodiment in the Roman empire. But I don't believe the beast of the sea in Revelation can be restricted to the Roman empire.[4] The fourth beast of Daniel 7 represented the Roman empire. If the beast of the sea were to represent just the Roman empire, it seems the description would have matched the fourth beast. But it is a composite of all the beasts which seems a reasonable way to represent the threat of persecution that confronts God's people from worldly governments wherever and whenever they exist. The challenge in the first century and for some time following was whether Christians would give their allegiance to Caesar or to Christ. And the enormous power of the Roman empire stood to enforce allegiance to Caesar. But Satan continues to tempt the Christian to choose government over God. And the Christian response must continue to be, "We must obey God rather than any human authority" (Acts 5:24).

But the sometimes seemingly invincible power of human governments can be overwhelmingly intimidating to the Christian. John said,

> One of its heads seemed to have received a death-blow, but its mortal wound had been healed. In amazement the whole earth followed the beast. They worshiped the dragon, for he had given his authority to the beast, and they worshiped the beast, saying, "Who is like the beast, and who can fight against it?" (Rev. 13:3-4).

A common phenomenon in human history has been a subjugated people rising up to overthrow tyrannical rulers, only to see those replaced by rulers as bad or worse than the ones before. The frustration of impotence in the face of governmental power has found expression in the proverb, "You can't fight city hall." And this has led to another proverb, "If you can't lick 'em, join 'em." Even the worst governments usually offer some benefits to the people. And for many people government becomes the presumed solution to all their problems. It becomes the object of their hopes, affections, and trust. In short, government becomes their god. And some rulers have received adoration that, for all practical purposes, can be described as worship.

But for all the benefit the beast might provide for some people, the fact remains that it is an enemy of God. Verse 5 says, "The beast was given a mouth uttering haughty and blasphemous words, and it was allowed to exercise authority for forty-two months." But in this statement there is also good news: the power of the beast is limited. He is allowed to exercise authority for only 42 months. But what does that mean? This time period (expressed also as 1,260 days, 3½ years, and "a time, and times, and half a time") is mentioned several times previously in the Bible. It appears in Dan. 12:7 to refer to a time of "the shattering of the power of the holy people." James refers to a period in the life of Elijah when it did not rain for "three years and six months" (Jas. 5:17). This seems to form the background for the time period first mentioned in Revelation in chapter 11:1-6 when the two witnesses were said to "have authority to shut the sky, so that no rain may fall during the days of their prophesying." A study of 1 Kings 17-19 reveals that the literal 3½ years of drought in Elijah's time was a period when God's people were persecuted by the rulers but protected by God. When Elijah thought he was the only one left, God encouraged him with the news that there were still 7,000 in Israel who had not bowed to Baal.

Revelation seems to use the literal 3½ years of persecution and protection in Elijah's time as a symbol of a period when God's people are persecuted but protected or preserved by God. This appears to be the situation in Revelation 11. In Revelation 12 the dragon persecutes God's people, but they are "nourished for a time, and times, and half a time."

So what is the period of time which carries the symbol of 42 months when Christians are persecuted by the beast, but protected by God? Paul assured Christians: "Indeed all who want to live a godly life in Christ Jesus will be persecuted" (2 Tim. 3:12). And Jesus said matter-of-factly, "In the world you face persecution" (Jn. 16:33). But Jesus also said, "I tell you, my friends, do not fear those who kill the body, and after that can do nothing more" (Lk. 12:4). Persecution may come. But,

> who will separate us from the love of Christ? Will hardship, or distress, or persecution, or famine, or nakedness, or peril, or sword?...No, in all these things we are more than conquerors through him who loved us (Rom. 3:35, 37).

Earlier in Revelation Jesus said to a church facing persecution, "Be faithful until death, and I will give you the crown of life....Whoever conquers will not be harmed by the second death" (Rev. 2:10-11). Persecution can harm the body, but God can protect the soul from harm. So when is the period of persecution and protection—the 42 months? It is the entire Christian age until Jesus comes again.[5] This is the ongoing experience of the church. It is no particular, literal 3½ year period during the Christian age. All who live a godly life in Christ Jesus will be persecuted, but the presence of Christ will be with them to the end of the age, protecting and preserving their souls.

John continued by saying of the beast,

> It opened its mouth to utter blasphemies against God, blas-pheming his name and his dwelling, that is, those who dwell in heaven. Also it was allowed to make war on the saints and to conquer them (Rev. 13:6-7).

This is one of only two times in Revelation where the word "conquer" is used of anyone other than God, Christ, and God's people. The previous instance is Rev. 11:7 which says, "When they had finished their testimony, the beast that came up from the bottomless pit will make war on them and conquer them and kill them." It looked like Satan had won. But his apparent victory was short-lived, for the next verse says "they went up to heaven." I am sure that Satan thought he had won when Jesus was nailed to the cross. But that appar-ent victory was short-lived because soon after that Jesus rose from the dead and ascended to heaven.

> What then are we to say about these things? If God is for us, who is against us? He who did not withhold his own Son, but gave him up for all of us, will he not with him also give us everything else? Who will bring any charge against God's elect? It is God who justifies. Who is to condemn? It is Christ Jesus, who died, yes, who was raised, who is at the right hand of God, who indeed intercedes for us" (Rom. 8:31-34).

And not only does he intercede for us now, even in the midst of persecu-tion, but he has gone to prepare a place for us. He said, "And if I go and prepare a place for you, I will come again and will take you to myself, so that where I am, there you may be also" (Jn. 14:3). The beast may separate our head from our body, but he cannot separate us from the love of God. From the world's perspective he may conquer, but we know that we are more than conquerors through him who loved us!

John said of the beast,

> It was given authority over every tribe and people and language and nation, and all the inhabitants of the earth will worship it, everyone whose name has not been written from the foundation of the world in the book of life of the Lamb that was slaughtered (Rev. 13:7-8).

Throughout the book of Revelation humanity is divided into two categories. One is "the inhabitants of the earth." This expression always refers to the ungodly. Paul expressed it in Phil. 3:19-20, "their minds are set on earthly things. But our citizenship is in heaven, and it is from there that we are expecting a Savior, the Lord Jesus Christ." For us, Jesus is Lord. He is the object of our worship. He is king of our lives. But there is little room in earthly kingdoms for two kings. The chief priests said to Pilate, "We have no king but the emperor" (Jn. 19:15). And they handed Jesus over to be crucified. Jesus said earlier, "If they persecuted me, they will persecute you" (Jn. 15:20). Sooner or later, in one form or another it will come.

So John said, "Let anyone who has an ear listen: If you are to be taken captive, into captivity you go; if you kill with the sword, with the sword you must be killed. Here is a call for the endurance and faith of the saints" (Rev. 13:9-10). So how is the Christian to face the prospect of persecution? What John says here is underscored by previous teaching of Jesus: "All who take the sword will perish by the sword" (Mt. 26:52). "My kingdom is not from this world. If my kingdom were from this world, my followers would be fighting to keep me from being handed over to the Jews. But as it is, my kingdom is not from here" (Jn. 18:36). "Love your enemies and pray for those who persecute you" (Mt. 5:44). "Blessed are you when people revile you and persecute you and utter all kinds of evil against you falsely on my account. Rejoice and be glad, for your reward is great in heaven" (Mt. 5:11-12).

Of certain ones Jesus said, "Then they will hand you over to be tortured and will put you to death....But the one who endures to the end will be saved" (Mt. 24:9-13). Jesus never promised his way would be easy. It requires endurance. And that must be sustained by an ever-deepening faith.

We began with the words of Peter, "Like a roaring lion your adversary the devil prowls around looking for someone to devour." We end with his following words which provide a fitting conclusion:

> Resist him, steadfast in your faith, for you know that your
> brothers and sisters in all the world are undergoing the same kind
> of suffering. And after you have suffered for a little while, the God
> of all grace, who has called you to his eternal glory in Christ, will
> himself restore, support, strengthen, and establish you. To him be
> the power forever and ever. Amen. (1 Pet. 5:9-11).[6]

The Beast of the Earth (Rev. 13:11-18)[1]

In Rev. 13:1-10 we were introduced to a beast that came up out of the sea, one of the agents Satan uses in his effort to destroy God's people. If it were to be given a single name, I would call it "persecution." I believe it represents persecuting governments which in the first century existed in the form of the Roman empire. Following that we are introduced to a second agent Satan uses.[2]

In Rev. 13:11 John wrote, "Then I saw another beast that rose out of the earth." This is not a beast from above. Paul said, "Set your minds on things that are above, not on things that are on the earth" (Col. 3:2). Of others he said, "their minds are set on earthly things" (Phil. 3:19). And of this beast John said, "It exercises all the authority of the first beast on its behalf, and it makes the earth and its inhabitants worship the first beast, whose mortal wound had been healed" (Rev. 13:12). This beast holds sway over the inhabitants of the earth, but not those whose names have been written in "the book of life of the Lamb" mentioned in verse 8.

We were introduced to the Lamb in Rev. 5:6. It was an unusual Lamb having seven horns suggesting complete power and authority. It reminds us of Jesus' statement before he ascended to heaven, "All authority in heaven and on earth has been given to me" (Mt. 28:18). This is the one John the Baptist introduced as "the Lamb of God who takes away the sin of the world" (Jn. 1:29). But Satan provides the earth an alternative counterfeit. The only physical description given of the beast that rose out of the earth was that "it had two horns like a lamb" (Rev. 13:11). It appears harmless and innocent, and its power is limited. But, in reality, it is dangerous and deadly. "And it spoke like a dragon" (Rev. 13:11). The words of the Lamb of God "are spirit and life" (Jn. 6:63). But the message of Satan's lamb is deadly. This beast is later referred to as "the false prophet" (Rev. 16:13; 19:20; 20:10). It reminds us of Jesus' statement, "Beware of false prophets, who come to you in sheep's clothing but inwardly are ravenous wolves" (Mt. 7:15). Jesus spoke of wolves in sheep's clothing. John portrays a dragon in lamb's clothing.

Paul expressed the same idea when he spoke of

false apostles, deceitful workers, disguising themselves as apostles of Christ. And no wonder! Even Satan disguises himself as an angel of light. So it is not strange if his ministers also disguise themselves as ministers of righteousness (2 Cor. 11:13-14).

The beast appears harmless, but we are dealing with something very subtle here. The dragon was identified in the previous chapter as "that ancient serpent,…the deceiver of the whole world" (Rev. 12:9). This is the one who with clever words confused and deceived Eve. Offers of instant gratification and questions raising doubts about God's word were part of his arsenal. This serpent/dragon/Satan now has another agent. It is portrayed under the symbol of a seemingly harmless beast that actually has all the authority of the sea-beast described earlier in this chapter.

This beast causes people to divert their worship from the true God to the first beast.[3] This should be no easy task. Surely nothing less that the most highly sophisticated means and maneuvers could cause this. Governments and rulers can gain the allegiance of people through giving them what they want, and by demonstrating awesome and devastating power to convince people there is no realistic alternative to life's challenges than to turn to them for help and hope. The deification of earthly rulers was not only a phenomenon of the first century. It has occurred throughout history, including the twentieth century. And religions have sometimes overtly, and at other times subtly, supported such practices.[4]

But how can false religion gain credibility? Of the beast John said,

It performs great signs, even making fire come down from heaven to earth in the sight of all; and by the signs that it is allowed to perform on behalf of the beast, it deceives the inhabitants of earth, telling them to make an image for the beast that had been wounded by the sword and yet lived; and it was allowed to give breath to the image of the beast so that the image of the beast could even speak and cause those who would not worship the image of the beast to be killed (Rev. 13:13-15).

The beast could use "all power, signs, lying wonders, and every kind of wicked deception" (2 Thess. 2:9-10). This has been possible when people

> refused to love the truth and be saved. For this reason God sends
> them a powerful delusion, leading them to believe what is false,
> so that all who have not believed the truth but took pleasure in
> unrighteousness will be condemned (2 Thess. 2:10-12).

Are we to believe the "miracles" of false religions are real?[5] I think not. The magicians in Moses' time were able to mimic his miracles through their magic only up to a point. The prophets of Baal were unable to call fire down from heaven under controlled conditions. The efforts of the Jewish exorcists in Ephesus resulted in a fiasco. Paul spoke of "lying wonders" and "deception." I have done magic shows for half a century. And my minor magic has created the same effect in people exposed to obeah in Jamaica and Satanism in the United States. Deception can be as convincing to the gullible as a miracle to the skeptic. The beast does not need to do genuine miracles when deception works just as well.

It is easy for people to be deceived by religion. It is perhaps Satan's cruelest trick to center his deception in religion. That which is presumably a highway to heaven could be a path to perdition. Satan would like people to think one religion is as good as another. But earlier in Revelation Jesus commended the church in Ephesus because "you have tested those who claim to be apostles but are not, and have found them to be false" (Rev. 2:2). Warnings are given about other false religious leaders in Revelation 2 and 3.

False religion can tolerate no rivals, especially truth. So it may resort to force. Of the beast John said,

> Also it causes all, both small and great, both rich and poor,
> both free and slave, to be marked on the right hand or the forehead,
> so that no one may buy or sell who does not have the mark, that is,
> the name of the beast or the number of its name (Rev. 13:16-17).

Some have taken this passage to suggest that some "Antichrist" will someday arise and force a literal brand on people, and only those who have given their allegiance to this person and accepted the mark will be allowed to buy and sell.

However, in the context of Revelation being "marked on the right hand or the forehead" appears to be the Satanic equivalent to "having the seal of the living God" (Rev. 7:2). An angel spoke of a time when "we have marked the servants of our God with a seal on their foreheads" (Rev. 7:3). In fact, three verses after mention of those who bear the mark of the beast "on the right hand or forehead" we are shown standing with the Lamb on Mount Zion those "who had his name and his Father's name written on their foreheads" (Rev. 14:1). Of those who will "reign forever and ever" we are told "his name will be on their foreheads" (Rev. 22:4-5). To be sealed suggests ownership and protection. Those who are sealed with God's name on their foreheads suggests those whose minds have been brought into captivity to God, who belong to him and are protected by him. Similarly, those who bear the mark of the beast would be those who have given their allegiance to him. In contrast to the ones who are sealed on the forehead by God and reign forever and ever,

> Those who worship the beast and its image, and receive a mark on their foreheads or on their hands, they will also drink the wine of God's wrath, poured unmixed into the cup of his anger, and they will be tormented with fire and sulfur in the presence of the holy angels and in the presence of the Lamb. And the smoke of their torment goes up forever and ever. There is no rest day or night for those who worship the beast and its image and for anyone who receives the mark of its name (Rev. 14:9-11).

What a contrast and what an incentive to refuse the mark of the beast!

"This calls for wisdom: let anyone with understanding calculate the number of the beast, for it is the number of a person. Its number is six hundred sixty-six" (Rev. 13:18). What does this mean? There was a practice in the ancient world of assigning number values to letters of the alphabet. We can still see an example of this in our use of Roman numerals. There was a game played in which the numerical values of letters in a person's name would be added together to produce a number that could represent that person. Consequently, many have attempted to find a word which would produce a value of 666. The futility of such a procedure is suggested by the fact that literally hundreds of names and words have been proposed which yield that result. Nero has been a popular choice. However, it doesn't work. It doesn't work in Latin, Greek, or Hebrew. But if you have decided who you think it must be, with some ingenuity you can probably make that name, and many others, fit. So it is with Nero. Try adding a title. Make it Nero Caesar. That still won't work in Latin. It won't work in Greek. But…it works in Hebrew: So Nero Caesar is 666, the mark of the beast.

Well, I don't think so. It seems too contrived. I believe the book of Revelation provides its own background for appreciating the significance of the number. Revelation uses the number seven 54 times. It dominates the book. It is a number symbolizing completeness or perfection. The number seven is found repeatedly in Revelation up to this point. But suddenly one confronts six. Six falls short of completeness and perfection. It is attached to a beast that has authority and power, but limited authority and power. In fact, we learn that this beast, for all of its pretensions, is a loser. It is doomed. It is finally "thrown alive into the lake of fire that burns with sulfur" (Rev. 19:20).[6]

But this is also the number of man. There is no indefinite article "a" in the Greek language. Some translations may say it is the number of *a* man, or person, as though it refers to a particular individual. This is what led to a search for Nero or some other person. However, the text can be, and probably should be, translated "the number of man," as in "mankind." And what is the condition of man apart from God? He is not a seven; he is a six. He is incomplete, imperfect. He falls short of the completeness he could have in Christ. He is a failure. And his experience in life can be summarized as six, six, six—failure after failure after failure. That is the number of man. It is the number of the beast. And it is certainly the number of man who bears the mark of the beast, who has yielded his allegiance to the beast.[7]

Revelation 13 has introduced us to two beasts who are agents Satan uses to destroy God's people. The first appears to be persecuting governments opposed to God and his people. In the first century this was preeminently embodied in the Roman government and emperor. The second beast seems to be false religion deceiving people into opposing God and his people. In the first century this was preeminently embodied in the emperor cult. The cult supported the emperor and sought to cause all people to worship him. But if the first beast is not to be identified with a single ruler or government, but represents governments that continually arise in opposition to God and his people, then the second beast which is associated with the first must also be false religious leaders and religions that continually arise in opposition to God and his people.[8]

Satan will use whatever weapon it takes to destroy Christians. If persecution won't work, deception centered in religion might. Pagan idolatry threatened Israel for centuries. Counterfeit Christianity assumes many forms today and deceives many. Revelation 13:11-18 provides a reminder that "the serpent was more crafty than any other wild animal that the Lord God had made" (Gen. 3:11). So we will do well to take personally the warning and solution Paul gave to Timothy:

> But wicked people and imposters will go from bad to worse, deceiving others and being deceived. But as for you, continue in what you have learned and firmly believed, knowing from whom you learned it, and how from childhood you have known the sacred writings that are able to instruct you for salvation through faith in Christ Jesus (2 Tim. 3:13-15).

The Great Whore (Rev. 17:1-6a)[1]

In Rev. 14:8 an angel exclaimed, "Fallen, fallen is Babylon the great! She has made all nations drink the wine of the wrath of her fornication." Later in 16:17-19, after "the seventh angel poured his bowl into the air," John said, "God remembered great Babylon and gave her the wine-cup of the fury of his wrath." These are the only explicit references in the book of Revelation to Babylon before chapter 17.

Chapter 17 begins with the words:

> Then one of the seven angels who had the seven bowls came and said to me, "Come, I will show you the judgment of the great whore who is seated on many waters, with whom the kings of the earth have committed fornication, and with the wine of whose fornication the inhabitants of the earth have become drunk."

The chapter ends with the same angel saying, "The woman you saw is the great city that rules over the kings of the earth." In the only subsequent reference to "one of the seven angels" John wrote:

> Then one of the seven angels who had the seven bowls full of the seven last plagues came and said to me, "Come, I will show you the bride, the wife of the Lamb." And in the spirit he carried me away to a great high mountain and showed me the holy city Jerusalem coming down out of heaven from God (21:9-10).

In the first instance, the angel told John he would be shown an evil seductress, and then was told that what he saw was the great corrupting city that had been identified as Babylon (17:5). In the second instance, the angel told John he would be shown the bride, the wife of the Lamb, and then was shown the holy city Jerusalem. The first was evil, the second was holy. The first city had fallen; the second had endured. The visions of the whore and the bride reveal the consequences for the residents of the two cities.

Neither the whore nor the bride is to be understood as a single person. The bride represents the saints (19:7-8). The bride is Jerusalem which consists of "those who are written in the Lamb's book of life" (21:27). Similarly, the whore is a city the identity of which has not been developed as chapter 17 begins.

But who or what is the whore? She is "seated on many waters." The background for the "many waters" is probably Jer. 51:13 which speaks of Babylon as living by many, or mighty, waters. But the meaning of the "waters" is explained in Rev. 17:15, "The waters that you saw, where the whore is seated, are peoples and multitudes and nations and languages." Babylon had world-wide influence, and the whore is presented in this way. We saw in verse 2 that the whore is one "with whom the kings of the earth have committed fornication, and with the wine of whose fornication the inhabitants of the earth have become drunk." In 18:2-3 an angel spoke of the impact of Babylon and said, "All the nations have drunk of the wine of the wrath of her fornication, and the kings of the earth have committed fornication with her." The nations and their kings alike have succumbed to the corrupting influence of Babylon. Consequently, in the next verse God's people are told to come out of her "so that you do not take part in her sins."

Speaking of the whore, the angel said, "The woman you saw is the great city that rules over the kings of the earth" (17:18). In John's time that was Rome. So the great whore is Babylon/Rome. But this is not to speak of a literal city. To "come out" of Babylon was not to evacuate the city of Rome. The nations/tribes/inhabitants of the earth and their kings were already geographically "out" of Rome. But they were being corrupted by Rome/the great whore. So it seems that to "come out of her" was to separate oneself from the corrupting influences symbolized by the great whore/Babylon/Rome.

This becomes increasingly apparent as one continues to read the description of the great whore in Rev. 17:3-5:

> So he carried me away in the spirit into a wilderness, and I saw
> a woman sitting on a scarlet beast that was full of blasphemous
> names, and it had seven heads and ten horns. The woman was
> clothed in purple and scarlet, and adorned with gold and jewels
> and pearls, holding in her hand a golden cup full of abominations

and the impurities of her fornication and on her forehead was written a name, a mystery: "Babylon the great, mother of whores and of earth's abominations."

The most direct and obvious connection of this passage to the Old Testament is in Jeremiah 51. Verse 7 says, "Babylon was a golden cup in the Lord's hand, making all the earth drunken; the nations drank of her wine, and the nations went mad." Babylon was a corrupting influence. So the previous verse said, "Flee from the midst of Babylon, save your lives, each of you! Do not perish because of her guilt." One is reminded of 1 Cor. 6:18 which is often translated, "Flee fornication."[2] Babylon is described as a "lover of pleasures" (Is. 47:8). And the same chapter that says, "Flee from the midst of Babylon," also says she was "rich in treasures" (Jer. 51:13). Babylon could offer pleasures and treasures to seduce God's people from their loyalty to God. This is the picture in Rev. 17:4.

Now Rev. 17:6 says, "And I saw that the woman was drunk with the blood of the saints and the blood of the witnesses to Jesus." Babylon/Rome was "a mighty city" (Rev. 18:10), a city of power. But although its persecuting power is mentioned three times (17:6; 18:24; 19:2) in terms of the "blood of the saints," its seductive power is the focus. This centers in sensuality/sexuality and luxury. A dozen times sexual terms are associated with Babylon, and expressions of the allure of a luxurious lifestyle dominate the descriptions of Babylon. Almost the entire 18th chapter of Revelation involves description of the wealth and luxury of Babylon. Revelation is saying Babylon is attractive, but she is deadly—both physically and spiritually.

One might expect a woman characterized as volatile and violent being drunk with the blood of the saints. But how could a woman characterized in terms of seductive sensuality and a luxurious lifestyle end up in this way? In the same way Herodias was drunk with the blood of John the Baptist. The king (the government) performed the execution, but the driving force behind it was Herodias. The woman's influence drove the king. The woman was sitting on the beast. The great whore occupied a position of power and luxury, and her charm was enticing and seductive. But her effect on the inhabitants of the earth was to leave them drunk on the wine of her fornication, while she herself was drunk with the blood of the saints. Moral and physical carnage are the legacy of the drunken whore. Moral degeneration with its alienation from God cost the blood of the Savior. And the moral degeneration of the heathen with their alienation from God can cost the blood of his saints.

The ability of illicit sexual activity to entice is facilitated by its apparent relative harmlessness. It is a presumably "victimless" pleasure. And "no one will know" or be hurt. But a number of passages in the Bible point to the potential deadly consequences of intimacy with the wayward woman. One example: "For the lips of a loose woman drip honey, and her speech is smoother than oil, but in the end she is bitter as wormwood, sharp as a two-edged sword. Her feet go down to death; her steps follow the path to Sheol" (Prov. 5:3-5).

But on a larger scale Rome promised economic well-being and a life of enjoyments, "bread and circuses," treasures and pleasures. Yet for countless Christians Rome offered terrifying persecution and bloodshed.

Now let us put all of this in perspective. Revelation 12 shows us Satan attempting to destroy the church. Revelation 13 shows us two agents Satan uses to accomplish that. One is portrayed under the symbol of a beast arising from the sea. I believe it represents governments which persecute God's people. The second is portrayed under the symbol of a beast rising out of the earth. I believe it represents false religion that deceives people into turning from the true way of God.[3] Chapter 14 introduces us to a third agent of Satan, Babylon, portrayed in chapter 17 as the great whore. I believe this represents the seductive power of the world to lead people away from God. In summary, Satan has three powerful agents he employs in his effort to destroy the people of God: persecution, deception, and seduction.[4] He can attack the body, the mind, and the will or passions of people. I believe the message of Babylon, the great whore, has been expressed in simpler terms in 1 Jn. 2:15-17:

> Do not love the world or the things in the world. The love of
> the Father is not in those who love the world; for all that is in the
> world—the desire of the flesh, the desire of the eyes, the pride in

riches—comes not from the Father but from the world. And the world and its desire are passing away, but those who do the will of God live forever.

It is easy for the Christian to be caught in the trap of materialism and sensuality. The world seduces us with offers of instant gratification of our desires in pornography, prostitution, gambling, and a host of other vices. Not only are they seemingly concentrated in the great cities of the world, but from those great cities the world is influenced. In the ancient world it could be seen in Babylon and Rome. In our times it can be seen in places such as Hollywood, Las Vegas, and New York City. Movies, gambling, television, and fashion flowing from these cities influence the world and can seduce the Christian.

The vision of the great whore should cause us to be reminded of the seductive power of our world and of our own vulnerability. It should cause us to remember Paul's challenge in Rom. 12:2, "Do not be conformed to the world, but be transformed by the renewing of your minds so that you may discern what is the will of God—what is good and acceptable and perfect." It should remind us of the words of Jesus to his Father concerning his people:

> I have given them your word, and the world has hated them because they do not belong to the world, just as I do not belong to the world. I am not asking you to take them out of the world, but I ask you to protect them from the evil one. They do not belong to the world, just as I do not belong to the world (Jn. 17:14-16).

To those in Babylon the voice from heaven says: "Come out of her, my people, so that you do not take part in her sins, and so that you do not share in her plagues" (Rev. 18:4). To leave Babylon is to enter a greater city. Of those who have done that the writer of Hebrews says,

> But you have come to Mount Zion and to the city of the living God, the heavenly Jerusalem, and to innumerable angels in festal gathering, and to the assembly of the firstborn who are enrolled in heaven, and to God the judge of all, and to the spirits of the righteous made perfect, and to Jesus, the mediator of a new cove-

nant, and to the sprinkled blood that speaks a better word than the blood of Abel....Therefore, since we are receiving a kingdom that cannot be shaken, let us give thanks, by which we offer to God an acceptable worship with reverence and awe; for indeed our God is a consuming fire (Heb. 12:22-24; 28-29).

I believe James Weldon Johnson, the great African-American writer, captured the spirit of the message of Revelation 17 and 18 when he concluded his sermon on "The Prodigal Son" with these words,

Oh-o-oh, sinner,

When you're mingling with the crowd in Babylon—

Drinking the wine of Babylon—

Running with the women of Babylon—

You forget about God, and you laugh at Death.

Today you've got the strength of a bull in your neck

And the strength of a bear in your arms,

But some o' these days, some o' these days,

You'll have a hand-to-hand struggle with bony Death,

And Death is bound to win.

Young man, come away from Babylon,

That hell-border city of Babylon.

Leave the dancing and gambling of Babylon,

The wine and whisky of Babylon,

The hot-mouthed women of Babylon,

Fall down on your knees,

And say in your heart:

I will arise and go to my Father.[5]

CHAPTER 5:
Conclusion

The focus of this thesis is homiletics. But the task is not yet complete. There is still some work to do and there are some final reflections to offer. How has this thesis project affected my personal ministry? On the negative side, it has been disruptive. The time invested in this has necessarily diverted attention from other matters of importance. On the positive side, and on balance, it has been beneficial. It has taught me patience and diligence. I have learned more about hermeneutics, homiletics, and the book of Revelation. I believe the church benefitted from the series of sermons I preached from the book, and preachers received the benefit of my research. And insights I have gained from my research should continue to improve my preaching and, in turn, help the congregation.

I preached my first sermon 42 years ago. I have preached "full-time" for the past 26 years (almost always two different sermons each Sunday). Yet I never had a course in homiletics until after 30 years of preaching. I had only a general speech course my freshman year in college. My ideas on preaching came from the Bible, hearing preachers, and my own intuitions. I did not consciously imitate other preachers, and I did not use sermon outlines of other preachers. My "style" was not three-point sermons. My general approach to preaching took two directions. One was to try to assess the needs of the church, look into the Bible to see what help it provided to address the needs, then try to communicate that as effectively as possible. The other way was to study the Bible to see what message it had that would benefit the church, then try to communicate that message as effectively as possible. The method of presentation was simply to move from a description of the need to the way in which the Bible presented a solution.

Habits formed over many years are not easily changed. It is one thing to accept new theories and see the value in new practices. It is another thing to apply them. The complexities of the texts chosen make the challenge extremely difficult. The eventual form and content of the sermon will be affected by the realization that people must understand the text before application can be made. It is difficult to see how a sermon can do what the text does unless the hearer has understood what the text says.

The dominating concept that controlled the creation of the sermons in chapter 4 was that expressed by Craddock in the quote earlier in this thesis. When I first grasped what I believe to be the meaning of the texts from which the sermons of chapter 4 are developed, I was extremely excited. I experienced an exhilaration through seeing things as I had never seen them before that remains with me to this day. That is what I want the hearers of these sermons to experience. My assumption was if I can lead people through the process which brought me insight and exhilaration, it will accomplish the same for them. To me, to see how God is working in his world and to be convinced that he and his people are the final victors is exciting, inspiring, and builds in me a sense of well-being, security, confidence, and a determination to endure to the end. When I go back and reread these sermons they rekindle those feelings. They not only reinforce understanding, they do something to me. This is what I hoped would happen.

However, every preacher knows that any given sermon produces any number of reactions from hearers. The same sermon may be regarded as boring, stimulating, or exciting by different hearers. My sermons tend to be long on scripture and explanation. They tend to be short on stories, illustrations, and examples. It may be because of my nature. My college roommate and I used to take notes when we listened to sermons. I always came away with a list of scriptures. He always had a collection of illustrations. Now I wish I had his notes, even though I wouldn't want to part with my own.

Twenty years ago I preached a series of 22 sermons, one from each chapter of Revelation. In the process I read everything I could on Revelation. The dominating influence on my hermeneutical approach to Revelation came from William Hendriksen. In the intervening years, and especially during my research for this thesis, I read everything I could on Revelation. This has led to a modification of some of my views, but I have found nothing that has convinced me of a better fundamental hermeneutical approach than that of Hendriksen.

In the process of developing this thesis I preached a series of 23 sermons on Revelation in Newberg, Oregon. One sermon was developed from each chapter, except for two from chapter 13. The hermeneutical approach was similar. But even the homiletical approach was somewhat similar. This was because somewhat intuitively I had many years before approached the preaching of Revelation in some ways significantly similar to those described by narrative homileticians. My aim was to "run the story" to create the emotional impact the text might have had on the first listeners. It was not to extract points to preach. But because of the complexity of the imagery, it seemed essential to weave explanation, illustration, and application through the narrative.

The three sermons in the previous chapter were not transcripts from the sermons I preached. The attempt was to write them as if I were to preach them again. However, as I have reflected further on these written sermons, I have realized they are long on explanation and short on the impact I would like to create. I believe there are some valuable insights from narrative theologians that are not properly captured in these sermons.

The result of this reflection has been the determination to start over on the text of Rev. 13:1-10 and write a new sermon. I would attempt to produce focus and function statements in the manner of Thomas G. Long. From these I would attempt to create a sermon that would allow the hearer to experience the text in a fresh way. I would try to recreate in the hearer something of the effect the text might have created in the original hearers. At the same time I would still hope to produce understanding of the text. This is a tall order. It is not that I didn't try to do this in the previous three sermons. However, after examining the finished product, I believe I see a way to reduce explanation and create some of the mood and feeling of the text.

What follows are the focus and function statements and the sermon that grew out of them. It has been a stretch for my imagination and is a clear departure from my habits. A comparison of the two sermons from the text at least reveals the possibilities of various ways sermons can be developed. It has been an eye-opening experience for me. Perhaps it will challenge the reader to tackle this and other texts in Revelation to produce sermons that will more nearly approximate the ideal.

A preliminary note: The previous sermon on Rev. 13:1-10 was intended to follow someone else reading the text. This sermon begins with the preacher reading the text as the introduction of the sermon. This text carries its own dramatic impact, is arresting, and calls for a close connection to what follows. The text actually begins with what in the NRSV is Rev. 12:18.

In the written text of this sermon the scripture references are identified in parentheses. In the oral delivery of this sermon they are not intended to be given for the sake of the flow of ideas.

Finally, this sermon remains heavy in scripture quotation. In this sermon they are not intended so much as explanation. For the most part they have been selected to create the impact I believe the text itself was trying to create.

> Focus: Although in his effort to destroy God's people Satan uses governments that gain the allegiance of the world, but which oppose God and persecute his people, Christians are not to respond with violence, but with endurance and faith.

> Function: In a context of ultimate victory, to reinterpret the Christian's perception of this world's governing authorities and to produce a response of non-retaliation, endurance, and faith.

When the Beast Knocks (Rev. 13:1-10)

Then the dragon took his stand on the sand of the seashore. And I saw a beast rising out of the sea, having ten horns and seven heads; and on its horns were ten diadems, and on its heads were blasphemous names. And the beast that I saw was like a leopard, its feet were like a bear's, and its mouth was like a lion's mouth. And the dragon gave it his power and his throne and great authority. One of its heads seemed to have received a death-blow, but its mortal wound had been healed. In amazement the whole earth followed the beast. They worshiped the dragon, for he had given his authority to the beast, and they worshiped the beast saying, "Who is like the beast, and who can fight against it?"

The beast was given a mouth uttering haughty and blasphemous words, and it was allowed to exercise authority for forty-two months. It opened its mouth to utter blasphemies against God, blaspheming his name and his dwelling, that is, those who dwell in heaven. Also it was allowed to make war on the saints and to conquer them. It was given authority over every tribe and people and language and nation, and all the inhabitants of the earth will worship it, everyone whose name has not been written from the foundation of the world in the book of life of the Lamb that was slaughtered.

Let anyone who has an ear listen:

If you are to be taken captive,

into captivity you go;

if you kill with the sword,

with the sword you must be killed.

Here is a call for the endurance and faith of the saints.

A knock on the door in the middle of the night. "You are under arrest." Beaten. Unbearable pain. Torture. Terror. "Will I live?" "What has happened to my family?" "Oh, God, where are you?" "Why is this happening?" "When will this ever end?" "Will it ever end?" "Can life ever be normal again?" The beast has struck again.

Reality in ancient Rome, modern Russia, contemporary Somalia. Persecution. But that is not my reality. That is not my experience. My government builds my roads, delivers my mail, protects me from criminals, and provides social security. My government has kept the peace, provided an orderly society, and given unprecedented prosperity.

But wait a minute. Doesn't that sound a little like ancient Rome? Didn't Christianity flourish in Rome? Didn't Roman authorities rescue Paul from a mob intent on killing him? Didn't Paul say, "authorities that exist have been instituted by God"? (Rom. 13:1). Isn't government God's servant for your good? (Rom. 13:4). And didn't Peter say to "honor the emperor," and that governors are sent by God "to punish those who do wrong and to praise those who do right"? (1 Pet. 2:17, 13-14).

But wait another minute. Wasn't the serpent more subtle than any beast of the field God had made? (Gen. 3:1). And isn't the great dragon, "that ancient serpent, who is called the Devil and Satan, the deceiver of the whole world"? (Rev. 12:9). Through his deceptions Satan has often distorted God's designs. Paradise was lost, marriages have been destroyed, churches have been divided, and governments have become instruments of persecution.

The church was not, and has not, always been persecuted. It began in the Roman empire and had "the goodwill of all the people" (Acts 2:47). It took awhile for the beast to raise its ugly heads. But in time persecution struck. It always will. Jesus said, "If they persecuted me, they will persecute you" (Jn. 15:20). Paul assured Christians: "Indeed all who want to live a godly life in Christ Jesus will be persecuted" (2 Tim. 3:12). Not always. Not in the same ways. But persecution is a reasonable expectation for those who are perceived as a threat to opposing ways of life.

The power of Rome had benefitted people in many ways. It had brought peace, stability, security, and prosperity for many. The power of Rome—

awesome! Opposition had been crushed. "And they worshiped the beast, saying, 'Who is like the beast, and who can fight against it?'" Who would dare! And what kind of person would want to turn our allegiance to an invisible (imaginary?) king? "We have no king but Caesar." Caesar is Lord! Don't you remember the chaos, uncertainty, instability, the frightful economic unrest? We have a savior. We want no pretender. Wasn't your savior crucified by Rome? What has he done for you? Would you try to impose on us alien ideas and practices? Are you an insurrectionist?...A knock on the door in the middle of the night.

During the reign of Nero Paul said,

> I urge that supplications, prayers, intercessions, and thanksgivings be made for everyone, for kings and all who are in high positions, so that we may lead a quiet and peaceful life in all godliness and dignity (1 Tim. 2:1-2).

During the reign of Nero Paul traveled around the empire and preached the gospel. During the reign of Nero Paul was imprisoned and put to death. Sometimes the beast seems to have received a fatal wound. But it always seems to revive. Nebuchadnezzar enslaved God's people. Cyrus said, "You can go home now." Ahasuerus signed an edict to destroy the Jews. Ahasuerus signed an edict to protect the Jews. Pilate wanted to release Jesus. Pilate had him crucified. Soviet and Chinese constitutions have offered freedom of religion. Soviet and Chinese governments have persecuted people who have professed faith in Christ. And the beast has struck again.

So what do we do when government and society have conspired against us? The human instinct for survival calls for retaliation. Peter whips out his sword in a moment of desperation. But Jesus says,

> Put your sword back into its place; for all who take the sword will perish by the sword. Do you think that I cannot appeal to my Father, and he will at once send me more than twelve legions of angels? But how then would the scriptures be fulfilled, which say it must happen in this way? (Mt. 26:52-54).

Which scriptures? Perhaps from Gen. 49:9-10 and Micah 5:8 Peter had formed an image of Jesus as the lion of the tribe of Judah. A clash between the beast and the king of beasts. Peter had seen the power of Jesus displayed in stunning miracles. Power against power. That was one way. But it was not the only way. There was another. There was another image from scriptures. Another beast. Harmless. Helpless. Gentle. "A lamb that is led to the slaughter" (Is. 53:7). Not the image of choice. Not the beastly image I'm looking for.

Jesus may be perceived as the lion king. But he must also be seen as the lowly lamb. That is how John the Baptist introduced Jesus to the world: "Here is the Lamb of God who takes away the sin of the world!" (Jn. 1:29). And when the other John heard one of the elders say, "See, the Lion of the tribe of Judah," he looked and saw "a Lamb standing as if it had been slaughtered" (Rev. 5:5-6). The Lamb was slaughtered. He who could have called ten thousand angels chose another way, the way of the cross.

John later reminds us that all the inhabitants of the earth will worship the ghastly beast. But there is another category of people: those who are in the world but not of the world. These have seen things differently. They also have seen, and perhaps felt, the power of the beast. But they have something else, something more. They have seen another kind of beast—and loved him. They have seen a lamb. Not just any lamb. They have seen the Lamb of God. And they are numbered among those whose names have been "written from the foundation of the world in the book of life of the Lamb that was slaughtered." They have heard the words: "If you are to be taken captive, into captivity you go; if you kill with the sword, with the sword you must be killed." They have heard the call "for the endurance and faith of the saints."

These are people who understand the message of Peter:

> If you endure when you do right and suffer for it, you have God's approval. For to this you have been called, because Christ also suffered for you, leaving you an example, so that you should follow his steps....When he was abused, he did not return abuse;

when he suffered, he did not threaten; but he entrusted himself to the one who judges justly (1 Pet. 2:20-21, 23).

These are people who know the Lamb had been slaughtered on a cross. The dragon had conquered—or so it seemed. They knew the dragon gave authority to the beast to "make war on the saints and to conquer them"—or so it seems. But they have done something about it. They have not taken up swords as though they could destroy the beast, much less the dragon. But "they have washed their robes and made them white in the blood of the Lamb" (Rev. 7:14), because they know the time is coming when "the Lamb at the center of the throne will be their shepherd, and he will guide them to springs of the water of life, and God will wipe away every tear from their eyes" (Rev. 7:17). They know that all the inhabitants of the earth will worship the beast. But they refuse to say, "Caesar is Lord." They will gladly go to their deaths singing the song of Moses and the Lamb. The dragon had offered the Lamb all the kingdoms of the world, but he turned him down. And the followers of the Lamb, like great people of faith before them, "confessed that they were strangers and foreigners on the earth.... They desire a better country, that is, a heavenly one" (Heb. 11:13, 16).

We know that "our citizenship is in heaven" (Phil. 3:20). We know the destiny of the beast:

> And the beast was captured, and with it the false prophet who had performed in its presence the signs by which he deceived those who had received the mark of the beast and those who worshiped its image. These two were thrown alive into the lake of fire that burns with sulfur (Rev. 19:20).

We know our destiny. We have seen the final vision of the Lamb and the heavenly land, and we know

> the throne of God and of the Lamb will be in it, and his servants will worship him; they will see his face, and his name will be on their foreheads. And there will be no more night; they need no light of lamp or sun, for the Lord God will be their light, and they will reign forever and ever (Rev. 22:3-5).

The Christian need not fear the ominous knock on the door in the middle of the night, for he has heard the gentle knocking on the door of his heart, and responded to the voice of the one who said,

> If you hear my voice and open the door, I will come in to you and eat with you, and you with me. To the one who conquers I will give a place with me on my throne, just as I myself conquered and sat down with my Father on his throne (Rev. 3:20-21).

> What then are we to say about these things?...Who will separate us from the love of Christ? Will hardship, or distress, or persecution, or famine, or nakedness, or peril, or sword?...No, in all these things we are more than conquerors through him who loved us. For I am convinced that neither death, nor life, nor angels, nor rulers, nor things present, nor things to come, nor powers, nor height, nor depth, nor anything else in all creation, will be able to separate us from the love of God in Christ Jesus our Lord (Rom. 8:31, 35, 37-39).

Final Observations

This sermon is considerably different from the previous one from the same text. The first attempted to lead the hearer through the text, explaining the text along the way while attempting to suggest its significance and application for us. The focus was providing understanding of a complicated text with the hope that insight would provide encouragement.

This sermon has not led the hearer sequentially through the text. Nor has it attempted to bring to bear much of the Old Testament background that might sharpen the understanding of the text. Instead it focuses on the reality that is fairly obvious in the text: Christians can expect persecution. It attempts to suggest why this can be a reasonable expectation for people who may not be currently experiencing it. And it attempts to fortify those who might experience that eventuality. It is designed to create a stronger emotional impact by constructing the experience of persecution, using linguistic devices, juxtaposing ideas, and using scriptures to inspire the believer.

One thing I tried to avoid in the sermons was place and time-sensitive illustrations. The use of current events and local happenings is valuable and enhances the relevance of sermons. Such would reasonably be incorporated in the actual delivery of the sermon at a particular time and place. The sermons in this thesis are intentionally generic for adaptation in specific settings.

The two sermons from the same text may reflect the difference between an expository and narrative approach to preaching. The former tries to enhance understanding while the latter seeks to create emotional impact and enable the experiencing of the text. Neither needs to be devoid of elements of the other.

This thesis has attempted to provide help in preaching the messages of Revelation. It has tried to emphasize that the construction of a sermon must move from hermeneutics to homiletics. It has attempted to demonstrate how that can be done. There is much more that could be done. Perhaps others can take up the challenge. For example, it could be very helpful to see a text from some of the more difficult portions of Revelation followed by an exegetical study followed by a sermon reflecting that study. Even better would be to see the entire book of Revelation treated in this way.

An additional project that could be beneficial would be to have several different homileticians assigned the same text from Revelation. The variety of resulting sermons could provide helpful insights for the preacher struggling to make sense of the text and how to apply it.

What has been presented in this thesis is a modest attempt to clarify and stimulate more effective ways of preaching from Revelation on my part. Perhaps it will benefit others as well.

APPENDIX 1:

Listener Response to Sermons

Following the research for this thesis I preached a series of 23 sermons on Revelation at the Newberg church of Christ in Newberg, Oregon. One sermon was preached on each of 21 chapters. Two sermons were preached from chapter 13. These were from 13:1-10 and 13:11-18.

A feedback group was selected from the congregation. This was composed of those willing to remain for 30 minutes following five randomly selected sermons to critique them. The goal was to have a group of six to eight that would represent a cross-section of the congregation. The congregation of nearly 200 was narrowed to 50 whose attendance patterns indicated the greatest likelihood of their being present for each sermon. These were narrowed to a group that would include an age range from teen to senior citizen. It included male and female, well-educated and less-educated, single and married. I had someone else select the individuals to avoid any possibility of choosing ones who might be most favorably disposed to my preaching. The final choices included eight from the core group plus two others to fill in if some were absent.

A "Questionnaire for Feedback Group" was prepared to provide some guidance for evaluation. Each person was encouraged to complete these and return them signed or unsigned. (Only eight were signed.) The participants were not required to return them immediately following the group meetings, but there was a total of 33 questionnaires returned. These responded to sermons on Revelation 7; 10; 13:1-10; 13:11-18; and 17.

The feedback group met in a room with me a few minutes after each of the selected sermons. Each person gave their reactions, both positive and negative, to the sermons, and there was general discussion and an exchange of thoughts. It was a very valuable experience for me, and the group seemed to appreciate the fact that their thoughts were heard. I took notes on the comments expressed to impress on my mind points that might help me improve future sermons.

Several observations from the oral response of the group were of particular interest to me. Some noted a tendency to repeat myself. Others felt the repetition was helpful. Some thought some of the sermons were too long. Others felt I should take as much time as necessary to cover the material. Some suggested breaking the longer sermons into two sermons. Some thought I rushed through some things to get everything said. It became clear to me that I needed to give more attention to time management in my sermons.

Some thought I was long on scripture but short on application. But others liked that. There was much discussion about this, but no consensus. It did make me more conscious of the need and importance of not assuming that the applications of a sermon are always obvious. My main concern in preaching has been to be like Apollos in being "well-versed in the scriptures" and teaching "accurately the things concerning Jesus" (Acts 18:24-25). The group at least made me conscious that there is a need to blend accuracy and application.

The results of the questionnaire revealed several things. No one stated that the sermons incorrectly presented the teaching of the Scriptures. None indicated the sermons were boring, offensive, disorganized, hard to follow, or irrelevant. One thought a sermon was confusing and another thought one was partly confusing. Of the 33 questionnaires returned, six noted that the sermon was too long, but half of those applied to one sermon in particular. In choosing words to describe the sermons 97% checked interesting, 97% informative, 82% helpful, 73% thought-provoking, 61% encouraging, 33% inspiring, and 27% practical.

When asked to grade the sermons, 23 marked A, 9 B, and 1 C. No one gave a lower grade on any sermon. Overall the experience was helpful and encouraging to me as a preacher.

The second part of the "listener response" application of the thesis was to produce a questionnaire to provide the entire congregation at the end of the series of sermons on Revelation. Altogether 40 questionnaires were returned. Only four were signed. There were two who did not indicate how many of the sermons they heard. The rest heard most of them, and six heard all of them.

The results of the survey were very encouraging to me. No one indicated a belief that I had incorrectly presented the teaching of the Scriptures. No one indicated the series was offensive. In fact, 70% thought the series was inspiring, and 86% gave the series an A. The most prominent negative criticism came from 25% who thought it was too long.

APPENDIX 2:

Preacher Response to Seminar

In the middle of my series of sermons on Revelation I attended meetings of preachers of churches of Christ in two areas of Oregon and Washington. I distributed a "Questionnaire on Preaching the Book of Revelation" and had 21 returned. One purpose was to learn the extent to which they had preached from Revelation. The men who returned the questionnaires had preached an average of 27 years. Based on other research I had expected to discover more neglect in preaching from Revelation. However, only two had never preached from a text in the book. Twelve had preached a series from Revelation, with the average length being nine sermons. Seven of the series covered the entire book. These were the only ones that covered chapters 4-19. Five had never preached from a text in those chapters.

I invited the preachers to attend a seminar I would conduct on preaching from the book of Revelation. In my lifetime I had already preached about 80 sermons from Revelation, covering every chapter. I had also completed my research for this thesis, and believed I could contribute something that would benefit them.

I conducted a 4-hour seminar, and 19 preachers attended. I divided it into three sessions: Introduction to Preaching Revelation, Hermeneutical Principles and Insights for Preaching Revelation, and Homiletical Principles and Insights for Preaching Revelation.

I prepared a questionnaire on the seminar to give to the preachers. I forgot to hand it out until it was over and some had left. So I only had 11 returned. Nine said they were more likely to preach from Revelation after having attended the seminar. One said, "Maybe," and another, "I think so." The general response concerning the benefit of the seminar was in seeing different views, and a better understanding through an overview of the entire book. The basic improvement suggested was simply that it needed to be longer. The most helpful part of the seminar was expressed in terms of the excitement created for preaching from the book and the sermon suggestions.

The grades I was given by the preachers were: 7, B, A-, A+, 99%, A, A, B, and A-. One gave no grade. Instead of giving a grade, one preacher said the most important thing he got was "enthusiasm about <u>GOD</u>!!"

The major benefit of the seminar for me was simply the joy of seeing others share the excitement and enthusiasm I have for the message of the book of Revelation.

End Notes

Term Paper

1   Donald Guthrie, *The Relevance of John's Apocalypse* (Grand Rapids: William B. Eerdmans Publishing Company, 1987), 11.

2   *Religion Index One: Periodicals RIO: A Subject Index to Periodical Literature Including an Author/Editor Index and a Scripture Index*, vols. 22-25 (Evanston, Ill.: American Theological Library Association, 1990-94).

3   Danny Drewry Clymer and Robert Allen Lowery, *Index to Periodical Literature on the Book of Revelation* (So. Hamilton, Mass.: Gordon-Conwell Theological Seminary, 1975), 73-86.

4   Daniel Russell, *Preaching the Apocalypse* (New York: The Abingdon Press, 1935), 9.

5   Fred B. Craddock, "Preaching the Book of Revelation," *Interpretation* 40 (July 1986): 270-71.

6   Thomas G. Long, "Preaching Apocalyptic Literature," *Review & Expositor* 90 (Summer 1993): 371.

7   Eugene H. Peterson, *Reversed Thunder: The Revelation of John and the Praying Imagination* (San Francisco: Harper & Row, Publisher, 1988), 187.

8   Craddock, 279.

9   Robert H. Mounce, *The Book of Revelation*, The New International Commentary on the New Testament (Grand Rapids: William B. Eerdmans Publishing Company, 1977), 12.

10   Guthrie, 31.

11   Michael Wilcock, *I Saw Heaven Opened: The Message of Revelation*, The Bible Speaks Today (Downers Grove, Ill.: InterVarsity Press, 1975), 20.

12   *The New Testament in the Original Greek*, rev. by Brooke Foss Westcott and Fenton John Anthony Hort (New York: The Macmillan Company, 1925), 612-18.

13   Wilcock, 24.

14   William Hendriksen, *More Than Conquerors: An Interpretation of the Book of Revelation* (Grand Rapids: Baker Book House, 1940).

15   Elisabeth Fiorenza, "The Eschatology and Composition of the Apocalypse," *The Catholic Biblical Quarterly* 30 (October 1968): 554.

16   David L. Barr, "Elephants and Holograms: From Metaphor to Methodology in the Study of John's Apocalypse," *Society of Biblical Literature Seminar Papers Series* 25 (1986): 411.

17   Eugene H. Peterson, "Learning to Worship from Saint John's Revelation," *Christianity Today* 35 (Oct. 28, 1991): 24.

18   Paul S. Minear, *I Saw a New Earth: An Introduction to the Visions of the Apocalypse* (Washington, D.C.: Corpus Books, 1968), 213.

19   David A. deSilva, "The 'Image of the Beast' and the Christians in Asia Minor: Escalation of Sectarian Tension in Revelation 13," *Trinity Journal* 12 (Fall 1991): 186.

20   Ibid., 200.

21   Ibid., 192.

22 Craig A. Loscalzo, *Preaching Sermons that Connect: Effective Communication through Identification* (Downers Grove, Ill.: InterVarsity Press, 1982), 118.

23 Craddock, 279.

24 Peterson, *Thunder*, xiii.

25 Ibid., xi-xii.

26 William H. Willimon, *Peculiar Speech: Preaching to the Baptized* (Grand Rapids: William B. Eerdmans Publishing Company, 1992), 55.

27 Long, 377.

28 Ibid.

29 Adela Yarbro Collins, "'What the Spirit Says to the Churches': Preaching the Apocalypse," *Quarterly Review: A Scholarly Journal for Reflection on Ministry* 4 (Fall 1984): 80.

30 Ibid., 83.

31 Long, 379.

32 Long, 381.

33 Craddock, 274-78.

34 Collins, 70.

35 Wilcock, 24.

36 Peterson, *Thunder*, 5.

37 Cornish R. Rogers, "Images of Christian Victory: Notes for Preaching from the Book of Revelation," *Quarterly Review: A Scholarly Journal for Reflection on Ministry* 10 (Fall 1990): 73.

38 Ibid., 76.

39 Craddock, 278-79.

Chapter 1

1   Scattered articles can be found dealing with certain aspects of the
    subject. The few books include: Daniel Russell, *Preaching the Apocalypse*
    (New York: The Abingdon Press, 1935); Merrill C. Tenney, *The Book of
    Revelation*, Proclaiming the New Testament (Grand Rapids: Baker Book
    House, 1963); Owen L. Crouch, *Expository Preaching and Teaching:
    Revelation* (Joplin, Mo.: College Press Publishing Company, 1985); and
    M. Eugene Boring, *Revelation*, Interpretation Commentaries (Louisville:
    Westminster/John Knox Press, 1989).

2   John MacArthur, Jr. and the Master's Seminary Faculty, *Rediscovering
    Expository Preaching* (Dallas: Word Publishing, 1992), 23-24.

3   John Bright, *The Authority of the Old Testament* (Nashville: Abingdon
    Press, 1967), 42-43.

4   A significant body of literature has developed in response to Hirsch's
    writing. Some of this response is found in: Walter C. Kaiser and Moises
    Silva, *An Introduction to Biblical Hermeneutics: The Search for Meaning*
    (Grand Rapids: Zondervan Publishing House, 1994); D. A. Carson
    and John D. Woodbridge, eds., *Hermeneutics, Authority and Canon*
    (Grand Rapids: Zondervan Publishing House, 1986); Peter Cotterell
    and Max Turner, *Linguistics and Biblical Interpretation* (Downers Grove,
    Ill.: InterVarsity Press, 1989); Norman L. Geisler, ed., *Inerrancy* (Grand
    Rapids: Zondervan Publishing House, 1979); and David Alan Black
    and David S. Dockery, eds., *New Testament Criticism and Interpretation*
    (Grand Rapids: Zondervan Publishing House, 1991).

5   E. D. Hirsch, Jr., *Validity in Interpretation* (New Haven: Yale University
    Press, 1967), 1.

6   Vern Sheridan Poythress, "Divine Meaning of Scripture," *Westminster
    Theological Journal* 48 (1986): 245.

7   Millard J. Erickson, *Evangelical Interpretation: Perspectives on
    Hermeneutical Issues*, (Grand Rapids: Baker Books, 1993), 118.

8   Elisabeth Fiorenza, "The Eschatology and Composition of the
    Apocalypse," *The Catholic Biblical Quarterly* 30 (October 1968): 554.

9   David L. Barr, "The Apocalypse as a Symbolic Transformation of the World," *Interpretation* 38 (January 1984): p. 39, n.1.

10   David L. Barr, "Elephants and Holograms: From Metaphor to Methodology in the Study of John's Apocalypse," *Society of Biblical Literature: Seminar Papers* 25 (1986): 411.

11   Richard Bauckham, *The Theology of the Book of Revelation*, New Testament Theology (Cambridge, England: Cambridge University Press, 1993), 16.

12   Ibid.

13   Paul S. Minear, *I Saw a New Earth: An Introduction to the Visions of the Apocalypse* (Washington, D.C.: Corpus Books, 1968), 213.

14   Adela Yarbro Collins, "Reading the Book of Revelation in the Twentieth Century," *Interpretation* 40 (July 1986): 242.

15   Wilfrid J. Harrington, *Revelation*, Sacra Pagina Series, vol. 16 (Collegeville, Minn.: The Liturgical Press, 1993), 13.

16   Barr, "Transformation," 49-50.

17   Arthur W. Wainwright, *Mysterious Apocalypse: Interpreting the Book of Revelation* (Nashville: Abingdon Press, 1993), 230.

18   Michael Wilcock, *I Saw Heaven Opened: The Message of Revelation*, The Bible Speaks Today (Downers Grove, Ill.: InterVarsity Press, 1975), 222.

19   David A. deSilva, "The 'Image of the Beast' and the Christians in Asia Minor: Escalation of Sectarian Tension in Revelation 13," *Trinity Journal* 12 (Fall 1991): 186.

20   William Hendriksen, *More Than Conquerors: An Interpretation of the Book of Revelation* (Grand Rapids: Baker Book House, 1940), 11.

21   Ibid., 26-27. On page 58 Hendriksen points out that persecution was only one struggle the Christians faced that had to be addressed. He also mentions false religion, lust, false teachers and sects, superstition, unbelief, and the struggle between truth and error.

Chapter 2

1   Wilcock, 24.

2   E.g., Morris, 16-18.

3   Ibid., 17.

4   All biblical references in this thesis are taken from the New Revised Standard Version.

5   David A. Hubbard and Glenn W. Barker, eds., *Word Biblical Commentary* (Dallas: Word Book, Publisher, 1997), vol. 52A, *Revelation 1-5*, by David Aune, xci.

6   Hendriksen, 28.

7   Robert W. Wall, *Revelation*, New International Biblical Commentary (Peabody, Mass.: Hendrikson Publishers, 1991), 38.

8   George Eldon Ladd, *A Commentary on the Revelation of John* (Grand Rapids: William B. Eerdmans Publishing Company, 1972), 11-12.

9   Collins, "Reading," 235.

10 Ibid.

11 Ibid., 236.

12 Ibid., 239.

13 Wall, 4.

14 Collins, "Reading," 238.

15 Morris, 23.

16 Boring, 28.

17 *The New Testament in the Original Greek*, rev. by Brooke Foss Westcott and Fenton John Anthony Hort (New York: The Macmillan Company, 1925), 612-18.

18　Henry Barclay Swete, *Commentary on Revelation* (Grand Rapids: Kregel Publications, 1977), ccxvi.

19　James L. Blevins, "Book of Revelation," in *Mercer Dictionary of the Bible*, ed. Watson E. Mills (Macon, Ga.: Mercer University Press, 1990), 761.

20　Ibid., 759.

21　Ibid.

22　Ibid.

23　Ibid., 760.

24　Craddock, 272.

25　Blevins, 761.

26　Hal Lindsay, *The Late Great Planet Earth* (Grand Rapids: Zondervan Publishing House, 1970).

27　Blevins, 761.

28　Boring, vii.

29　Ibid.

30　Craddock, 278-82.

31　Hendriksen, 22-48.

32　It is against this background that the sermons in chapter 4 are developed. See Hendriksen, especially pp. 22-43.

33　C. S. Lewis, *Mere Christianity* (New York: The Macmillan Company, 1960), 121. Lewis is not quoted as a New Testament scholar, but as a literary critic competent to comment on the meaning of symbolism in literature.

34　Boring, 47.

35   Wilbur Smith, "Revelation," in *The Wycliffe Bible Commentary*, eds. Charles F. Pfeiffer and Everett F. Harrison (Chicago: Moody Press, 1962), 1500.

36   Craddock, 279.

37   J. Ramsey Michaels, *Interpreting the Book of Revelation*, Guides to New Testament Exegesis (Grand Rapids: Baker Book House, 1992), 10.

38   Ibid., 146.

39   Ibid., 147.

40   Westcott, 612-18.

41   David L. Larsen, *The Anatomy of Preaching: Identifying the Issues in Preaching Today* (Grand Rapids: Baker Book House, 1989), 65.

Chapter 3

1   Wilcock, 24.

2   Cornish R. Rogers, "Images of Christian Victory: Notes for Preaching from the Book of Revelation," *Quarterly Review: A Scholarly Journal for Reflection on Ministry* 10 (Fall 1990): 73.

3   Ibid., 76.

4   Hendriksen, 49.

5   Peterson, xiii.

6   Hendriksen, 12.

7   Craddock, 279.

8   Craig A. Loscalzo, *Preaching Sermons that Connect: Effective Communication through Identification* (Downers Grove, Ill.: InterVarsity Press, 1982), 118.

9   Walter Brueggemann, *Finally Comes the Poet: Daring Speech for Proclamation* (Minneapolis: Fortress Press, 1989), 85.

10   William H. Willimon, *Peculiar Speech: Preaching to the Baptized* (Grand Rapids: William B. Eerdmans Publishing Company, 1992), 55.

11   Long, "Apocalyptic," 377.

12   Ibid.

13   Ibid. See Acts 7:56.

14   Adela Yarbro Collins, "'What the Spirit Says to the Churches': Preaching the Apocalypse," *Quarterly Review: A Scholarly Journal for Reflection on Ministry* 4 (Fall 1984): 80.

15   Eugene L. Lowry, *How to Preach a Parable: Designs for Narrative Sermons* (Nashville: Abingdon Press, 1989), 22.

16   Thomas G. Long, *The Witness of Preaching* (Louisville, Ky.: Westminster/John Knox Press, 1989), 84.

17   Long, "Apocalyptic," 371-81.

18   Charles L. Campbell, *Preaching Jesus: New Directions for Homiletics in Hans Frei's Postliberal Theology* (Grand Rapids: William B. Eerdmans Publishing Company, 1997), 119.

19   Long, *Witness*, 37.

20   *Random House Webster's College Dictionary*, rev. 3d. (1996), s.v. "Narrative."

21   Campbell, 122.

22   Peterson, 5.

23   Collins, "Spirit," 70.

24   Campbell, 138.

25   Ibid., 129.

26   Neil Postman, *Amusing Ourselves to Death: Public Discourse in the Age of Show Business* (New York: Viking Penguin Inc., 1985), 54.

27   Campbell, 118-20.

28   Ibid., 217-18.

29   Craddock, 278-79.

30   Richard A. Jensen, *Thinking in Story: Preaching in a Post-Literate Age* (Lima, Ohio: C. S. S. Publishing Co., Inc., 1993), 77.

31   Campbell, 256.

32   Long, *Witness*, 86-87.

33   Ibid., 86.

34   Ibid., 87.

35   Lowry, 38.

36   Campbell, 197.

37   Long, 74.

Chapter 4
The Beast of the Sea Annotations

1   Pre-sermon strategy: I would have someone read the text before I begin the sermon. Some texts in the Bible are so clear, the meaning is so plain, that the preacher's task is primarily to find proper application. Rev. 13:1-10 poses a greater challenge. The average listener of the text would probably think, "What is this all about? What is going on here?" The first task is simply to help the listener to understand the text. However, I believe when the light of the biblical background illuminates the text it reveals the truth of the Christian's circumstances in the world, its relevance becomes self-evident, and it has transforming power by reorienting our perspective on our place in our world. So the plan for this sermon is to lead the listener through the text while attempting to illuminate it with relevant biblical background.

2   This is a rather grim text that features a beast making war on the saints. Revelation intersperses terrifying scenes with scenes of victory and encouragement. This sermon focuses on a particular text that may suggest little of encouragement to the casual listener. But it would be an injustice

to keep from the listener the message in its larger context which is one of ultimate victory for God's people. So I thought it appropriate to preface a look at the text with a reminder that we have both an adversary and an advocate. The quote from 1 Peter is to prepare the listener for the dragon imagery by noting the imagery of the roaring lion. It parallels the dragon imagery, but it also provides a way to conclude the sermon by the rest of the quote providing a note of hope and victory justifying the call for endurance found at the end of the Revelation text.

3   If it can be said that Jews flourished under the reign of the Persians, it can also be said Christianity flourished under the reign of the Romans. But it is still true that Romans persecuted Christians and Persians persecuted Jews. Biblical evidence is found in the edict of Xerxes that called for the extermination of every Jew in the empire (Esther 3:6-4:4). Further evidence comes from Daniel 7. The second beast in verse 5, representing the Persian empire, is portrayed as a bear tearing the ribs out of another creature. Certainly the fourth beast was terrifying. But the second beast would strike terror in the heart of anyone who confronted him. If the fourth beast was different from the others, it was not because it alone persecuted God's people. It is known that the first one did. And when Revelation 13 presents a beast persecuting God's people it is a composite of all four beasts, not a replica of the fourth.

4   The limited time the sermon affords does not permit an explanation and evaluation of the many competing views regarding the meaning of all the symbols and details of the text. I am presenting an interpretation that among scholars perhaps more nearly reflects that of William Hendriksen. I obviously believe the interpretation I am giving is correct for the reasons given plus others there is simply not time to include. However, I think it is important to say, "I don't believe" with emphasis on "believe." I wish to distinguish certain, dogmatic truths from what "I believe" in dealing with Revelation. I have confidence in my interpretation, and my intent is to share that with the listener with the hope that he or she will gain insight that will be true and provide hope, confidence, and encouragement that I have experienced through this study. At the same time I want to avoid an unbecoming dogmatism concerning difficult texts.

5 This is not a novel interpretation. Although he did not accept it, Pieters called it "a favorite explanation." See Albertus Pieters, *Studies in the Revelation of St. John* (Grand Rapids: Wm. B. Eerdmans Publishing Company, 1954), 229. It is a view held by Hendriksen, Wilcock, and Harrington, among others.

6 Post-sermon reflections: This text could be developed in many different ways. No claim is made that this is the best way. Priority was given to help the listener understand the text and its relationship to the teachings of scripture. I recognize there is more information about the beast in chapter 17. Time restraints would not permit justice to be done to developing insights that might be gained from that very complex passage. That might be done in an additional sermon or class.

The Beast of the Earth Annotations

1 Pre-sermon strategy: Literally hundreds of different ideas have been proposed concerning the details of this passage. It would be impossible in a single sermon to even mention all of them, much less analyze and evaluate them. This sermon will be simply an attempt to present what I believe is the truth about the meaning of this text and why I believe it. Its relevance should be self-evident within the explanation of its meaning. If there is transforming power here, it should come through a reorientation of thought concerning the subtlety and danger of seemingly harmless false religion.

2 Although this sermon has been developed to stand on its own, the listener would be better served if he or she would hear it in connection with a sermon on the previous verses. Because this text speaks of the previous beast, an identification must be made of that beast. Due to time constraints there can only be a statement of identification without development of the reasons for the conclusion. The listener is left to assume the identification is valid. The "I believe" statement avoids the dogmatic "It is" to assure the listener that this is a conclusion that need not be accepted uncritically.

3   While the initiative for the Roman Imperial cult in Asia Minor came from denizens, and not from Rome, the cult still demanded emperor worship from reluctant citizens.

4   Examples could certainly be included here, but it might be as well to allow the listener to fill in the blank.

5   This question and the answer given are included here to emphasize the extent to which deception is practiced, and how powerful it can be.

6   Hendriksen and many other scholars agree with this view. It is true one must "add up" the number of the beast because it is "six hundreds sixty six." But when those three are added up, the resulting number is 666 (six hundred sixty-six). Is that number then to be treated as a symbol, or must one play the gematria game? The fact that a number was derived by adding other numbers together does not mean the resulting number cannot be a symbol. The number 144,000 is derived by adding up twelve 12,000's. But the gematria game is not played with 144,000. It is clearly a symbol. It is true that gematria can explain 616, which is a variant reading. But gematria can explain any number, given enough ingenuity. There is not always an explanation for scribal error. For example, I can understand how I copied 1983 as 1933 in one draft of this thesis. But I have no idea how I copied 1986 as 1984, which I also did. And it is not true that the simple name Nero equals 616. A title must still be added to achieve the desired result. In this case, add Caesar and use the Latin form. And it is not true that Nero equals 666 in Hebrew. Caesar must still be added. A good, brief discussion of this can be found in Bruce M. Metzger, *A Textual Commentary on the Greek New Testament* (Stuttgart: United Bible Societies, 1975), 749-50.

7   To translate "number of man" in Rev. 13:18 does not violate anything that is known concerning the anarthrous noun in Greek. The Greek scholars who translated the NIV say "it is man's number," not "a man's number." Translating this "man" rather than "a man" is as legitimate as translating "God" rather than "a god" in Jn. 1:1.

8   Hendriksen and others do not think this is a large leap. It does not seem that the second beast has to overtly and intentionally promote worship

of the first beast. It did in the case of Rome. But false religion inevitably tends to promote the first beast.

The Great Whore Annotations

1.   Pre-sermon strategy: I would have someone read Rev. 17:1-6a before beginning the sermon. The vision of the great whore/Babylon extends into chapter 19. Time would not permit developing everything said in the larger context. Some decision and choice must be made on how to approach this. The intent of the sermon is to identify the great whore, and help the listener understand its significance for us. The decision is to focus on Rev. 17:1-6a on the belief that an understanding of that text when informed by other scriptures will accomplish the purpose. Many commentators have identified the great whore with the Roman Catholic Church. I could mention that and take time to explain why I believe that is not true. The decision has been made, largely in the interest of time, to simply explain what I believe the text means, and why. Even then I cannot give all the reasons. Most of these can be found in many commentaries. William Hendriksen's provides a good explanation of the view expressed in this sermon.

2.   I have consistently used the NRSV in quotations except for here. The NRSV says "shun" here rather than "flee" even though it translates the Greek word as "flee" elsewhere. I believe "flee" is better.

3.   The Roman Imperial cult was a false religion that turned people from the true way of God. But even scholars who believe the beast of the earth refers exclusively to the Imperial cult acknowledge there is no evidence that all of the specifics concerning the activities of the beast as described in Rev. 13:11ff. have been found in the practice of the Roman Imperial cult. This adds to the reasons for believing the beast encompasses much more, a view held by Hendriksen and others.

4.   Interpreters have referred to Satan and the two beasts as John's unholy Trinity. Certainly they are. But Satan employs Babylon as well as the beasts to accomplish his purposes. In fact, there are at least five enemies of God's people in Revelation: Satan, the inhabitants of the earth, the two beasts, and Babylon.

5   James Weldon Johnson, *God's Trombones: Seven Negro Sermons in Verse* (New York: Viking Penguin, 1927; repr. New York: The Viking Press, 1955), 25.